HALF A BILLION RISING

HALF
A BILLION
RISING

*The Emergence of
the Indian Woman*

Anirudha Dutta

RAINLIGHT
RUPA

First published in RAINLIGHT by
Rupa Publications India Pvt. Ltd 2015
7/16, Ansari Road, Daryaganj
New Delhi 110002

Sales centres:
Allahabad Bengaluru Chennai
Hyderabad Jaipur Kathmandu
Kolkata Mumbai

ISBN: 978-81-291-3658-9

First impression 2015

10 9 8 7 6 5 4 3 2 1

Typeset by SÜRYA, New Delhi

Printed by Parksons Graphics Pvt. Ltd, Mumbai

Dedicated to my parents,
who dreamt for us; and to Siddhant and Avantika,
for whom I dream

SHE RISES WITH HOPE

—Tina Vajpeyi

She rises each morning to the call of her mother
A woman who dreams for and empowers her
Who clothes and who feeds her

She rises at school to the voice of her teacher
A woman who moulds and emboldens her
Who informs and instructs her

She rises at the office to the orders of her senior
A woman who tasks and trains her
Who enlightens and develops her

She rises in the evening to the chatter of her family
Women who share with and care with her
Who cook and who clean with her

She rises in the night to the touch of her husband
A man who demands from and dares her
Who cares for and loves her

She rises in hope that each day she will hear
Of women living more equally and happily than her
Women living with hope and not fear

CONTENTS

PARICHAY—AN INTRODUCTION

Girls and women in India have had eminent status and positions of power from ancient to modern times, in mythology and in real life. Consider this: the gods of learning, wealth and power are all women. Indian mythology is replete with references to princesses and queens who were not only the embodiment of beauty but also of valour, bravery, state craft and wisdom. During the independence movement and after independence we have had some very powerful and successful women political leaders like Sarojini Naidu, Vijay Lakshmi Pandit and Indira Gandhi. Unlike most of their male counterparts, and irrespective of whether we agree with their politics or not, leaders like Jayalalithaa, Mayawati and Mamata Banerjee who have emerged over the last three decades are self-made. And it is not just in the field of politics. Take corporate India as well. In recent years many of the large financial institutions and banks, both in the private and public sector, have been led by women CEOs, a record that is globally unprecedented.

It would be easy to conclude that women in India enjoy an exalted status of respect and equality. But this is far from the truth. There is a wide gulf in the power, esteem and respect that women deities in the Hindu pantheon and a few women in different walks of public life enjoy and what an average girl or woman has to endure through her life. The life of an average girl or woman in India is very different; it is one of drudgery, back breaking hard work, relentless discrimination and a continuous cycle of violence and abuse. An average woman in India is not worshipped, she is beaten and subjugated; she is not empowered, but disenfranchised

1

and discriminated against. This cycle of discrimination, violence and abuse starts even before birth.

But this cycle is changing and breaking down for good. We are at the cusp of a once-in-a-lifetime change. What is increasingly evident is the rise of woman power in India as women get more educated, better informed, more empowered and traditional barriers collapse to give them near equal, if not equal, opportunities. Increasingly one sees and hears of women taking up formal corporate roles in managerial and technical positions as against traditional jobs like teachers and office assistants. This change has been long overdue.

This multi-decadal, once-in-a-lifetime change I believe is an incredibly powerful trend with wide ranging implications over the next decade due to the sheer size of the opportunity. India is home to 586 million women, just over 17 per cent of the world's total number of women. India is also home to 173 million young women below the age of fifteen, which is about 20 per cent of the world's young women.[1] So the developments and changes in the lives of women, socially and economically, are of import not only to India but to the world at large.

Below the age of twenty-five years, just over 270 million girls and women account for 47 per cent of India's youth and education, economic development and empowerment of women is necessary to reap the benefits of demographic dividend. If India is to realize its demographic dividend then it is imperative that the gender schism is reduced. Some studies estimate that if the workforce participation of women and men becomes level in India then India's GDP will rise by 27 per cent.[2] The World Bank's World Development Report (2012) says, 'Gender equality is a core development objective in its own right. It is also smart economics. Greater gender equality can enhance productivity, improve

---

[1]Available at: http://en.worldstat.info/; World and Population Reference Bureau (www.prb.org).

[2]Booz & Co., (2012), *Empowering the Third Billion: Women and the World of Work.*

development outcomes for the next generation, and make institutions more representative.'

This is work in progress. Meanwhile, there are many gaps. Participation of women in the workforce in India is very low at 29 per cent, as against 51 per cent in the world and 81 per cent for men in India.[3] Literacy levels for women in India are only 65.5 per cent as against 82.1 per cent for men.[4] Not surprisingly, but certainly disappointingly, is India's ranking in the Global Gender Gap Index 2012, which is a low 105 out of 135 countries[5] and is among the worst in the world. The Third Billion Index developed by Booz & Co, ranked India 115 out of 128 countries.[6] At every level in society, India is characterized by gender biases, gender stereotypes and widespread crime and violence against women. This was brought to the fore in December 2012.

The abduction, brutal rape and subsequent death of Nirbhaya in December 2012 in the heart of the capital of India shocked and shook the conscience of the entire country and brought global spotlight on the issues of gender violence and women's safety in India. Nirbhaya would have remained just another statistic, one of the sixty-eight girls who get raped every day, but for the gruesomeness of the rapists and the young age of one of them. In 2012, the number of rapes reported indicated that sixty-eight girls and women were being raped every day—2.85 rapes every hour. Nirbhaya's brutal rape happened at a time when the country was frustrated with slowing economic growth and rising corruption and the anger of a seemingly impotent nation seething with rage against the

---

[3]The World Bank, (2013), *The Little Data Book of Gender*.

[4]Census of India, (2011), Provisional Population Totals, Dr C. Chandramouli of the Indian Administrative Service, Registrar General & Census Commissioner, India, 2011. Government of India.

[5]World Economic Forum, (2012), *The Global Gender Gap Report*.

[6]Booz & Co., (2012), *Empowering the Third Billion: Women and the World of Work*. The Third Billion Index ranks countries in terms of their effectiveness in empowering women as economic agents in the marketplace.

system and the ruling elites burst out on to the streets of Delhi and in different parts of the country.

Of the many paradoxes that abound in India, one is the status of women in society. In the Hindu pantheon of gods, there are many goddesses and often *shakti* or power is represented by women. Even the gods of wealth and learning—Lakshmi and Saraswati—are women. It is paradoxical that India was the second country in the world to have a democratically elected woman leader as the head of the government in Indira Gandhi, even as the suppression of women's voices and the unrelenting cycle of gender-based violence garners headlines. Violence against women starting from the womb is very high and high female foeticide is leading to severe gender imbalances.

The adverse gender ratio at the state and country levels is usually blamed on the economic costs of bringing up a daughter. First, is the high cost of marriage because of the practice of giving dowry. In many states marriage expenses can be crippling for a girl's family and unfortunately the practice of giving dowry endures till this day in many states and communities, although it is illegal. Apart from dowry, there is also the issue of division of property if girls demand their share of the family property. Second, it is believed, in many cases erroneously, that sons will take care of their parents in their old age whereas daughters will be married off; hence, it is worthwhile to equip sons with education in preference to daughters and thus improve the future earning potential of sons.

But it is interesting to note that the so-called economic costs cannot be the only reason for this skewed gender ratio. Otherwise how does one explain the differences in gender ratio patterns in states like Bihar and Andhra Pradesh on the one hand and states like Haryana, Rajasthan and Maharashtra on the other, as the practice of dowry is prevalent in all these states. And then there is a state like Gujarat where the practice of dowry is less prevalent but the gender ratio is still poor.

Society it seems is horribly schizophrenic with double standards and this is not a recent development. Look at Indian mythology for instance. Lord Rama, who is considered as the embodiment of an ideal man (*maryada purushottam Rama*) disfigures Surpanakha because she expresses her love and desire for him, a married man, even though it was very normal for a king to have many wives, including Lord Rama's father who had three. While Rama was perfectly within his rights to spurn the advances of Surpanakha, did he really have a right to physically disfigure her? And then his treatment of Sita—guided by the whims and fancies and the complaints of one of his subjects, he had Sita undergo tests to prove her fidelity. This is undesirable and not worthy of an ideal man in today's context. I have used the words 'Indian mythology' and 'Hindu mythology' interchangeably. While it is true that the treatment of the feminine and women in many religions and ancient societies leaves much to be desired and remains regressive by today's standards, I have given a few examples from Hindu mythology because it is the dominant religion of the people of India.

Then there is the image of the ideal Indian woman or *adarsh bhartiya naari*, who is pure and virginal and does not stray or express her desires and feelings in public and mostly not even at home. Her feelings and desires are subservient to those of her father, brother, husband, in-laws, uncles and sundry male relations. She is usually never the vamp, although temptresses abound in Indian mythology and the villainous mother-in-law or step-mother is a staple in mythology and in popular culture like films and TV serials. As a result vamps in Indian films or the extras dancing to item numbers in skimpy clothes are depicted with fair skin and blonde hair. I mention Hindi films because they are a good barometer of Indian society. But why only films? The cheerleaders in the Indian Premier League are all, barring none, western or Caucasian white-skinned girls. How can Indian girls be cheerleaders wearing skimpy clothes and gyrating to loud music? These cheerleaders clearly work well with a largely male audience that is obsessed with fair skin.

In that 'glorious' tradition of our largely patriarchal society, which seeks to maintain the Indian culture and 'protect' the honour of the ideal Indian woman, the only publicly acknowledged porn movie star in India is also an import—Sunny Leone. Sunny Leone is her stage name and her real name is Karanjit Kaur Vohra, a lady of Indian descent, born in Canada who starred in American porn films before coming to India to search for her fortunes in the Hindi film industry. In a similar vein, India's biggest home grown porn star is Savita bhabhi (sister-in-law), a cartoon character. At the same time, millions of women and children in India are estimated to be victims of human trafficking, although no reliable estimates are available and only a few thousand official complaints are recorded every year. I am not sure whether we are schizophrenic or plain hypocritical or both.

This paradox can be seen elsewhere as well. More recently, India became one of the very few countries where women decisively broke the glass ceiling in the corporate world, primarily in financial services. None of these women leaders in financial services have inherited family businesses; they have all risen up the rungs of the corporate ladder from scratch in an industry which is globally dominated by alpha males. A global fund manager's remark in this context is pertinent. When I was telling him about my research, he told me that in his experience of analysing global financial companies, he found ICICI Bank to be the most gender friendly financial services company in the world. How did this happen?

In a country with strong religious and cultural traditions, the winds of change can be seen in the way some traditions are subtly changing. Karva Chauth is a festival which is primarily a tradition in north India but now with the media hype and frenzy that accompanies it, it is virtually an all-India festival. During Karva Chauth, a married woman fasts the whole day for the well-being and good health of her husband and has her first morsel of food and first sip of water of the day only after spotting the moon. Going by social media, many of my friends, rather people like us, find this tradition regressive. While women adhere to this tradition and smart marketers have ensured that husbands buy lavish gifts and organize massive parties, slowly many husbands too have started fasting in sympathy with their wives. Gender equality, Indian style.

I have thought about these issues over a period of time. The idea of this book was born as I travelled through India over the last many years in my job as an equity research analyst. The changes that I witnessed, intrigued and fascinated me. In the last two or three years, I started asking questions on the changing lives of girls and women in India and their potential socio-economic impact. Was there a real change taking place? Were women feeling more empowered? To me the answer was YES, in capital letters. At the same time there seems to have been an increase in violence and crime against girls and women, although we can keep debating whether the increase is due to better disclosure and reporting now than earlier.

There are multiple drivers of this change and foremost among them is education. There is a fair amount of economic research on how the education of girls and their participation in the workforce in larger numbers influences the socio-economic fortunes of a society and a country for the better. Much of this research, however, is focused on the developed economies and the tiger economies of Asia.

There is some work that I came across, which focuses on the impact of this trend on the Indian economy. But I have not come across any book or research that tells the story of the young girls today and how their lives are very different from their mothers' and their grandmothers' lives. I wanted to put faces to the names and tell the stories of these girls, their aspirations, their disappointments, their expectations, their struggles and the challenges that they face. These are girls from all segments of the socio-economic pyramid. I wanted to understand what or who was driving these changes, who were the role models for these girls and how was their immediate and larger society reacting to this rise of woman power and then tie the common threads from these stories to speak about the socio-economic implications of the same for India.

I am no economist and hence rely on the economic research done so far to take forward some of my arguments and clearly there is scope for a lot more research to be done on this subject going forward. There were two questions that I asked myself as I mulled over the idea of the book:

The changes and trends that I planned to write about, were they really new? Or was I just late in discovering them?

Who would read this book? Who would I like to see reading this book?

Rising education and increased participation by women in the workforce in corporate India is a trend that has been recognizable for some time. But for most part of the decade of the 1990s or even later it was a very urban metro-centric phenomena, possibly limited to a few big cities, particularly when it came to being employed or having a career. My sense was that led by the media, technology and various other changes that I will discuss later, we have reached a tipping point. Hence, the time was ripe to try and study this phenomenon and chronicle the changes, the change drivers and their implications.

The subject matter of this book was of interest to me and while there have been profiles and stories of the successes of young girls and women in the media I have not seen any major article or book on the subject. This interested me immensely and I was passionate enough to dream of writing this book.

I realize that this generation of girls is far more confident than their parents, not just in large cities, not just among middle class and affluent families, but pretty much across socio-economic strata and across the country. In 2009, along with my colleague Srini, I travelled nearly 22,000 kms across the country over a period of two months and I wrote:

> Although parents are more focused than ever on ensuring a good education for their children, including their daughters, they seem to be increasingly content to let their kids pursue their own dreams...Also encouraging is evidence of women increasingly going out to work, even in small-town India. This will be a major change driver as women become economically empowered and better educated...Throughout my journey of discovery across India, I realized time and again that it remains a country of

paradoxes. Any generalization is fraught with risk. In a region (the northern belt) notorious for female foeticide and infanticide, skewed sex ratios and high dowry demands, I didn't expect to hear people talk excitedly about educating their daughters, irrespective of their financial situation. Maybe things are changing for the better.[7]

My intention is to chronicle the changes as they are unfolding primarily through the voices of young girls and women across the country. The voices are important because numbers never tell the full story. At the same time the idea behind speaking to these young girls and women at random is to identify the change drivers in their own voices and also to understand the challenges that they face as they look towards a future that is different and in most ways better than what their mothers and grandmothers endured.

The first chapter starts by looking at women whose dreams were snuffed out at an early age or they never grew wings; and it lays the base to study and contrast with what is happening with today's generation. In the second and third chapters I look at the stories of girls of this generation from urban and rural areas—primarily from socio-economically challenged or middle class backgrounds to understand their goals, desires, role models, ambitions and how they are continuously overcoming challenges and discrimination.

In the fourth chapter I look at the change drivers. At every stage based on my interviews with the girls, I try to co-relate my conclusions or hypotheses with facts and data or research that have already been done. The fifth and sixth chapters take a look at how society is changing, where it is stagnant, what society's reaction is to the changes that are occurring and how these are reflected in films, TV serials and advertisements.

The seventh chapter discusses the dark or not so positive side of the changes that are taking place and tries to find answers to questions like whether the scourge of female foeticide is reducing

[7]Anirudha Dutta and Srinivas Radhakrishnan, (April 2009), *On the Road: India's people, power, politics and places.* CLSA Asia-Pacific Markets.

with education and prosperity? Are violence and discrimination against women reducing? Is trafficking of young women for marriage on the rise? In the eighth chapter I discuss the role of the government and NGOs, especially the role of grassroot NGOs and the importance of the role they are playing in this churn that is taking place in society.

In the ninth chapter I discuss the impact points, primarily from the economic viewpoint, of the changes and what boys and men need to learn and probably unlearn as they confront and live the changes that are taking place around them.

Even as I watched these changes unfold in front of my eyes during my travels, I was intrigued by not just the change drivers but also by how men were reacting to the changes and how old prejudices were being discarded: was the support or lack thereof for the girls from within the family and if so from whom, what kind of jobs did these girls want, would they compromise their morality to get ahead in life, what role, if any, were NGOs playing in these changes? The answers to these questions would not be available without speaking to the protagonists.

This is not my story, although some of the people featured in this book are related and/or well known to me. It is the story of the people I met and interviewed and hence, I preferred to write this book with lots of direct quotes. Given the nature of the conversations, sometimes the same subject does find mention in more than one chapter. Similarly the issue of violence against women has many different dimensions and layers to it, from gender-selective abortions to rape; these have, in some cases, been discussed in different chapters. Trying to compartmentalize in strict silos or any attempts to avoid any repetition of some subjects like violence, discrimination, role models and education would have spoilt the spontaneity of the conversations that I had with the girls featured in this book and disturbed the natural flow. I hope the reader indulges my style and approach here. It was a roller coaster emotional journey to listen to real life stories and I hope I have been able to capture part of this as I tell the stories. Some of it may have been lost in translation since the interviews were conducted in multiple languages, primarily Hindi, English and Bangla and were often interspersed with a smattering of the local dialect in Marathi, Gujarati, Bhojpuri, Maithili or Urdu.

I hope and dream that the stories of the girls in this book inspire other girls to follow their dreams, to challenge the status quo and make their lives better and more meaningful. If it helps even a few girls, I would say 'mission accomplished'. Last but not the least, boys and men should think about the changes and the likely new norms and make the best of them and be true sensitive partners of women in society's progress. Deep socio-cultural beliefs and practices will have to change for India to become a better country for girls and women.

As half a billion girls and women in India rise, it is a huge opportunity for corporates and various service providers. Imagine the boost to GDP and consumption when a few hundred million qualified and skilled women enter the workforce over a decade, the same women who are sitting out today. Every research house, every company and every institution should have an interest in the subject. I am sure many are already looking at the changes and the opportunities and challenges for them and I hope they find something useful in this book.

In today's world where self-publishing is quite common, I could have written to indulge my passion and follow my dreams. But I want the book to be read by a large audience because I hope it can help in the change process and also encourage more research and a better understanding of the underlying opportunities and challenges. I hope this is the starting point of a dialogue between various stakeholders like NGOs, social entrepreneurs, government officials, academic institutions, politicians, researchers, corporates and media on how to help drive the change and how to handle its implications, both good and bad.

Some of the changes and impact points can be anticipated, as I have tried and anticipated in this book. But I am equally certain that there will be impact points that I will miss and there will be surprises. As Tina, my co-interviewer/researcher in some of the interviews, remarked during one of our discussions, 'Indian mothers will have to start training their sons to change nappies.' Yes, Indian mothers who have coddled their sons for too long will have to start training their sons for a lot more than just changing nappies.

I hope the reader, who has been brash enough with his or her purse, to paraphrase Vikram Seth, will enjoy reading this book, will find something new and come to share some of the excitement and passion that I felt as I researched and wrote it. If nothing else, be assured that the money spent will go to a good cause since any royalty earned from the sale of this book will go to two deserving NGOs, Parivaar in Kolkata and Vidya & Child in Noida. Let the journey commence.

*

BAS, SAB KHATAM HO GAYA—IT'S ALL OVER

Chandra was born in...well she is not sure, but most likely it was in 1940. She was born on Pataldanga Street, a crowded dingy narrow lane in north Kolkata, where the azure sky is hardly visible thanks to the not very tall but very densely packed buildings that look like pencils. It was possibly a cold January day in Calcutta (now Kolkata), as it usually is at that time of the year. In 1940 the world was in turmoil and the German war machine was advancing; closer home the independence movement was gaining momentum. These thoughts, however, were far away from Debendra Kumar De's mind, an overseer (weaving master) at the Premchand Jute Mill. At his home was born his third daughter, Chandra. He would have one more daughter before the mandatory son was born a few years later.

Chandra's initial years were spent in Chengail, a small town a couple of hours from Calcutta. Chengail is one of those nondescript towns on the Kolkata-Kharagpur route between Nalpur and Uluberia, indistinguishable from any of the other few dozen stations along the route. This is where Chandra spent her early childhood. Her earliest memories are of a tutor coming home to teach the three sisters since Chengail did not have any schools. The nearest school was in Uluberia, which was two train stops away and girls were not allowed to travel 'that far'. Those days there were restrictions on travel from home especially for girls. By all accounts Chandra's family was a reasonably well-to-do middle class one and they lived in a comfortable bungalow with a small garden in the front. Maybe colourful flowers grew there in the winter as this entire region is quite fertile.

When Chandra was in Class V, she and her elder sister moved to Calcutta to stay in their maternal uncle's house on Pataldanga Street to continue their education. In her words, 'We took admission in Mitra Institution Balika Vidyalaya and studied there till Class IX. The school had opened that year.' According to Chandra, Debendra De had acquiesced to the move because Chandra was good in studies. Chandra was also good in music and arts and had a knack for both and like in most Bengali families there was reasonable encouragement to pursue these interests.

Then her father changed his job and joined Prabartak Jute Mill in Kamarhati. Kamarhati is a separate municipality situated outside the limits of the Kolkata Municipal Corporation at the northern fringes of the city on the banks of River Ganga. Today it is a very crowded extension of the city with residential houses jostling with small and dilapidated industrial units. It reflects the overall industrial degradation of the city and the state. Open sewers, a strong smell of cooking, smoky and run down industrial units, garbage dumps by the roadside and open fish and vegetable markets give a very depressed feeling to an outsider. Middle class residential neighbourhoods and private schools have also cropped up alongside. There are only imaginary boundaries between the two as cycle rickshaws, cars and two-wheelers create an unimaginable cacophony. If one can picture that area without the haphazard cheek by jowl construction and the dirt and filth spilling over from overcrowded shanties and small industrial units, it is possible to picture a pretty idyllic rural suburb overlooking the Ganges with boats ferrying passengers to and fro with its banks fronted by coconut trees and banana plantations.

Chandra moved back with her parents and appeared for her Class X board exams privately. This was around the time when her eldest sister got married. Soon thereafter her father fell seriously ill; he was to be operated for haemorrhoids but later the doctors diagnosed it as cancer. Meanwhile Chandra was informed by the board that her geography answer paper had been lost and she had to sit for a re-exam which she did on 6 June 1959 and the same night her father passed away. '*Bas, shob shesh hoye geylo* (It was all over; everything was finished),' she told me more than half a century later as we sat talking in her house in Ariadaha, which could not have been too far away from her father's then residence in Kamarhati. When we met she was dressed in a customary red bordered cream coloured saree and had the red, white and iron bangles on her wrist, the kind that Bengali married women wear. Her strong jawline spoke of her steely determination, but she is a frail lady today battling numerous illnesses and scars from the decades gone by.

For Chandra, the world as she knew ended when her father died an untimely death. Even after fifty-four years, she breaks down as she talks about her father's death and how it changed the course of her future. Her father died in June and her marriage was solemnized in December the same year without waiting for the mandatory twelve-month period of mourning when usually no auspicious events are held in a Hindu family. 'A mother's friend brought the marriage proposal and therefore, no one ever looked at either the boy or his family and the marriage was fixed.' Chandra was just over the legal age of eighteen when she got married.

What happened to her Class X results? The geography paper?

'I don't know. No one bothered to find out my results. If my father had been alive, our studies would have continued. But my mother's side of the family was very conservative.'

No one could be bothered about the studies or results of a 19-year-old whose father had just passed away, certainly not if she was a girl and if her family was conservative. Her mother's side of the family was not only conservative but like most Indian (or I should say Asian) families valued boys more than girls. Chandra's son remembers how when they visited his dida's (maternal grandmother) house, he was showered with praise and gifts whereas his sisters were berated or had barbs directed at them. One of the barbs would go something like this: '*Chele ra hochche sonar chanda, meye ra hochche kaadar dhela*'. Loosely translated it means, boys are like gold coins and girls are like a lump of clay. Looking back Chandra's son feels that some of this may have been said in jest, but surely it had some negative impact on his sisters and cousins. At that young impressionable age, he actually believed that he was superior to his sisters and cousins! Gender stereotyping and discrimination in a typical Indian family starts early.

Within two or three years of Chandra's marriage, her youngest sister was also married. This was a very different India. Overall literacy level during the first Census in 1951 was 18.33 per cent and among women it was a much lower 8.86 per cent;[8] average life expectancy for Indians in 1951 was thirty-one years.[9] Marriages happened at a very early age and child marriages were fairly common. To address this social issue, in 1929 the Child Marriage Restraint Act[10] was introduced and it became law on 1 April 1930. However, child marriages remained fairly commonplace even after that and children, including boys, had no say in their marriage and often met their spouse only during the marriage ceremony. In 2006, the government brought in the Prohibition of Child Marriage Act[11] to address the shortcomings of the Child Marriage Restraint Act and also to focus on prevention and prohibition rather than on restraining child marriages.

Have the laws helped? Going by anecdotal evidence they most certainly have. Enforcement of the laws and education too has

---

[8]Literacy level during the first Census (1951): Dr C. Chandramouli, *Provisional Population Totals* (Paper 1 of 2011, India Series 1), Statement 20—Literacy rate in India 1951–2011.

[9]I found various numbers ranging from twenty-nine to thirty-seven for life expectancy in 1951. Average life expectancy at birth for men and women in India is now 66.7 and 69.1 years (the World Factbook, CIA).

[10]Child Marriage Restraint Act (1930), Ruchira Goswami, (2010), 'Child Marriage in India: Mapping the Trajectory of Legal Reforms', available at: http://sanhati.com/excerpted/2207/.

[11]Prohibition of Child Marriage Act (2006), Government of India: Ministry of Women and Child Development; UNICEF, 'The Prohibition of Child Marriage Act, 2006,' available at: http://www.unicef.org/india/Child_Marriage_handbook.pdf.

helped. Equally importantly social consciousness against child marriages has grown, but the problem has not yet been eradicated. Incidences of child marriages have come down but still continue to be very high. While the problem of child marriages is not limited to India, it is certainly most widespread with an estimated 40 per cent of child marriages in the world taking place here. A study estimates that 39,000 child marriages[12] take place in India every day. Today India ranks a low thirteenth in the world in child marriages, with 47 per cent of the girls getting married before the age of eighteen years.[13]

At that young age neither the boy nor the girl are mature enough to know their rights, duties and responsibilities. Young brides are particularly vulnerable with devastating consequences in terms of maternal mortality, fertility outcomes, domestic violence and infant health and well-being. Pregnancy related deaths are a major cause of mortality in young married girls in the 15–19 years age group[14] and they are twice as likely to die during childbirth as compared to girls in the 20–24 years age bracket. Girls below fifteen are five times as likely to die in childbirth.[15] Young illiterate or semi-literate girls are more likely to experience domestic violence and harassment and have virtually no empowerment within their family circles.

Chandra faced a lot of harassment at her in-laws place after her marriage. A young fatherless girl had to bear the taunts and harassment with fortitude. In the first year of her marriage, her husband was hundreds of miles away from the joint family. Even if he had been living with Chandra, it is doubtful how much he

---

[12]Number of Child Marriages in India: 'The Curse of Child Marriage', Socialscribblers (21 June 2013).

[13]United Nations, available at: http://www.icrw.org/child-marriage-facts-and-figures.

[14]Childinfo, (2009), 'Statistics by Area—Child Marriage', UNICEF, available at: http://www.childinfo.org/marriage.html.

[15]International Center for Research on Women, 'Child Marriage Facts and Figures', available at: http://www.icrw.org/child-marriage-facts-and-figures.

would have been able to help, even if he wanted to, given the deferential treatment to family elders in Indian families. Chandra had to do all the household work—cooking, washing etc. for a joint family of over ten members. The rest of her life has also been spent in cooking, cleaning, sewing, taking care of her husband and bringing up her three children. Nobody ever asked her what she wanted and what she liked. In her words, 'I was quite good in music and drawing. So who knows what I would have pursued if fate had willed otherwise.' Her dreams died young and later in life she tried to live her dreams through her children. She fought for their interests and well-being fiercely, particularly those of her son and younger daughter and it resulted in her son and younger daughter doing well professionally.

However, in the twilight of her life bitterness at her own fate has multiplied manifold. It increased as her health faltered from years of backbreaking work. She often rants against the cards that fate dealt her and her object of ire varies from her mother, and her family members, to her husband and her in-laws. She has found solace and anchor in religion and has become a devout person. As the empty nest syndrome hit her, she found sanctuary in gods, goddesses, temples and rituals. Loneliness at home has been replaced by friends made in the temples and ashrams that she frequents.

This is the life of millions of women in India—undereducated, disempowered and exploited; machines to cook, sew, wash clothes and utensils and produce children. A tiny minority have led different lives and a majority of them came from well-off or upper middle class backgrounds and families that were enlightened. Like Chandra, Daksha's mother is not one of this tiny minority.

Daksha lives in Bhavnagar, a small sleepy town on the coast of Gujarat. I was visiting Shaishav, a NGO that works with slum children in after-school hours. On a cool February morning I landed in Bhavnagar along with my friend Satindra after a very early morning flight from Mumbai. Parulji, the co-founder of Shaishav, had come to pick us up at the airport in an auto-rickshaw; for most parts the ride to the Shaishav office was bumpy along half paved roads or roads that had huge speed breakers. Initially after leaving the airport we passed through what were wetlands—large stretches of nothing. The landscape told us that we were not far from the coast. As we entered the city, the roads were decent and wide, but the town was dusty like most small Indian towns and cities; the old jostled with the new and traffic was chaotic.

The same evening I met Daksha for the first time as a part of a session that Satindra was holding for Shaishav's employees. It must have been a group of 15-20 youngsters and Daksha clearly stood out. Daksha had a nice round face, dark in complexion, but it was her eyes, bright with a twinkle in them, and her sing-song voice which held my attention. She was among the most articulate and exuded a confidence which was refreshing. She didn't hesitate even once to articulate her viewpoint and often broke into a bright smile or loud laughter at what she said. She exhibited a curiosity, thirst for knowledge and confidence as she asked us questions. I decided then that I had to speak to Daksha because she was different; she was unmistakably bright. Not just Daksha but a few of the other girls too were far more articulate and confident than the boys in the group. As the meeting ended, Satindra echoed my thoughts and we discussed how we were seeing this in different spheres of life—girls were invariably performing better than their male counterparts.

The next day when I visited Daksha's house I met her mother and her grandmother. Daksha was twenty years old and her mother was most likely in her forties, but she appeared much older. She was corpulent and her head was covered with one end of the saree as she sat on the floor playing with her grandson and listening to my conversation with Daksha. Once in a while she added something to what Daksha had said. The grandmother wore thick prescription glasses, kept her head covered in the traditional manner and didn't speak a word during my entire visit, quite possibly because she may have been hard of hearing or more likely because she had rarely spoken to an outsider in her life.

Daksha's mother didn't remember the age when she got married, probably fourteen or fifteen, maybe even younger. She had given birth to eight children of which five had died. High child mortality, particularly among poor and rural families, means that families typically want to produce more children so that at least a few will survive. Often more children are also produced if the first few are daughters. Contraception or family planning is rarely practiced and women certainly have no say in that matter. Daksha's mother wanted to get herself sterilized but her mother-in-law would not hear of it till a son was born. Forget about Daksha's mother, even her father had no say in the family planning decision. When she told me the story, Daksha's mother pointed to her mother-in-law and had no hesitation in blaming her in front of a complete stranger. Clearly age, her own children growing up and the ageing of her mother-in-law had given voice to Daksha's mother.

Daksha's mother is not an exception in the pressures that she faced from her mother-in-law. Abhijit Banerjee and Esther Duflo, economists at MIT, write, 'Their (poor people) fertility decisions are the product of a choice...At the same time, what leads them to make these choices maybe in part factors that are outside their immediate control: women, in particular, maybe pressured by their husbands, their mothers-in-law, or social norms to bear more children than they would like.'[16]

I asked Daksha about her mother's life. Did she speak to her about her childhood and her early days of marriage? 'My mother sometimes tells me stories of her life till late in the night when everyone is asleep. And whatever happens in my life, I tell my mother—sometimes till 2 or 3 a.m. She tells me that she was married at a very young age. And she hadn't ever done any household work before marriage. But after marriage lots of responsibilities fell on her and she had to even start cooking. She tells me a lot of stories about her in-laws. For ten years she was tortured a lot. That is one of the reasons why I don't want to get married. When my mother was young, she was brought up by her mama (maternal

---

[16]Abhijit V Banerjee and Esther Duflo, (2011), *Poor Economics: A Radical Rethinking of the Way to fight global Poverty*, pp. 118–19 (First Edition).

uncle who was in the police) since they did not have any children. She was kept like a princess. She says her childhood was more luxurious than mine. Her life was very good till her marriage.'

Every young woman looks forward to her marriage, relationships and a home of her own; so does every young man. But listening to their mothers' life stories and seeing what happens around them, many young girls also say what Daksha told me matter of factly, 'If I can exercise my choice, I will never get married.'

I worry about a very different issue. Will Daksha find a husband from her immediate community who will be of similar calibre, have similar ambitions and a similar worldview—someone who will be able to be her partner, if not equal at least substantially so? This is an issue that is confronting even girls from upper middle class and affluent sections of society as I gathered during my research.

Daksha's mother's life was very good till her marriage. Daksha's mother and Chandra are separated not only by thousands of miles but they also belong to two different generations, from two different socio-economic strata, but their life experiences are not very different. The only difference is that Chandra never worked outside her home, whereas Daksha's mother had worked for twenty-three years. Poor economic conditions and her husband's ill-health meant that she was a bread winner for the family, although not the sole bread winner. She worked in a local school as a cleaner and her job involved sweeping the premises, every single day for the last twenty-three years. She left home very early in the morning and was back in the afternoon to complete her chores at home. Mesmerized as I was by her story, I completely forgot to ask her name. To me she remains Daksha's mother.

What struck me during my conversation with Chandra and Daksha's mother was how feisty both women were when they discussed their daughters and what they wanted for them. While Chandra is literate, Daksha's mother is not, but both put a very high premium on education and economic independence for their daughters. Daksha will pursue a career come what may and Chandra's younger daughter already has a very successful corporate career spanning different countries under her belt. If the lives of young girls and women over the next ten and twenty years is going to be any different from their mothers, then it will be because of education, economic independence and the resultant empowerment. When this happens, there will be an additional dimension to the India story which is still under-appreciated and little understood. Nearly 49 per cent of India's 1.27 billion people[17] are women; 47 per cent of India's population is under twenty-five years of age and of this 47 per cent are girls.[18] The number of girls under twenty-five years of age is 270 million, which is more than the population of UK. As per the sixty-eighth round of NSSO survey the labour force participation rate (LFPR)[19] for women in India is only 23 per cent, while the comparable number for men is 56 per cent.[20] If this 47 per cent of the population becomes better educated and economically empowered, then the socio-economic implications for India will be huge. When a significant part of this potential workforce is brought into economic activity, then India's productivity and output will both receive a significant boost.

About America, billionaire investor and philanthropist Warren Buffett says:

> It has to do with America's future, about which—here's a familiar opinion from me—I'm an unqualified optimist. Now entertain another opinion of mine: Women are a major reason we will do so well. Start with the fact that our country's progress since 1776 has been mind-blowing, like nothing the world has ever seen. Our secret sauce has been a political and economic system that unleashes human potential to an extraordinary degree. As a

---

[17]Census, (2011).

[18]Census, (2011).

[19]LFPR: Labour force participation rate is the proportion of the population aged fifteen and older that is economically active: all people who supply labour for the production of goods and services during a specified period.

[20]Sixty-eighth round NSSO Survey, Key Indicators of Employment and Unemployment in India, 2011-12, available at: http://pib.nic.in/newsite/erelease.aspx?relid=96641.

result Americans today enjoy an abundance of goods and services that no one could have dreamed of just a few centuries ago.

But that's not the half of it—or, rather, it's just about the half of it. America has forged this success while utilizing, in large part, only half of the country's talent. For most of our history, women—whatever their abilities—have been relegated to the sidelines. Only in recent years have we begun to correct that problem.[21]

We can replace USA with India and 1776 with 1947 and the statements will be as valid. America is far ahead in women's participation in the workforce and women's empowerment. In 2012 in the US, women's share in wage employment in the non-agricultural sector was 48 per cent and the female adult unemployment rate was 9 per cent.[22] In the Gender Gap Index, USA was twenty-two out of 135 countries. In educational attainment it was number 1, in economic participation number eight, but in political empowerment it was only at fifty-five. In comparison, in India women's share in wage employment in the non-agricultural sector was only 18 per cent. Its rank in the Gender Gap Index was a low 105 out of 135 countries and the only area where it scored well was a rank of seventeen in political empowerment.[23] The high rank in political empowerment is justified given the success that women have achieved at all levels in politics starting from the national level to the panchayat at the village level. The success at the village level has also been aided by affirmative action policies.

I believe that things have started changing in India. This change is all set to accelerate over the next decade and its socio-economic impact will be significant and felt all around. Most of this change will be for the better; and then there will be some consequences that will be for the worse in the near term as the existing power structures of a patriarchal society feel threatened and are challenged.

---

[21]*Fortune Magazine*, available at: http://money.cnn.com/2013/05/02/leadership/ warren-buffett-women.pr.fortune/.

[22]World Economic Forum, (2012), *The Global Gender Gap Report 2012*.

[23]Ibid.

It seems ironical that when I started interviewing young girls and women from across the country on their education, empowerment and dreams, it was in the immediate aftermath of the brutal rape and subsequent death of the 23-year-old physiotherapy intern in New Delhi. In some ways it is possible to understand how part of the violence perpetrated on women and girls is a reaction of a patriarchal male dominated society to the challenges thrown by girls and women, their covert and overt demands for changes in the status quo and the exposure of these men to a world far removed from their reality through various forms of the media. These are not the only reasons—and this is not to justify in any way what happened on that fateful night—but I believe these are some of the reasons for part of the violence that we are witnessing.

Reading everyday stories of violence, rape and killings of girls and women, I was briefly assailed with doubts whether things are indeed changing. But the more I travelled and the more I interviewed girls across the country, the more convinced I was that a monumental change is underway. The change did not start yesterday and it will not end tomorrow. The fact remains that the place and role of women in our society has been changing over a period of time but earlier it was changing very slowly. I believe that the pace of change has accelerated over the last few years and it has moved beyond cities and large towns to smaller towns and villages; the change today is also cutting across socio-economic strata.

The physiotherapy intern dubbed variously as Damini, Nirbhaya, Amanat and the Delhi Braveheart by the media represented this change. She was probably the first woman in her family who had graduated and was looking forward to a career in an academic institution or with a corporate. Damini's parents hailed from a small village in Ballia, Uttar Pradesh, the largest state in India and lived in Delhi. Her father worked as a loader and sold his ancestral agricultural land to educate his daughter. She was on her way home after watching a movie with her friend, a software engineer. She went to a movie with a boy who was not related to her by birth or marriage. Damini's education and independence must have been a giant leap for her and her family and she was a role model in the commune of daily wage labourers in Delhi where the family lived.

Role models both inside and outside homes are very critical. In meeting after meeting I realized the importance of the right role models. I was rudely reminded of this in a village in Karjat, about a three hour drive from Mumbai, in Maharashtra. I was in my car, being driven, and as usual I was fiddling with my phone. Suddenly I looked up and saw a man sitting on a motorcycle at a distance, pulling the hair of a woman standing next to him and giving her a few slaps. The woman reeled under the impact. On getting slightly closer I saw that there were two children—one girl and one boy, around 8-10 years old sitting on the bike. The family, for it was a family, was dressed in fine clothes as this was a day after Diwali. By the time my car crossed the couple, a reconciliation was in progress, although the woman's body was raked by sobs.

The children were mute spectators. Consider the impact of what happened and if what happened on the road on that day frequently occurred in their home, as it may well have—the girl would grow up thinking that being beaten by her husband was normal, a part of the conjugal rights and probably women deserved it, while the boy would grow up thinking that he could beat his wife. It is not as strange as it sounds. Surveys have shown that 47 per cent women think that being beaten by their husbands is justified and acceptable.[24] According to the National Family Health Survey-3, 33 per cent of women in India in the age group of 15-49 years have experienced physical violence. On the other hand children brought up in households where women are treated as equals and with respect grow up believing that this is normal. The right role models are important not only for gender equality and gender sensitization but also in making correct and rational choices regarding education, career and personal lives.

---

[24]'Percentage of women who believe that wife beatings are justified', available at: http://www.childinfo.org/attitudes.html.

Damini's journey towards a professional career was not smooth.[25] From Class XI she started tutoring children to meet part of her education expenses. When she got into a college outside Delhi to study physiotherapy, she simultaneously worked in a call centre. She was clearly very hard working, ambitious and a dreamer. She dreamt big and saw her education as the passport for raising her family out of penury and towards financial stability.

Like Chandra, Damini's dreams died young. So did the dreams of her parents. But there are millions of Daminis living in India today—Daminis who are dreaming big, who are working hard and who are challenging the status quo. I want to chronicle the stories of some of those young girls and women and try to understand the socio-economic impact that it will have over the next decade. Chandra's struggles, Daksha's mother's struggles and Damini's untimely, unwarranted and brutal death cannot go in vain.

This book may never have been written but for serendipity. I remember about fifteen years back on a trip to Himachal Pradesh when I had walked down verdant slopes enraptured by the scenery around me till I reached a tiny village where a woman was working behind her house. Seeing an unknown man, she started shouting and waving and flailing her hands. While I could not understand her language, it was obvious that I was unwanted; the intrusion was certainly not welcome. I indicated the camera slung around my neck and requested her for one picture, which I was harshly refused and the woman covered her face immediately closing any prospects of any further requests.

However, in the last five or six years whenever I have travelled with my camera in tow, I have noticed a distinct change. In towns and villages, girls and women are no longer refusing to be photographed by a male stranger. They are in fact happy to pose—some would say brazenly—for my camera. This was a Eureka moment for me. I could also see other changes in behaviour and appearances.

---

[25]'Delhi gang rape victim's family remembers her as a dreamer', available at: http://indiatoday.intoday.in/story/delhi-gangrape-victim-village-ballia-remembers-her-as-a-dreamer-damini/1/241354.html.

In village after village any woman over forty was dressed traditionally in sarees and would have her head covered, if not her face; but anyone below that was experimenting with her clothes and could be seen frequently dressed in a salwar kameez. And anyone under fifteen was often dressed in denims or trousers and there was no question of covering her face. Many a times they were perfectly happy and comfortable to have a chat with a stranger.

I experienced this in villages in Madhya Pradesh, Gujarat, Maharashtra, Uttar Pradesh, Bihar, West Bengal, Tamil Nadu, Jammu & Kashmir, pretty much across the country. I mention villages specifically because they are the last bastions of conservative traditions. If these changes are taking place in villages, they must be happening in towns and cities at a much faster pace. I must mention an incident here. Priyanka, a girl I interviewed in Patna, Bihar took my cell phone number and started keeping in touch with me asking for career advice and introductions to people who could help her. At one level she was being brave in asking and also sharing her phone number with a virtual stranger, and at another level she was exhibiting a confidence that would be unimaginable even a decade earlier.

I remember that after India's economy was opened in the early 1990s, there were huge expectations of a consumer boom driven by the oft estimated middle class number somewhere between 100 to 200 million. Investments were made by consumer companies, primarily multinationals, on the back of those projections and forecasts. Most of those forecasts proved to be spurious. But then about a decade later—sometime in the early to middle part of the first decade of the new millennium—the India consumer story took off. Consultancies wrote paeans to the Indian consumer as did investment banks and brokerage houses as everything from car sales to motorcycles to diamond jewellery, art and international travel boomed.

What had changed in these ten years between 1995 and 2005? The Indian economy was certainly doing very well—in sync with the global economy. But the big change was that a new generation had come into the consuming class. This was a generation unfettered by decades of socialism and had not grown up in an economy chronically short of everything, where choices were few and far between. Instead it had grown up in a country which was increasingly inter-linked to the global economy, where information was available at the press of a button or a remote control or the click of a mouse. This generation's propensity to consume and take risks was unlike that of any other generation in India's independent history. Economic cycles can slow down growth rates, but the consumption trajectory will go only one way for a decade and more, and that is up. My friend Suprio calls this cohort of post-liberalization children 'responsible hedonists'.

A similar change with equally, if not more, far reaching impact will be witnessed as 49 per cent of the population starts participating in mainstream economic activities and becomes better educated and empowered; 20 per cent girls below the age of fifteen in the world are in India[26] and if nothing else, then this is a big enough reason to be interested in this megatrend of education, empowerment, aspirations and ambitions of young women in the second most populous nation on earth.

This is just the beginning of the journey, exciting, full of hope and some heart breaks along the way. The clock has started ticking and the tick tock will get louder by the day. There is no turning back now. Chandra and Daksha's mother's future generations will have it much better.

---

[26]Population Reference Bureau, 'The World's Women and Girls: 2011 Data Sheet', available at: http://www.prb.org/pdf11/world-women-girls-2011-data-sheet.pdf.

SIRF HARVARD HI JANA HAI—TO HARVARD, AND NOTHING LESS

'My name is Saira and I am fifteen years old. I study in Class IX in Aseema, which is a BMC (Brihanmumbai Municipal Corporation or Municipal Corporation of Greater Mumbai) school, but run by the NGO Aseema. It is located in Santacruz. My mummy is a housewife. My father is an auto-rickshaw driver. First he drove a car.' While saying the last sentence Saira started laughing at the incongruous thought of someone who drove a car coming down the ladder of automobiles to start driving an auto-rickshaw. I was meeting Saira at the American School in the Bandra Kurla Complex. She was small in appearance, her hair well oiled, neatly tied in a pony tail and she exuded oodles of self-confidence. She was certainly the best in spoken English among the kids from her background that I have met. After school she, along with other girls coming from different parts of Mumbai, attends a programme by the NGO Avasara called Leadership Academy, which is run from the premises of the American School.

Santacruz, where Saira lived, is a western suburb of Mumbai and one of the affluent suburbs popular with corporate types, those associated with the film and TV industry and well to do local businessmen. But dotted between the sky rises and bungalows are sprawling slums, part of the ecosystem that caters to the requirements of its affluent denizens. Saira lived in one of these slums with her parents and two brothers—eighteen and fourteen years old.

Saira started her studies in an Urdu medium school in Mumbai. Students from different age groups were herded into one classroom, with the older girls and boys getting benches to sit on and the younger kids sitting on the floor. From her description it seemed that the education was at least partially on religious matters. If they passed, they got a packet of rice but they were also often beaten for reasons they could not understand and were never told.

Then life changed for Saira. One of her aunts (father's sister) who worked for a NGO took her out of the Urdu school and put her into a residential school in Goa. Saira started learning English under good tutors and started flourishing academically. 'I started coming first. I stayed there for five years before moving back to Mumbai. I was twelve years old when I moved back to Mumbai.'

In Class VII her dad wanted her to stop her studies. Saira fought back and with her mother and aunt's support she got admission in the Aseema school. Saira's mother had studied till Class VII only and was married within two years of completing her studies. She must have been fifteen or sixteen then and Saira's father about twenty. Her aunt also studied till Class VII but one of her daughters has completed her graduation and her younger daughter is in Class XII.

I asked Saira what inspired her mother to support her when she, Saira, wanted to continue her school education. 'In my mom's generation they did not study much. But now we are studying more. My bua (father's sister) studied till VII but she wants her daughters to study a lot. My mother is also influenced by my aunt's daughters. She says that if they can do this (graduation) then you can also do it; but sometimes she does get influenced by people around her.' Saira added the last bit as an afterthought. This underscores the importance of right role models and the much needed grassroots intervention of NGOs almost continuously.

Saira wants to become a psychiatrist. Why psychiatry? 'Psychiatry is something related to mind. My chacha (dad's younger brother) is mad; any dispute or fight and he starts cutting himself. Yesterday he came and started cutting himself. I don't understand why he does this; I get scared. I heard from my madam that psychiatry is about the study of mind. I have seen this also on Discovery Channel.

For me there will be many opportunities to think about later; right now I am trying for the school scholarship.'

What are your ambitions and dreams?

'First I will buy one home for my mother; not for my dad. I mean my father will also stay if my mother comes. My mother is very sweet and easily influenced. So I will take care of her.'

Saira is ambitious. She is working hard and at the same time her dreams and aspirations are within the realms of reality. It is not surprising that the first thing that she wants to buy when she starts working is a home for her mother, to take her out of the slums. Even at her age, Saira is already more educated than a significant number of girls in her immediate vicinity and she knows how much the environment can influence choices. Hence she hates the gossiping that goes on among women in the neighbourhood for a large part of the day.

What do the women talk about and discuss?

'People in my area do not discuss anything useful in their leisure, not even politics; their thinking is very low, they just discuss about their sons and daughters. They try to influence my mother by saying do not educate your daughter and give the example of some girl who ran away with her boyfriend. If people are more educated their level of thinking will change.' Her mother's biggest worry is that Saira may fall in love and run away with some boy bringing 'dishonour' to the family. These fears are primarily fuelled by what her neighbours tell her.

What is Saira's biggest worry?

'I get worried by women sitting in a circle and gossiping. It scares me because I don't want to end up like that.' Saira doesn't want to end up like that and the fear that she may become like her mother is spurring her to work hard at her studies and make good her escape from the life she otherwise will be condemned to live.

Saira's story is fascinating at multiple levels. Her story is also not typical because unlike many families where boys' education is always given priority, in Saira's home, Saira seems to be getting ahead of her brothers. Saira's older brother failed in Class IX and is now working as a mechanic repairing television sets and other electronic gadgets. He studied in an Urdu medium school. 'We are Muslims, na,' she tells me as if that is the most natural thing to do for Muslims. Her younger brother is also studying in the same Urdu school and it is difficult to envisage that his future will be very different from that of his elder brother.

Saira's brothers have not only been deprived of any quality education, but they also have no skills in English, a language in which proficiency is a must for better opportunities in India. Is English really that important? Saira said, 'I think it is important to study English because the importance of Hindi is going down. If you speak to someone in Hindi, they may not respond, but if you speak to them in English, they will always respond. It gives good impression and even for jobs English is very important.' This view about the importance of English is repeated again and again by many.

Whether we like it or not English has become the language of aspirational India represented by Saira and hundreds of millions like her. Nandan Nilekani, co-founder of Infosys and former chairperson of the Unique Identification Authority of India (UIDAI) in his book *Imagining India* wrote:

> Through the early days of independent India, many saw English as a language of the imperialists and did everything possible to marginalize the tongue. This included attempts to make Hindi the sole national language, and restricting or banning outright the teaching of English in state schools. But once outsourcing made English the entry ticket to a global economy and higher incomes, the language rapidly became a popular aspiration, a ladder to upward mobility for both the middle class and India's poor. As a result state governments across the country are now reversing historically anti-English policies where Hindi-language nationalism was trenchant.[27]

---

[27]Nandan Nilekani, (2009), *Imagining India: Ideas for the New Century*, p. 9 (revised and updated).

Not surprisingly Saira is already emerging as a role model. Once in a while her brothers ask her to teach them English. Recently a boy living in the neighbourhood and studying in Class VI approached her to help him with his studies. But everybody is not appreciative of this emerging role model in the neighbourhood, where girls rarely study beyond Class VI or VII and are co-opted into domestic work at the first given opportunity. Her mother is often criticized by her neighbours for letting her daughter study 'so much'.

While Saira is emerging as a role model for some, she herself doesn't have too many role models other than different teachers at different points of time. Her worldview is also very limited unlike that of a fifteen year old from a middle income or affluent background. She wants to be a psychiatrist because her uncle exhibits some extreme self-inflicting violent behaviour, but doesn't really know what a career in psychiatry means. Girls like Saira need a lot of hand holding and guidance and since this is usually unavailable in their homes or in the immediate neighbourhood, it usually comes from NGOs.

I spoke to Tamara Philip, Academic Director at the Avasara Leadership Institute. Tamara, a science teacher from the UK, is of average build, good looking with a rectangular face, black hair; she was dressed in salwar kameez. She was clearly at home in the sophisticated environs of the American School and spoke with a British accent. She obtained a degree in Molecular Cell Biology and a PhD in Biochemistry from University College London. Tamara is passionate about teaching, and hence, instead of pursuing research, she got a PGCE in science education from the Oxford Brookes University. She moved to India in 2006, taught at Woodstock School in Mussoorie and then moved to Mumbai to join Avasara in 2012.

I asked Tamara about who or what influences the career choices of the girls she interacts with. 'The big influencers—TV serials. There was this whole bunch of girls who said they wanted to be airhostesses. That is fine. But then we realized that they were influenced by a serial of the same name. The other big influence is their parents. They want to do it for their parents—like become an engineer or a teacher because her mum couldn't become one.'

With time I am certain that Saira and her fellow students' career choices will, to a very large extent, be determined by the advice they get at Aseema and Avasara. Saira's current role model was Mangala madam at Avasara: 'At different stages my role model changes. First it was my principal, then my science teacher and now it is Mangala madam. It keeps changing as every day I meet new people and I get influenced by them.' This means that she is in good hands and far luckier than we can ever imagine.

Many girls with a background similar to Saira's are married off by the time they are eighteen or nineteen, if not earlier. Saira stopped attending marriages when during one such ceremony one of her aunts chose her as a bride for her son. This was when she was in Class VIII. Saira refused and it resulted in tension and soured relations within the family. Saira then decided to stop attending marriages to avoid getting into further trouble.

Sitting in the American School and talking to this fifteen year old, it was difficult to imagine that someone actually wanted her to be married off two years back; one shudders to think what fate would have befallen her if by now the marriage had been solemnized.

Saira may be lucky, but what cannot be denied is that she is also brilliant. She consistently comes first in her class and speaks English in a near flawless manner. I mention English not only because it is important but also because in the environment that she is in, Saira has no exposure to the language whether at home or in the media that she has access to or among her peer group. Imagine how difficult it must be to pick up a skill that you cannot practise once you leave your school and go home at the end of the day. Apart from being brilliant, Saira has a steely determination to succeed and with a little bit of luck in a few years' time she will be one of the most educated persons in her extended family.

Saira represents the changing face of the Indian girl today. She is confident, she is aspirational and ambitious and she is working hard to further her education. Education is the passport to a better tomorrow whether it is for boys or girls. Very often access to education also means moving to a large city or town from the village. I digress a little to tell Manisha's story. Manisha, who hails from Allahabad, a city in the state of Uttar Pradesh known for the kumbh mela[28] that is held every twelve years and as the home town of the first prime minister of India, works for the Hindi edition of one of the leading weekly news magazines in India which is published from New Delhi. She is about five feet four or five inches tall, has a round friendly face and is slightly plump. She was wearing a pale yellow sleeveless top and a red ankle length skirt with black patterns on it. From her demeanour and often colourful language it is obvious that Manisha is confident in her skin and lives life on her own terms. After her college, Manisha completed her education in Mumbai and the city was liberating for her.

However, Manisha may never have made it even to Allahabad if her father had not been educated. He was born in a very poor farming family in Uttar Pradesh and the family did not have enough land to make ends meet. So Manisha's grandfather, who was very keen that his children—or at least his sons—studied moved to Allahabad and started working as an electrician. Manisha's father and his elder brother studied, went to the university, did their PhDs and became professors.

We conversed in the living room of her small colourfully decorated apartment in central Delhi, sipping red wine and sharing a few Marlboro Lights. Two of the walls were adorned with film posters and photographs of world famous film directors from Kurosawa, Woody Allen and Francis Ford Coppola to India's own Satyajit Ray and many others which I was not able to identify. There was another poster, actually a collage of pictures of Che Guevara that occupied a prominent position on one of the walls. Probably that is where Manisha draws her revolutionary inspiration

---

[28]Kumbh mela is a religious gathering held once every twelve years in Allahabad at the confluence of the holy rivers Ganga, Yamuna and the mythical Saraswati. In 2013 more than 120 million people reportedly visited Allahabad during the period of the kumbh mela to take a dip in the holy rivers.

from. A third wall was lined with a bookshelf filled with an enviable collection ranging from poetry and politics to fiction and biographies in both Hindi and English. Given her interests and her profession, Manisha's tastes were understandably eclectic. In Manisha's words, 'The thing that changed my father's life was education. If he had not been sent to the university, he would still be tilling a small parcel of family land in the village and reading religious scriptures.' What she doesn't say is that had her father not studied, her future too would have been very different.

In the midst of all this there was one person in her father's family whose life started and ended within the boundaries of the village—her father's sister, Manisha's bua. While her grandfather educated his two sons, he married off his daughter after Class X to a farmer in the village. 'For the rest of her life my bua belonged to the village. She cooked in the chulha (earthen oven primarily used in villages that uses cow dung cakes as the primary fuel), gave fodder to the cattle and swept the house clean every single day of her life,' said Manisha with a deep sigh. She elaborated:

'My father travelled all over the world; bua's world was limited to four rooms in her husband's village house.

'My mother wore sleeveless blouses; bua would keep her head covered and also half her face even within the confines of her house.

'My father knew about America, Chile, Japan and Brazil, whereas my bua thought the world started at Tunda tehsil and ended at Allahabad.

'My father learnt to live with self-respect, his head held high and with pride; bua learnt to live a life governed by the abuses and beatings of her husband and her mother-in-law.

'My father read books; bua cooked rice properly.

'My father discussed Cuba's politics; bua fasted for her husband's long life.

'For my father, life is an open blue sky; for my bua, life is nothing but a dungeon.'

For Manisha life will not be a dungeon, she will never tolerate abuse, let alone beatings from her husband or mother-in-law; she will travel the world on her own terms and she will tell other girls to do so.

Education is empowering women and girls and giving them confidence. I remember growing up in the 1970s and 1980s and our diffidence when it came to dealing with people or circumstances that were outside our comfort zone. I still recall how I admired a friend who could walk confidently into the lobby of a five star hotel (in those days Calcutta had only one), use the toilet and walk out nonchalantly. It was decades before I gained the same confidence and I know that I was not really an exception.

In contrast, Saira's confidence was so refreshingly different. The American School with its charts, fancy chairs, tables, air-conditioned nice smelling classrooms, science models and access to the internet must be a world and a half removed from her own world where Saira spends most of her day. But she was not overawed by anything. As we sat there discussing her life, there was soft lilting music in the background and the sound of a student practicing tabla in one of the classrooms. Other students of the school, mostly children from expat western households, walked past the open area where we were sitting. I did not discern any signs of diffidence or discomfort or resentment at her lot and fate. Instead there was optimism and determination. Apart from education, access and exposure to information is also driving this confidence and empowerment.

Saira's drive, grit and determination are not an exception. Girls are fighting huge odds stacked against them. A few thousand kilometres from Mumbai, I visited one of the day centres operated by the NGO Vidya & Child in Noida, part of the National Capital Region (NCR). This was at the end of March and as I navigated the last few hundred metres on foot, I could feel that the weather had already started turning warm. The lanes were narrow, with open drains and at best one could squeeze through in a two-wheeler. But all the houses were pucca. The slum, situated right next to a middle income colony with nice painted three-four storeyed houses, presented a bustling picture of activity and chaos to an outsider. Almost everything was being sold in open makeshift stores, clothes hanging outside houses, old colourful cotton and chiffon sarees substituting for curtains and small children running around. It was not just the sight, but the smell of the locality which also assaulted you, if you were not used to it.

I asked my way to the centre, located in the temple complex. Once inside I saw a large well-swept compound, not surprising given it was within the temple complex, and classes were in progress. I met Supriya, the founder of Vidya & Child. Supriya has a long face, large black eyes and always wears a welcoming smile. She was wearing her trademark dull red cotton saree and a large red bindi on her forehead. What struck me about her was that her face was serene and radiated happiness. This probably came from the work she did.

This centre, I was informed, had been in operation for fourteen years. What changes had Supriya seen in these fourteen years? 'About 50 per cent are girls in our centres. Earlier there used to be reluctance to send girls to the centre. Now that reluctance is no longer there.' Why and how did this change occur?

'I feel that this slum is right in the middle of an urbanized locality. So they see all the changes around them. Like they see the child of a middle-income household studying, learning, growing and working; they understand the value of education. The challenge comes when the girl becomes fifteen or sixteen and there is pressure from other family members, especially those in the village, to get the girl married and the parents may not be able to resist or handle this pressure. Or if there are a large number of siblings, then the education of the girl child takes a backseat. At an overall level awareness is very high and that is why the intervention with the parents is very important. We have to pre-empt such situations from developing. What we have seen is that if a child completes her school education, then she can do a lot by herself as well. The first barrier that needs to be crossed is completing school education.'

It is evident that awareness about what is happening around us has increased either because of one's neighbourhood or because of access to media. At the same time interventions at the grassroots by social entrepreneurs are critical and cannot be overemphasized.

Without these interventions, awareness will not translate into change for many and the revolution will remain half-baked. How is the nature of the girls changing? Supriya said, 'I think in this centre the girls are very confident. Confidence is not an issue; also their ability to voice their needs and aspirations when they go home is much higher. It is directly proportional to the exposure they are given.'

Does she see similar changes with girls not associated with the centre?

'Yes, at an overall level that is there. But there are girls in the centre who are making and editing films. That level of exposure even we did not receive. So there are some differences between siblings when one attends a centre and another doesn't.'

Are these girls very aspirational and ambitious?

'By the time they reach Class IX and X, they know their capabilities. But it is very clear that they want to do something. We start talking to them at a very early age.'

What about girls outside Vidya & Child?

'The awareness levels are low but the aspirations are there. They are thinking big, which can sometimes be a problem. The challenge is to manage the expectations within your comfort zone as an individual. That is our challenge as well.' This once again highlights the need for interventions at a personal level by grassroot NGOs and also the challenges of aspirations running far ahead of reality and the realms of what is possible.

The rise of children, particularly girls, from humble backgrounds is visible in the results of schools, colleges and various entrance exams. In 2013, 136 Indian Police Service (IPS) probationers passed out of the 65th batch from the academy in Hyderabad.[29] Out of these, twenty-two (just over 16 per cent) were women officers. This is a record of sorts, I am told. At the top of the batch was Shalini Agnihotri of Himachal Pradesh whose father is a bus conductor.

---

[29]'Bus conductor's daughter tops IPS training batch', available at: http://www.firstpost.com/india/bus-conductors-daughter-tops-ips-training-batch-1212089.html.

This increase in the percentage of both girls and women is visible in almost every field. But at only 16 per cent of the total batch size, it is still not good enough. Similarly women account for only 18 per cent of the total entrants in the civil services (IAS, IPS and IFS), and about 17 per cent (less than 3 per cent at executive levels) of the total workforce in public sector banks.[30] The representation of women among elected representatives is worse. Women made up less than 10 per cent of MPs in the fourteenth Lok Sabha, and less than 7 per cent of all MLAs in state assemblies.[31]

In the IIT Joint Entrance Exam (JEE), one of the toughest entrance exams globally for admissions to the most prestigious engineering institutions in the country, the percentage of female candidates to total registered went up from 10.8 per cent in 1997 to 33.3 per cent in 2012. Part of the sharp jump in 2012 can be explained by the exemption from fees for girls; but it must be noted that since 2007 the percentage of girl candidates was consistently in the range of 23–25 per cent. However, the percentage of girls among qualified candidates in 2012 was only 12 per cent, fitting into the stereotype that girls do not like math. In management education the percentage of girls is much higher. Between FY13 and FY15, the representation of women among passing out batches in fourteen leading business schools went up from 17 per cent to 28 per cent, with their proportion reaching almost 50 per cent in a few schools.[32]

Another interesting fact is that in 2011, 92.4 per cent of the registered candidates (both boys and girls) for the IIT entrance exam had declared their parents' annual income as less than Rs 6 lakh (US$10,000) and 79.3 per cent of the candidates who qualified had parents whose annual income was less than Rs 6 lakh. Nearly 50 per cent of the qualified candidates came from households with

---

[30]ICICI Group, *Women in Leadership*. Human Resource Research Desk.

[31]'Vital Stats: Women in Parliament and State Legislatures', 30 June 2008, PRS Legislative Research.

[32]ICICI Group, *Women in Leadership*.Human Resource Research Desk.

parents' annual income less than Rs 3 lakh (US$5,000). It is evident that children from lower middle income and middle income families are aspiring and working hard to get into one of the most prestigious institutes in the country. When I studied in one of the IITs in the mid-1980s an overwhelming majority of the students came from metro cities and a fair number of them came from affluent households who had studied in elite English medium schools. To gauge the extent of the change, look no further than one of the most popular events in Spring Fest at IIT Kharagpur[33]— *hasya kavita sammelan* (humorous poetry recitation in Hindi), an event that has traditionally been very popular in the Hindi heartland. A generation back this would have been considered infra-dig for an elite institute.

I met Sunita Gautam at the centre run by Vidya & Child. Sunita, seventeen, has been associated with Vidya & Child from a very early age. Sunita was tall and slim and was slightly hesitant initially to open up. She was wearing a loose bright orange T-shirt over her faded denim trousers. She kept switching from English to Hindi during our conversation making it pretty clear that Hindi was the comfort language for her. She wanted to be an engineer and was a Class XII student of Amity School in Noida, an upmarket school in the National Capital Region. Sunita did very well in her Class X board exams and this opened the doors of Amity School for her.

Can you tell me something about your background and family?

'We are five brothers and sisters (three sisters and two brothers) and my mother; my father passed away in 2004. My younger sister is in Class XI and younger brother is in Class VIII. My elder sister has completed her BA. And my elder brother is not doing...he has not completed his education. He left his studies when my father passed away. He is now a fruit seller near Sector 34 (Noida). Right now my didi (elder sister) is teaching and also takes tuitions for around ten

---

[33]Spring Festival is an inter-college cultural and performing arts festival held annually at IIT Kharagpur in January.

students. We have our own house that has five rooms. We live in one room and the other four rooms are rented out. The household runs on my didi's income and the rental income.'

What did your father do?

'My father was in the fruit business and he had quite a large business. He was mainly trading in bananas and in mangoes in summer. He got raw bananas and ripened them in the godown here. Papa passed away and he had no savings.'

How did your father pass away? Was he ill?

'No, it was not due to any disease. Actually a friend of my father shot him dead.' At this point she broke down and I felt miserable at having asked her whether her father died of some illness; I offered her some water and we took a small break. The silence for a few seconds was funereal. Sunita was in Class II when her father was killed.

Father dead, shot by a friend; elder brother leaves home leaving behind his mother and her four children of whom three are girls to fend for themselves. But during my nearly two hour conversation with Sunita, she never once complained although she was very kind in candidly discussing her life.

What do you want to do after Class XII?

'My aim is to become an engineer. In the Class X board exams I got ten CGPA (this is the maximum you can get in a CBSE or Central Board of Secondary Education exam). And now I am taking coaching classes for engineering. I study at Amity on a scholarship so my education is free. No one forced me to do anything at home. Right from the beginning I had this thing about studying, studying. I forced my mother to let me join Vidya & Child. I was in Class I then and joined the evening classes. Apart from my eldest sister and brother, my other brother and sisters come here. In my school I got a fee waiver of Rs 100 and the remaining Rs 800 was paid by Vidya & Child till Class X. I stood first in my school in the Class X exams.'

Why engineering?

'During career counselling we went through a lot of tests. There were two-three options that came out and given my interest in science and math, I decided to do engineering. Before this I used to think of becoming a teacher or a doctor. But I do not like studying biology. My aim is to get into the IITs. If not, then NITs. I do not want to go to a private college, I want to go to a good college. I am yet to decide which field of engineering. I will think about that after my board exams.' This once again illustrates how right guidance at an appropriate time can help a child make appropriate choices and set the right goals and targets.

How important is English?

'I think if you go out of this country, then English is very important. But in our country you can do well without being too good in English. I now study science and other subjects in English only.'

How is your life different from your mother's?

'My life is very different from my mother's. My mother had to struggle a lot. As she says they were eight siblings—four brothers and four sisters. The brothers went to school and the sisters stayed behind and did household work. They also took the cows and goats for grazing; they got new clothes only during festivals. For food they did not have any problems because that came from their own fields. Compared to that, our life is very different. I am getting educated; I by and large get what I want.'

Who are your role models?

'My role models are Supriyaji and Saritaji at Vidya & Child. I have been lucky to meet good people.'

What are your material goals?

'I want to have my own house in a society, away from the slum.'

This is exactly what Saira had also told me. This is what Damini might have said if anyone had interviewed her when she was in Class X or XII. There is a pattern here that is easily discernible. Sunita is confident, aspirational and ambitious and she is working hard to achieve her goals. While thinking of engineering, she is thinking of the best colleges in the country, no less. She doesn't feel the burden of her background even for a minute. Her role models are from her immediate vicinity, mostly a teacher or someone from a NGO she goes to. With a modicum of support and a helping hand from Vidya & Child, Sunita's future will be very different. What is evident is that the lives of gen next will be very different from those of the previous generation.

Isn't this ambition, this hunger for success, very natural for girls from socially or economically challenged backgrounds? After all they want to get ahead in life. What about girls from more privileged backgrounds? Are they as driven, ambitious, career oriented? To find out I met Meghna in Mumbai to discuss these issues and more. Meghna is a student of Cathedral & John Connon School in south Mumbai, one of the most sought after and elite schools of Mumbai. She joined Cathedral in Class XI, after completing Class X from Bombay Scottish, another well-known school in Mumbai.

Meghna, born in 1996, was seventeen when I met her. A tall slim girl, she sported waist length straight black hair, had bright eyes and spoke in a very soft but sure voice. She was most comfortable speaking in English and had a habit of repeating words for greater emphasis. She had an excellent academic record and was planning to pursue her undergraduate dreams in USA like most children from similar backgrounds in India today. After completing her undergraduation, she wanted to do her MBA from Harvard; more recently she had been thinking about Stanford as well. Maybe a certain Steve Jobs whose biography she was reading had something to do with it or maybe it was her cousin already at Stanford. When I interviewed her she was wearing a casual T-shirt and skin-hugging jeans, the uniform for teenagers the world over. Her clothes were branded unlike Sunita's or Saira's. Meghna's parents are well educated, her dad is the CEO of a financial services firm and her mother used to be a full time teacher in school and now is a sometimes on-sometimes off teacher. Meghna's worldview and her goals reflect her background and upbringing and clearly she is no less ambitious or aspirational than her peer group from less privileged backgrounds.

Meghna's privileged background and upbringing could not be

more different from Sunita's or Saira's. If Sunita wants to study in one of the IITs, Meghna's eyes are set on MIT, Harvard, Berkeley or Stanford. While Sunita prepares for IIT JEE, Meghna prepares for SAT. Outside Delhi, Sunita has only travelled to her village in Uttar Pradesh, Meghna has seen a large part of the world and in mid-2013 went on a week's trip to Japan on an exchange programme.

Thanks to her access to information and counselling, Meghna eschewed the conventional career choices of engineering or medicine that most bright students like her usually make in India. Or maybe they used to. In her words, 'As of now I am planning to major in economics and minor in either math or statistics. I am also interested in psychology (it sounds interesting) and actuarial science (combination of math and stats—an abbreviated form for Statistics commonly used by students).' My best friend is planning to do actuarial science and that's how I got interested. Subsequently I spoke to my dad. I really really like both math and stats. During a career fair in school, a friend's mother was speaking on finance. She told me that if you love math and stats then you must definitely do actuarial science because it is an interesting job and she really regrets not doing it. Then there is a dearth of actuarial scientists. I am for sure going to do an MBA after that and then go into finance although I do not know which area of finance.'

I never knew anyone who wanted to study actuarial science when I was in school. I doubt if any of us even knew that such a subject could be studied. The most esoteric career that the brightest person in my class had was his desire to become an astro-physicist—you see he loved physics, astronomy and the space. It is another matter that he went on to become a very successful oncological surgeon. To this day he wonders what would have happened if he had proper career advice and guidance at that formative stage.

Meghna has no dearth of advice. She is lucky. Like the other children I met, her role model is also from her immediate vicinity—her father; she has also been influenced by her teachers and cousin brother. 'My dad definitely (is my role model). He had a hard time when his mother was unwell. But he has done quite well for himself. Despite that he is also a person who doesn't talk about his achievements. He never tells us about any interviews on TV or in the press that he gives. I think it is a big deal. We come to know from others and my mum gets quite pissed.'

How did she get interested in economics? 'My cousin brother inspired me to do Eco. He did his Eco major from Delhi University. He spoke to me about the subject and what he does. His work interested me a lot. Plus my Eco teacher in school is very good; she has really helped me a lot. She really created my interest by going through the concepts again and again. For me she is the best teacher.'

Meghna's choice of subject is driven by deep thinking and is not an adhoc decision based on what her best friend is going to study, although that certainly must have influenced her. I asked her why she is straightaway not choosing a more conventional subject of study like engineering since she likes math. She told me, 'I was thinking of doing engineering. Engineering and doctors were conventional jobs maybe ten to fifteen years back, but no more. Most guys still want to do engineering. It is generally between engineering and finance. I too wanted to do engineering and hence I took physics and chemistry. Then I realized that I loved Eco more. I also considered doing a double major in Engineering and Eco. There are some colleges that offer that. Then I realized that I am eventually going to do finance and engineering really isn't going to help me unless I start my own engineering firm or something.'

Meghna's choice of finance as a career has been influenced by the fact that her dad is a finance professional and also by the fact that she has seen or read about many successful women finance professionals in India. She specifically mentioned Shikha Sharma, CEO and Managing Director of Axis Bank and a career banker with the ICICI group before that, during our conversation. 'She has done sooo well for herself in spite of being a woman and without ignoring her kids. I really admire her.'

I was intrigued by her choice of the phrase 'in spite'. I asked her to explain it. Do you think there is discrimination even today? 'It is not that. There is pressure from the family to look after kids so what

I have seen is that women tend to take off for a year or so after their kids are born. After that...like my mom—she was working and then she stopped when I was born. Then Malini was born. She started working quite a few years after that. In Shikha aunty's case a mid-career break did not happen. What helped her was the support she had from her parents and her in-laws. That was a plus. Usually it is expected that the mom will look after the kids and not the dad. So it puts women at a disadvantage when it comes to career and work.'

Is that changing or will it change in your generation?

'I think, yeah (and she broke into a big smile and laughed as if almost amused at her own articulation of what many boys of her generation will do). I think more guys will be staying at home. I am sure.'

For a seventeen-year-old, I found Meghna's views crystal clear and based on observations of the world around her. There was clarity in her thinking and a maturity in her response. Sheryl Sandberg, COO of Facebook and author of *Lean In* would be proud of Meghna. Sheryl wrote:

> Fathers who want to drop out of the workforce entirely and devote themselves to childcare can face extremely negative social pressure. Currently, fathers make up less than four percent of parents who work full-time inside the home...When looking for a life partner, my advice to women is date all of them: the bad boys, the cool boys, the commitment phobic boys, the crazy boys. But do not marry them. When it comes time to settle down, find someone who wants an equal partner. Someone who thinks women should be smart, opinionated, and ambitious. Someone who values fairness and expects, or even better, wants to do his share in the home...We need more men to sit at the table...the kitchen table.[34]

What is true of USA is true of India as well. We do need more men to sit at the kitchen table. More men in India, irrespective of how

[34]Sheryl Sandberg, (2013 edition) *Lean In: Women, Work and the Will to Lead*, pp. 114, 115, 116, 121.

small that number is in the overall scheme of things, will likely become stay at home husbands over the next ten and twenty years or they will start working from SoHos as their wives pursue demanding corporate careers; more men will also take mid-career breaks. At least the first signs of this trend are visible in urban India and role models are emerging.

Onler, celebrated boxer Mary Kom's husband, is one such role model. Mary Kom is a household name in India thanks to her well-known and stupendous achievements. A daughter of a rice farmer in Manipur, Mary rose to become a five-time world champion in boxing, a bronze medal winner at the London Olympics in 2012 and a gold medal winner at the Incheon Asian Games in 2014. But the story that is not as well known is that her husband, Onler, encouraged Mary to return to boxing to realize her full potential after they had twin sons and he looked after their upbringing so that Mary could concentrate on her boxing. Without Onler's support Mary's talents may have been lost.

It is quite possible that some working men will be asked: 'How will you balance your professional commitments with your personal ones?' when they announce that they are about to become fathers. It's also possible that working men will start sharing parenting responsibilities, and supporting their partner's dreams. I have no idea how fast that will happen. But what I am pretty certain about is that Meghna is unlikely to do what her mother did—allow her career to take a backseat. Said she, 'Earlier I wanted to get married at twenty-four. But now that seems impractical and therefore, I would like to get married around twenty-six, twenty-seven and have two children, preferably twins—one boy and one girl.'

Why twins?

'Because then they will grow up together and they will be of the same age. Age difference will not come into play. There was a time when my sister and me were not very close. Now we are like friends. To get married at twenty-four is impractical because four years of undergraduation and I will be twenty-two, then one year work experience and two years MBA, then I will be get married earliest at twenty-six, twenty-seven. I will get married only after I have completed my education—that's very clear.'

If you are in a relationship and the boy wants to get married before that, then what will you do?

'It depends on the guy. If I really think he is worth it, then maybe I will get married. But I will make it very clear that I will finish my MBA before having kids etc. As long as he is clear about that I will be happy to get married because both of us can complete our education together.'

Your mother took a break when you were born. Do you think it will happen with you as well when you have children?

'No, I don't think so (there is no iota of doubt here in her mind; she is absolutely firm that she will not take a career break after having children). I think both of us will continue to work. In my generation, most people—women who will work and do really well, will not stay at home. Women and men will find a way of balancing their lives. We will find a balance between us or we will find a crèche or help.'

Meghna is so focused on her education and career, but are there girls she knows who would get married early and not work?

'I have this friend—she comes from a very conservative Marwari family and if they are not married by twenty-four, then they go in for arranged marriages, which I think is really really stupid (I am not very sure whether it was the marriage age or the arranged marriage concept that Meghna found stupid). They just think that twenty-four is the age for a girl to get married and they marry them off into any family. Everyone teases this friend that she will be married and will become a housewife, but she says that she is going to work and have a proper job. She is really really motivated. She is very clear that she wants a career.'

Will Meghna's friend put her foot down if her husband asks her not to work?

'I am not completely sure. She would put her foot down if her in-laws do not want her to work, but her parents support her desire to work and I don't think her husband will ask her not to work. I mean this is a different time, he can't do that and if he does then it means that it has not been a correct family choice.' Meghna finds it difficult to believe that any boy will ask his wife not to work in this day and age.

Saira's father is an auto-rickshaw driver, Sunita's father was murdered and Meghna's father is a top corporate honcho. Saira, Sunita, Meghna—different castes, different religions, different socio-economic backgrounds, studying in very different schools, growing up in very different neighbourhoods—but they all have something in common. They are ambitious, striving hard to do well in academics and have reasonably well set goals. Each one of them wants to have a career and is likely to continue pursuing her career even after marriage and starting a family.

Saira is willing to protest and do whatever is necessary to study and start a career. She, like other girls of her generation, will pick and choose her battles. This is something that I heard repeatedly during the course of the interviews I conducted and it is refreshingly different from what it was a generation ago.

Chandra's eldest daughter, Rachita, did not protest or fight for her desires and rights, whether it was before or after marriage. Decades of back breaking work in a joint family from the young age of nineteen had taken a toll on Rachita's health. She appeared very slim but on closer inspection it was obvious that she had a number of health issues that restricted her activities and diet very heavily. She walked with a slightly stooped gait and was wearing a very simple lightly coloured cotton saree. Sitting in her tastefully decorated small three-room apartment in Kolkata, Rachita told me she wanted to study bio-science and wanted to be a teacher. She ended up graduating in arts and getting married at nineteen. Why? 'I think my father said that I should study arts; he said that there would be problems if I studied bio.'

What problems?

'I don't know; I never asked him.' This was a time when children didn't demand any explanations from their parents; they just obeyed them.

Did you think of teaching after your graduation? Why did you get married so early?

'Yes, I told my mother that I did not want to get married early. But before my graduation, my marriage had been fixed and this was the time when my mother's health was quite poor. I got married at the age of nineteen. After marriage I got involved in matters of the family. We lived in a joint family, but I did complete my graduation immediately after that.'

Rachita did not live her dream, but she inculcated a fierce desire for economic independence in her daughter. 'When my daughter was a small child, I injected into her mind the thought that she will have to be economically independent. Initially there was some objection to sending the children to an English medium school, but I put my foot down. It happened. I always told Riki, my daughter, that she has to stand on her feet. I told her that women have to face so many problems because they are economically dependent; an economically independent woman can stand up for her rights and protest against injustice.' Here is a familiar story again—a mother fighting for her daughter, for an English medium school and economic independence, thereby giving her the empowerment that has been denied for generations.

Rachita's daughter completed her engineering, joined the information technology workforce and now works for a well-known MNC for a six figure monthly salary. Is she different from her mother? Will she tolerate injustice? Says Rachita, 'Absolutely not (tolerate any kind of injustice). My daughter lives life on her own terms. If her in-laws do not approve of the way she dresses etc., she doesn't care. She sticks to her stand without being disrespectful as long as she thinks it is reasonable. She can do this because she is economically independent. And she also says and acknowledges that she can do this today because of her job.'

Not just Riki, but Meghna, Sunita, Saira and millions like them will live life on their own terms and challenge the existing power equations and social mores with metronomic regularity. It is already happening all around us and is nothing short of a revolution. But is what is true of large towns, cities and metropolises, also true of small towns and villages?

MAIN ISKI UMMEED RAKHTA HOON—
I HAVE HOPE

It was 2009 and I was in a village near Seohar in Madhya Pradesh. Seohar is well known because of the wheat that grows in this district. During harvesting season the fields look as though covered with a patina of gold and it is one of the most beautiful sights that I have seen in rural India. There is not a speck of green or brown or any other colour to break the cover of gold. The other equally enchanting sight that I have seen are the mustard fields in Punjab when the yellow flowers boom. As I walked around the village I was happily shooting pictures even as I discussed the lives and times of the villagers accompanying me.

As is common in a rural area, a gaggle of children and young men followed me. Given tradition and culture young girls and women from the village are rarely a part of the group unless one stops and speaks to them specifically. More often than not they are busy at work. Boys and men have more time for leisure.

But that is another story. In Seohar I wanted to click a picture of a group of young girls of ages ranging between thirteen and twenty years. I asked them for permission and they happily posed for me. None of the girls covered their faces and none of them were wearing the traditional saree. Everyone in that group was wearing a salwar kameez and some of the younger ones were wearing denim trousers and kurtas or T-shirts. They exuded a mix of confidence, exuberance and sense of freedom that is difficult for me to describe. But it was something that I sensed immediately and intimately and it is a feeling that stayed with me for a long time.

To many readers there may be nothing out of the ordinary in this scenario. For me it was a Eureka moment. About a decade back when I had approached a lady in a village in Himachal Pradesh to take a picture I had been shooed away with angry words and furiously gesticulating hands. Standing in the middle of this village in Madhya Pradesh as the winter sun started setting my mind went back to that lady in Himachal Pradesh. How much times had changed. Was this a sign of a new confident generation of girls and women rising?

I could not put the two images out of my mind and I have used them as examples many times to illustrate how lives of girls and women are changing in small towns and in rural India. The confidence of these women and girls is reflected in their clothes and in the way they interact with others, particularly with male members from outside their society. But is it just an outward change of appearance or is there more to it? My conviction is that they are breaching the mores and boundaries of femininity—all drawn by men, of course—and challenging established norms, talking back and demanding their rights, speaking out about their desires and goals. There is no better way to gauge this than to speak to a random selection of people, primarily girls, from different parts of the country.

> The red-light district in the town of Forbesgunge does not actually have any red lights. Indeed, there is no electricity. The brothels are simply mud-walled family compounds along a dirt path, with thatch-roof shacks set aside for customers. Children play and scurry along the dirt paths, and a one-room shop on the corner sells cooking oil, rice, and bit of candy. Here, in the impoverished northern Indian state of Bihar, near the Nepalese border, there's not much else available commercially—except sex.

This is how Nicholas D Kristof and Sheryl WuDunn describe Forbesgunge, a town in Bihar situated on India's border with Nepal, in their book *Half the Sky*.[35]

---

[35]Nicolas D Kristoff and Shery WuDunn, (2010), *Half the Sky: Turning Oppression into Opportunity for Women Worldwide*, p. 3, First Vintage Books Edition, June.

When I met Tanvi (name changed on request), who hails from Forbesgunge, I had not read *Half the Sky*. Tanvi—in her looks and appearance a next door girl you would take home to mom—was in her thirties, dressed in jeans and a T-shirt. She had shoulder length curly hair. Tanvi grew up in Forbesgunge where her father, a doctor, worked. I asked Tanvi about her memories of the town but there were very few. In Tanvi's words, 'We were not allowed to go anywhere outside our house. It was not a good place. My father said you will get into bad company. So we played with the three or four helps in the house. I never visited any of my friends' houses. I never went to any friend's birthday party. Even for the school bus we were escorted by the compounder.' As I read *Half the Sky* I understood why Forbesgunge was 'not a good place' for Tanvi or her brother to grow up in.

I met Tanvi in her two-bedroom nicely decorated house in central Mumbai, where she lived with her banker husband and one-year-old son. The skyline was dominated by skyscrapers in ways one would not have imagined even a decade back. It signalled the rise of a prosperous India and an end of another era when textile mills till the 1980s and then their locked gates and small scale enterprises in industrial galas that came up dominated the landscape.

The industrial galas are still there but the chimneys are the only structures that reminded one of the bygone era when textile mills thrived in Mumbai. The chimneys could not be brought down because somewhere in the government records they are classified as heritage structures. Preservation of the chimneys was a contribution of the Mumbai real estate developers to conserve and preserve the heritage of the city. The occupants of industrial galas are now mostly an eclectic mix and a part of the new age economy or new age consumers—dot com businesses, furniture stores, linen, bathroom fittings for the million dollar apartments in the city, tony restaurants and pubs.

The French windows in Tanvi's house were tightly shut, as much to keep the heat out as the noise coming from some celebration that the Shiv Sena Youth Wing had arranged for the entertainment

Half a Billion Rising 55

of the local lads. The hum of the air conditioners was not heard; complete silence, as the Daikin brand advertises.

Tanvi studied to become a doctor at Patna Medical College & Hospital (PMCH) and then specialized in pathology. What or who inspired Tanvi to study in a district where even today the literacy level for women is just 26.9 per cent[36] as against the national average of 65.5 per cent?[37] Who were her role models? 'It was my mother,' said Tanvi. From Kolkata to Bhavnagar to Forbesgunge, the story was the same. What made her mother different? Tanvi told me, 'My maternal grandfather lived in cities so she (Tanvi's mother) always had a different attitude. My mother got married at sixteen or seventeen, as was the custom in those days, but she wanted to study. She said that in her in-laws house she saw that whenever a girl was born people would say start saving for her dowry. She would tell me that when she had a girl child she thought that her daughter should not go through the same things that she had gone through. Therefore she wanted me to study and stand on my two feet. My mother thought that even if my brother did not study much it would be fine since we had a lot of property.'

Tanvi's mother instilled a strong desire for higher education in her daughter as she wanted Tanvi's life to be different from hers, in spite of the fact that it was Tanvi's father who was far more educated. Tanvi's father never discriminated between her and her brother but Tanvi is even today very sure that her father would not have been very patient and would have considered marrying her by the time she turned twenty-five if she had not got admission in a medical college. Her father's word, after all, was the law in their house.

Tanvi belongs to a very prominent family in Bihar. She told me, 'I belong to the family of Jagannath Mishra (former chief minister

[36]'Female Literacy Rate in Forbesgunge', available at: http://www.forbesganj.com/statistics.htm.

[37]'Female Literacy Rate in India', Dr C. Chandramouli, *Provisional Population Totals* (Paper 1 of 2011, India Series 1), Statement 20—Literacy rate in India 1951–2011.

of Bihar). We had a lot of landed property. We have three sisters (cousins) in the family—my didi (elder sister; first cousin) is eight years older to me. And they would say *"Arre*, if a girl is born in this house, then it is very good and there is nothing to worry as there is enough property and wealth for her marriage." My sister was married off at the age of seventeen. But by the time I came of age, my parents told me that I was good in studies and they did not want to marry me off early. "Do well in studies and you will study further. We will give you a certain timeframe, otherwise we will get you married off early," they told me. I started studying hard with the fear that otherwise I will be married off *(main to isi darr se padti thee)*.'

Tanvi's family was also progressive. Her father was a doctor so it is fair to assume that she faced lesser hurdles when it came to pursuing her studies. Her parents were supportive of her education. But does her example influence the life of other girls? This is a question that has interested me a lot. What at the end of the day is the impact of one small revolution inside one household? Does it change the lives of other girls in the same society? Is she an example that is emulated or is her example ignored?

I asked Tanvi how things had changed within her extended family after her marriage. Tanvi became a doctor and post-marriage came to Mumbai to work. She is financially independent and she has got married to a person who is very supportive of her work and profession. Therefore, Tanvi is a role model for many in her family and immediate social network in Bihar. Or so I thought. But like many other things in life, the law of unintended consequences works and although she is a role model, she is one for very different reasons.

When Tanvi got married, her parents did not have to pay any dowry. She married a very accomplished person who was one of the top rankers in the extremely tough entrance exams to the Indian Institutes of Technology (IITs) and who now works for a global investment bank. Narayana Murthy, co-founder of Infosys, once said in a TV interview that his son went to study at Cornell because he could not get admission to the IITs.[38]

---

[38] Available at: http://www.cbsnews.com/news/imported-from-india/.

Maybe Tanvi's husband Neel was different and an exception when he opted for no dowry; he may well be an exception rather than a rule. But many parents in Tanvi's circle of relatives and acquaintances believe that Tanvi got a 'good catch' because she was so educated. To top it all no dowry when dowry demands can easily cripple the financial well-being of a family. The only condition that her would-be husband put to her parents was that Tanvi should be allowed to complete her studies.

Tanvi told me, 'All my uncles and aunts thought that once a girl studies then there is no tension about marriage. So now they want their daughters to study even if they have to pay donations to get them admission. This is driving the education of girls.' This is something that I heard in other towns and cities as well. The scourge of dowry still exists but there are more boys like Tanvi's husband and their tribe is increasing. If nothing else, the demand for dowry is substantially scaled back depending on the academic qualifications of the girl. I did not ask Tanvi how much dowry was taken by her father's family when he got married.

Is your husband different from your father or are they very similar? Tanvi said, 'Neel is very different. My dad never did any work in the house. I told my father once that I will never marry a person like him: "You are a good father, you are a good husband, but I do not want a husband like you." He is very authoritarian and dominant. My father was progressive but his word was law in the house. We did not have any say over and above that. He would decide what colour of dress I would buy, which dress I should wear. I do not get along very well with my father. It is always his way or the highway. My mother has never been able to express her feelings or desires. This is the way of life for her. But my life is different. I got married in my final year of MBBS. Let me tell you a story. My younger cousin sister who is also a doctor is getting married to another doctor. She got engaged and her fiancé told her something which completely shocked me. Her fiancé told her not to address him as "tum" but use "aap". After marrying Neel I cannot think anyone can do this. Neel gave me so much freedom. But women

accept certain things as normal and think this is the way of life.'
'Tum' and 'aap' both mean 'you' in English but 'aap' is usually used
for elders and signifies respect, whereas 'tum' and 'tu' are used to
address younger people and one's peer group. Clearly all men are
not changing and many are finding it difficult to deal with the
changes.

Of course, there are exceptions. One such exception is Muskan's
father. Muskan is a young girl associated with Vidya & Child.
When I asked Supriya whether men were changing she said that I
must meet Muskan's father. He was a tailor and had difficulties
making both ends meet, as people were increasingly switching to
readymade garments. Muskan's father wants to educate his daughters
as much as possible and is willing to make all kinds of sacrifices for
this. To one of my questions asking him about his progressive
attitude towards his daughters' education, he said, '*Hum Tughlaqi
nahin hain* (literally it means I am not like Tughlaq referring to
Mughal ruler Muhammad Bin Tughlaq who was known for his
conservative and intolerant ways.)'

All traditions are also not being thrown out of the window.
Strange as it may sound in this day and age, Neel and Tanvi did not
meet before their marriage; they just spoke to each other over the
phone. But this in itself is a big change. In the early 1990s, one of
my batch mates from Muzaffarpur, Bihar, first spoke and saw the
girl he married during the wedding ceremony. This friend of mine
was a doctor who had spent all his life outside Bihar, in cities like
Kolkata and Delhi, but when it came to marriage he acquiesced to
his parents' wishes.

Neel lends a helping hand around the house and shares the
workload with Tanvi. This enables Tanvi to pursue her career. But
she is willing to make certain compromises, if necessary, of her own
volition. For further studies, Tanvi decided to specialize in pathology,
as against the more conventional choice of gynaecology or paediatrics.
Her father was not very happy that she chose pathology because he
thinks she has taken a backseat in her career by not choosing
something more active like gynaecology. Tanvi chose pathology

because Neel's working hours were very long and if she too spent long hours working which she would have to if she specialized as a gynaecologist, what would happen to her family and family life? She emphasized that it was her choice and was not influenced by Neel or his family.

I am still intrigued by the fact that Neel and Tanvi met for the first time during their engagement. Both of them were told by their respective parents that they were free to call off the marriage if they did not like each other. Even Tanvi's father was meeting Neel for the first time on the same day. Tanvi and Neel now have a good laugh thinking what would have happened if they had indeed called off the marriage, given that elaborate arrangements had been made for the engagement ceremony and relatives from all over the country had come in. From Forbesgunge, Tanvi landed in Taipei after her marriage and her first holiday was in Antarctica. The very much in love couple do not regret not calling off the marriage.

The sign of changing times was evident when Tanvi told me that if she has a daughter she would have no issues who she gets married to and what she studies. But did Tanvi ever think of an inter-caste marriage? She studied in a medical school where she could have met and fallen in love with another student. Tanvi told me, 'Never thought of it, never thought of it. My father would have never allowed that. No, he wouldn't have killed me but I would have been boycotted.' In Tanvi's batch, a Hindu-Muslim couple fell in love and got married and went on to live happily, at least so far.

Tanvi's brother, who is a few years younger than her, is going to marry someone who is an 'outsider'—a girl he went to college and fell in love with. She is not really from a different caste. She is also from Bihar and a Brahmin, but from a different sub-caste—while Tanvi's family belongs to the Maithili Brahmin caste-group, her brother's girlfriend's family is Kanyakubja Brahmin. Therefore, Tanvi's father does not approve; he is not going to compromise on his principles and beliefs even though he has only one son. Tanvi told me, 'He (my father) is not going to attend his son's marriage. I do not know what his principal objection is. In our family all my cousin brothers have had inter-caste or inter-religion marriages. This girl is also a doctor. My mom has no choice and will follow my father. She will not do anything behind his back. She will also tell my brother that if your father says so, then you must do accordingly.' In many such instances of love marriages, as opposed to the very Indian concept of arranged marriages where parents fix up a match, the problem is not just about the caste or religion but the fact that the parents did not get to choose the bride or the groom.

Will Tanvi and Neel be fine with inter-caste marriages for their children? Without any hesitation Tanvi told me, '*Arre*, yeah, yeah. We have no issues. I don't even think he will get married according to our choice. In fact Neel and I joke that we will be very happy if our son gets married to a girl (and not a boy).' And she breaks into laughter at the thought of this; I have had this same light-hearted conversation with my wife and friends, although it sounds politically very incorrect to object to or have reservations about same-sex marriages in today's day and age.

Tanvi's husband's attitude towards dowry and women can possibly be explained because of his education and the subsequent few years of working abroad, but that is an easy and lazy explanation. Priyanka's would be husband has neither studied in an IIT nor has he worked overseas; he has not been influenced by Mumbai or Bengaluru or Kolkata. Yet he is like Neel in many ways.

Before Priyanka's husband, it is Priyanka's story that is absolutely riveting. If Tanvi had a comfortable childhood in an upper middle class milieu, Priyanka was born into a poor family. Forbesgunge's red-light district did not have any electricity; Priyanka's home in Munger also did not have any electricity. And then one day her father was charged with theft of electricity and the police came visiting their house.

In Priyanka's words, 'We never had electricity in our home and obviously we did not have a TV or radio. Till Class X we wanted those things, then we all got conscious of our careers and future. We used a generator to get electricity from 6 p.m. to 10 p.m. for our studies. Then there was a case of theft of power against us. My father's name was dragged into the power theft when we did not even have power in our house; the neighbour who was caught stealing power was asked for his guardian's name and he gave my father's name, Rajinder Sharma. Thus, we got dragged into it. When I heard this I said, "How is this possible? How can anyone say anything and no one is protesting?" Then I went to the police station. I knew that what was happening was incorrect and unjust. At the police station I was informed that the case had gone to the electricity office and they would not be able to help me. I went there. There was one Rashmi madam (Rashmi Sinha) who was in charge. I told her that whatever had happened was incorrect and unjust. The people in the electricity office said that my father's name would be removed but after two days we realized that his name was still there. Then I spoke to Rama madam in school (the principal of the school she studied in). Also at that time I was giving tuitions to a girl whose father was a police officer. They guided me to go and speak to the DIG, a senior ranking police officer in the district. This was in 2008. Rama madam came with me to meet the DIG, spoke to him and said that she had visited our home, knew what our problems were and the fact that there had not been any theft. Next day I met the DSP at the advice of the DIG. My family members were aghast at my behaviour and they thought that this matter could have been resolved by paying some money. Then the DSP told me that he would do the final inspection based on court orders and my father's name was removed from the case.'

It did help that a principal is held in high regard in society and Priyanka's principal was on her side and they had access to the DIG. Power theft is punishable by imprisonment in India and the police can harass an innocent person no end to extract money or to settle personal scores on someone else's behalf. Priyanka's uncle had earlier said that if her intervention was successful he would shave his head off. So I asked her if he did. Priyanka broke into peals of laughter as she imagined her uncle with a shaved head.

Priyanka embodies the changing face of Indian women and perhaps even as I write this, her story maybe more mainstream unlike what it seems to me. Priyanka had an underprivileged and economically challenged background. She was born and brought up in Jamalpur, Munger. Munger is known as the gun capital of India. The production of firearms is no cloak and dagger affair but is carried out openly right in the heart of town. Some of the gun factories are very sophisticated and the clients range from dacoits and gangsters to politicians and policemen. Munger's other export is yoga. The Bihar School of Yoga was founded in 1964 on the banks of the River Ganges, the holiest of holy rivers in India and teachers from this institute are now spread all over India. Socialites from Mumbai often travel to Munger to attend yoga classes or yoga conventions.

Born in 1986 Priyanka's life was very far from yoga gurus, gods and guns. Priyanka told me, 'I do not belong to a very well-to-do family. My father had a small shop selling audio cassettes. We are four sisters and one brother. My brother is the fourth child. My father has seven brothers and one sister with my father being the second eldest. It was challenging for him because he had four daughters. Everyone told him that he would have to get four daughters married, which would entail a lot of expenditure and therefore, why should he spend a lot of money on their education. My mother, a home maker, is from Arha district and is illiterate; but she is much greater than any literate woman. She has been an inspiration for me. She taught me how to sustain myself in the difficult environment and to get ahead in life.'

How did your mother become interested in education? I asked Priyanka. 'The story that we have heard from our mother is that her early married life was very difficult. There was the usual story of her being a daughter-in-law and therefore, being beaten. She also had to do all the household work. My parents were told that there was no point in educating their children. My father is matric pass. Initially he agreed with his family. But when he saw that we were eager to learn, he supported us.'

If the story sounds familiar, then it is. An illiterate woman who was married off early inspires her daughter to study as it is the only possible gateway to a better life, and from a life that would otherwise mirror hers. In many households in India, while the wife or mother is economically not independent, she does have some say and/or control over the finances of the household, especially in nuclear families, and that is making a big difference. As the World Development Report (2012) notes:

> Greater control over household resources by women leads to more investment in children's human capital, with dynamic positive effects on human growth. Evidence from a range of countries (such as Bangladesh, Brazil, Cote dÍvoire, Mexico, South Africa, and the United Kingdom) shows that increasing the share of household income controlled by women, either through their own earnings or cash transfers, changes spending in ways that benefit children. In Ghana, the share of assets and the share of land owned by women are positively associated with better food expenditures. In Brazil, women's own non labour income has a positive impact on the height of their daughters. In China, increasing adult female income by 10 per cent of the average household income increased the fraction of surviving girls by 1 percentage point and increased years of schooling for both boys and girls...In India, a woman's higher earned income increases her children's years of schooling.[39]

When I met Priyanka in Patna she was studying for her MBA at the International School of Management (ISM). Priyanka was small built and could easily pass off as a high school girl. She was dressed in a white shirt and blue jeans. ISM, Patna is one of the thousands of MBA colleges that have mushroomed all over India to sell the promises and dreams of a career that comes with a MBA degree. Irrespective of whether India harnesses its demographic dividend or not, intrepid and sometimes unscrupulous entrepreneurs in the field of education are harnessing it for sure as they cater to the dreams of the young. ISM, Patna claims to be Bihar's first AICTE

---

[39]The World Bank, (2012), *Gender Equality and Development, World Development Report 2012*, p. 5.

approved unaided MBA institute. It was started by a few IITians and funded by a real estate developer and in my view is unlikely to remain in business for long.

In Bihar almost every child grows up wanting to be an engineer, doctor or a bureaucrat. The state has had so little to offer in terms of opportunities that the best and the brightest go to other states. By some estimates students from Bihar make up as much as 50 per cent of students in other popular centres of learning like Delhi and Pune. The day before I met Priyanka, I had visited the Asian Development Research Institute (ADRI). To reach ADRI from my hotel, I travelled the length of Boring Canal Road. It is one of the most prominent roads in the city and is dotted with various commercial and retail establishments. As I approached the A N College end of Boring Road, the crowded streets and by-lanes were dotted with coaching centres offering guaranteed success in all kinds of entrance exams to different courses across India. One could not miss the coaching centres even if one looked skywards since the entire street is festooned with colourful advertisements strung across the road.

Priyanka is a product of the same system although she never had a shot at going to one of these coaching centres in Patna. Priyanka studied in N C Ghose Balika Ucch Vidyalaya, a government run school under the Bihar board in Munger till she completed her matriculation (Class X). Then she finished her high school from Munger and graduation from JRS College, Munger under Bhagalpur University in English Honours. As she was a Hindi medium student it was very difficult and challenging for her to take English as her Honours paper. Why did she choose English? 'All my friends studied in CBSE; I always heard that there is no future for Bihar board students and they are not able to project themselves because of lack of English.'

At every step Priyanka had to struggle against her extended family and against society. When her elder sister travelled to Mumbai to study fashion design, Priyanka was nearly married off. But before that she had already taken steps to become indispensable to her father in his business. In her words, 'When I was in Class V, it was financially very difficult for my family to continue our studies. We were seven members in the family and my father then was handling his business alone. That is when I took my first step towards my career. My father was visiting Patna to buy goods, a regular Sunday affair. Every fifteen days he would also visit Kolkata. And he was worried that the shop would remain closed when he was out. So this particular Sunday I took the shop keys and told my mother that I was going to the shop (*hum dukan ja rahein hain*). All my family members were shocked. I forced the family to let me go. My mother supported me and so did a friend of my father's. That day I became my father's right hand. That was the beginning of my career and till Class XII I regularly worked with my father and I knew each and every aspect of his business.'

Coming back to her sister's studies, Priyanka said, 'It was a very critical situation for the family when my sister got admission into the National Institute of Fashion Technology (NIFT), Mumbai. My uncles told my father that rather than spending Rs 4 lakh on her studies, the same money could be used for her marriage. What was the point of studying further? It was the simplest solution for them. However, inspired by her drawing teacher my sister was very keen to pursue further studies. But there was a big possibility that her studies would be stopped. We both were in the same class and for my parents it was a dilemma about which daughter should continue her studies since at that stage the financial situation of the family was such that both of us could not have continued our studies. They asked me what should be done. And I told them that since they were to be the final decision makers, it was up to them to decide what was to be done. But my view was that my sister should continue with her studies and I would drop out and start earning. Since I had finished Class XII, I started teaching in the English medium Path Bhavan School. So my sister managed to go to Mumbai. But before that there was again a war in my family. Just before her departure a family meeting was held at home—a kind of family council in which everyone participated. It was not just about the financial situation of the family. For a middle class or lower middle class family, sending a daughter away from home to such a far-off location was a very big decision. The conclusion was that Babita would go to Mumbai for further studies and Priyanka would get married—this was one of my uncle's suggestions.'

Why the two decisions were linked is also difficult to fathom. Priyanka protested against that. '*Yeh to achchi baat hai...woh padegi aur main kya ghaans gaad rahin hoon* (this is very good; she will study and am I so useless that I will be engaged in planting grass?) My mother was also against this decision. I told my uncle to find a boy within six months but he would have to bear all the expenses and my father would not be involved but let Babita go to Mumbai first. Somewhere my offer resulted in a change of heart in my uncle and he said that he would bear the expenses for my studies, if necessary. So I started teaching in the school and sponsored my own studies with my earnings. I was getting Rs 1,000 per month. My sister got a scholarship—Rs 2 lakh—as well and it was a big financial help for my father.'

Priyanka's feisty side was evident as she narrated this; there was firmness in her steely voice which reflected determination and which I thought would stand her in good stead in the future.

Even today, all over India, the extended family has a lot of say in family decisions although with more nuclear families, this is now slowly reducing. Apart from girls from nuclear families, other girls like Priyanka are also putting their foot down and taking their destiny in their own hands. They are no longer willing to accept the decision of family elders without protesting or putting up a fight.

Priyanka fought significant odds to come this far. Has Priyanka's story caused any ripple effects in her village? Is Priyanka an aberration, an isolated example or has her story influenced the lives of other girls? Priyanka told me that the effect of her standing up to the elders in the family for her rights and ambitions and the sisters pursuing their studies has had a huge impact on other families and girls in the neighbourhood. 'The first impact was that people started taking initiatives for educating girls. After my sister, seven or eight other girls went to NIFT. People started coming to our home and asking my dad for advice. After my graduation I took admission in Mass Communication & Journalism from Nalanda Open University. Now I will appear for my second year final exams for my MBA degree.'

Why are you doing journalism along with your MBA, I asked her. 'I realized that journalism can be a big support for my family because journalists have contacts and they can raise their voice against injustice. We realized the benefit of this when we had to open an account with the State Bank of India (SBI). He had been turned back many times by the bank. So I told him one Saturday that we would go and find out what the issue was. The manager told me to come back the next day and asked me which class I was studying in. I told him that I was doing my MA. And he asked me do you know the meaning of MA. I told him that I was doing MA in Journalism. His attitude immediately changed. He asked me to take a seat. The bank account was needed to withdraw my money from the Provident Fund (PF) that had accumulated from my teaching job. In two hours flat my account was opened.'

The bank manager's attitude towards Priyanka is the paternalistic misogynist attitude visible all across India. His attitude towards Priyanka's father is something that poor people across India face every day whenever they have an interaction with any government official. If at one end education is helping in smoother, dowry-less marriages, then at the other it is also helping many to know their rights and entitlements, and then demand and get them. It is empowering and liberating for hundreds and thousands of girls like Priyanka.

Our conversation moved to relationships and marriage. Priyanka is engaged to be married to Kamal Kishore, an engineer who is now studying for his Master's degree. They met fleetingly at her cousin's marriage and it was love at first sight. And as luck would have it they are from the same caste and that helped. Kamal Kishore's parents approached Priyanka's parents with the marriage proposal; some traditions are still strong and near non-negotiable, but what Priyanka will not tolerate is any injustice. Said she, 'There has been no talk of dowry and he is not going to accept any dowry. I now have the ability where no one will dare to behave badly with me. And if anyone does then I can take appropriate action. They, Kamal Kishore's family, have a family business in iron and steel. Sooner or later he may join the business. But I have told him that first get your own image and am insisting that he appear for his Union Public Services Commission (UPSC) (to become a bureaucrat).' Priyanka wants Kishore to establish himself independently before joining the family business.

Priyanka's mother got married when she was thirteen or fourteen. Priyanka is now twenty-six years old and will get married once she starts working. She expects her husband to help her around the house and share the chores. She would like to have only one child given that aspirations are high, costs are rising and life will not be a bed of roses. She would like to provide the best for her child. To paraphrase the cigarette ad from many decades back, you, the Indian woman, has come a long way.

Like Priyanka in Patna, Deepika has also come a long way. Deepika is thirty years old and works for a global multinational telecom equipment major in Bengaluru. Deepika was about five feet three, slightly stockily built with an average girl next door looks and wearing the trademark white T-shirt and blue jeans. She was not wearing any bangles or bindi. I met Deepika in her hostel and we sat in the open courtyard under a tree just outside the reception area, which had all its lights switched off probably to conserve electricity on a Sunday afternoon. Or maybe there was a power cut, a common occurrence in most cities in power starved India. Youngsters kept coming in and out of the hostel.

The weather was pleasant, as it is wont to be the whole year round in Bengaluru. Deepika had no hesitation in discussing her life with me, a complete stranger. Obviously the introduction through a person known to both of us helped. Deepika was born in Lahorijan, a small town in Assam near the border with Nagaland, to parents who had studied till Class VIII. Her mother's world was limited to the four walls of their home, but Deepika represents the modern peripatetic Indian. After Dimapur, where she studied till Class VI and travelled by cycle rickshaw daily, she did her schooling in Kerala, her college education in Chennai, Tamil Nadu and has already worked in Mumbai, Delhi and Bengaluru.

Along the way she picked up oodles of confidence and self-belief and also a little bit of anger and resentment against her conservative parents who do not understand what their daughter is pursuing instead of getting married, settling down and presumably having a few babies. Their baby has moved far away from the world she was born thirty years ago in Dimapur. They do not know or understand Deepika's world today and she doesn't want to be part of the world where she has come from.

Deepika had accompanied her father to Kerala where her younger brother and some other neighbourhood boys were to sit for an entrance exam to a boarding school. When she saw the school—Vidyaprakash Public School—she started pestering her father that she too wanted to study there and, for some reason to her eternal good fortune, her father agreed. This one decision probably changed Deepika's life. Even after all these years she told me, 'It was important that my brother studied and it was an accident that I ended up studying what I did.'

By the time Deepika finished her schooling she knew that she wanted to study engineering. But her father wanted her to study medicine since medicine is seen by many as a more suitable career for a woman and at this stage her father wanted her to return to Assam and continue her studies there. To satisfy her father she sat for medical entrance exams and unsurprisingly she did not qualify. Meanwhile she asked her brother to send her addresses and contact details of various engineering colleges in south India and started writing to these colleges seeking admission. In her words: 'I asked my brother for names of engineering colleges and also to scan the newspaper for addresses of engineering colleges and applied to them with my academic credentials. Many of them replied back. The Hindustan College of Engineering in Chennai asked me to meet them. Accompanied by my father, I went to Chennai. As I had not sat for the written test, I had asked for a management quota seat in engineering. The donation was Rs 1 lakh and my father agreed to pay that. So I did computer science for four years. After engineering, I did my internship with Sify Technologies and then did my MBA from ICFAI Business School in Chennai and partially in ICFAI's Hyderabad campus.'

Deepika's parents have also had a tough life. Her father was born in what is today Bangladesh. Facing discrimination on religious grounds, the family migrated to India. Her father had to discontinue his education as his parents could no longer afford to educate their children. They had left all their wealth in another country and were suddenly staring at stark poverty and difficult living conditions in refugee camps.

While there was no discrimination at home, educating Deepika was never a priority for her parents; her brother's education was. Even today Deepika believes that it was a fortuitous accident of fate that she ended up studying as much as she did.

Deepika's family is no different from the other families we have met so far when it comes to taking decisions. In Deepika's words, 'All decision making in the family is by my father. My mother has absolutely no say in any of the decisions taken.' In Deepika's case this was very good because it was her father who encouraged and supported her when she wanted to study more. Unlike most of the other families that I met during the course of this research, Deepika's mother is not too happy with her decision to study so much. In her view Deepika should have got married and settled down. She blames education for Deepika still being single and given a choice she would rather have seen Deepika married than educated.

Deepika never gave her the choice. Deepika's life is already far removed from her parents' lives. Said Deepika, 'There is a huge difference in the way my mother was brought up. Recently my father was travelling and there was no rice in the house. My mother did not eat anything because she was reluctant to go out. This will not happen with me. And anything she has to do, she has to consult my father and ask his permission. She does it out of sheer habit; she cannot go out alone, she has no confidence in taking any decision. It is not that my father insists on that.'

Will they approve if she wants to marry someone outside her caste or region? Deepika believes that they will approve even if not wholeheartedly since they would be relieved that she is finally getting married. '*Bhala tala shaadi ho gayee iski* (good that she got married at last),' is what they will think, according to Deepika.

Like the others girls I met Deepika would also like her husband to share the household work. She would like to manage her own kitchen, and then she smilingly added that most men like to cook these days and she would happy to have her husband in the kitchen helping her or cooking on his own. But she has two non-negotiable demands—first, she would like to continue working for as long as she wants and second, she wants her little personal space in her life; she would not like to be constantly monitored or be answerable to her husband about what she is doing, where and why. As she told me this I wondered whether boys and men in India were changing fast enough and in enough numbers to handle the new age Indian woman.

Are Deepika's parents looking for a groom for her? No, Deepika is looking for her own husband and has registered on a matrimonial website. Given her long working hours she has very few opportunities to socialize or meet eligible young men outside her office. She knows her family cannot support her here, and so far her experience has not been encouraging. Deepika told me, 'I put up my profile on one of the matrimonial sites. During that period I met many wrong people and I had a very bad experience with one of them. I met a guy, when I was working in Delhi, he was interested and I introduced him to my parents. He was from Rourkela and later on we got to know that he was already married. That influenced me to come back to Bengaluru.'

Deepika is still registered on the matrimonial website, but the problem is that when she speaks to the boy directly, he does not give her much importance. The boy and his parents give more attention only if her parents get involved. Some things are not changing fast enough yet.

Deepika was waiting for her passport application to be processed when I met her. Her employer wants her to travel to Europe and meet her colleagues there. But her application is caught in India's legendary bureaucratic mess. I wished her all the best, as I took her leave, and asked her one last question: Will she bring up her daughter, if she has one, differently? 'Yes, of course. I will give her freedom, I will be a friend to her.' Maybe that is all Deepika wanted her mother to be—a friend, which she could never be. She has been cast away in a different world to navigate on her own. But her daughter will not have to face the same issues.

While Deepika's mother will never become her friend, Daksha's mother is her friend, as was obvious during our interaction. It was late afternoon when I met Daksha at her house for the second time which I reached after a ten minute auto ride through the lanes and by-lanes of Bhavnagar. Daksha was wearing a tight yellow salwar kameez, which had faded over the years, but was not at all self-conscious. On the contrary she exuded a confidence that had first surprised me the previous evening. As I approached her house around 3 p.m, I saw some boys playing carrom. Daksha's house was modest and we sat in the outside room which was probably less than ten sq feet and overlooked a courtyard that belonged to the temple compound inside which the house was located. The roof of the house leaked during rains. From the room I could get a good view of the barren courtyard with one large tree with the mandatory crows squawking and the main road beyond.

Daksha had a lilting sing-song voice. She never stopped smiling during our conversation. She had bright eyes, and her eyebrows were shaped, something slightly unexpected. But then I shamefully realized my assumption was based on my prejudice that girls from economically challenged backgrounds in small town India do not visit salons and beauty parlours—another sign of change and assertion, which signals a generational shift in attitudes.

Daksha's father works as a chowkidar, a watchman. Prior to this, for three years he stayed at home unemployed because of poor health. Before that he worked in a diamond factory where he developed problems with his breathing and eyesight, most likely due to the unhygienic working conditions in these diamond cutting and polishing factories. But that is one of the only jobs available in the city in reasonably large numbers and most families have one or more members working in diamond factories. Daksha's elder sister and brother have studied till Class X and Daksha will be the first member of the family to go to college.

How has your life changed, I asked Daksha? 'Lot of things have changed when I look at my life and even my sister's. When my sister was eighteen (I am three years younger to her), she could not speak to any boy in the neighbourhood. When she was in diamond cutting, one day her bicycle was stolen. So her "brother" who used to work with her—they used to sit next to each other—said that since it was quite late he would drop her home. He also told her not to be afraid since his wife was also present. My sister said, "I cannot go on anyone else's bike because if my father sees me then I will get severe scolding." Her life worked to a routine—mornings go to school, afternoons go to the diamond cutting workshop and then by 7 p.m. be back at home. Wherever she went, either my mother or I would accompany her. My life has changed so much that even when I come back very late, anyone can drop me back home and my father doesn't say anything. He says if you work together then this is bound to happen. My elder sister would never speak up in front of my father but I do. That is the relationship I share with my father. So I put my foot down in a way that my brother and sister have never done.'

Daksha wants to do social work after finishing her studies. Having spent a large part of her time in Shaishav, Daksha was clearly influenced by Parul's thinking and philosophy. As I listened to Daksha's plans, I was once again struck by the fact that role models are so important in one's life. Or an excuse or an opportunity or a chance to break out of their comfort zones, as Priyanka in Munger or Deepika from Dimapur did.

Priya Raju Sirodkar of Aurangabad, a student of first year BA, is not very different from Daksha or the other girls we have met so far. Priya was a square-faced girl with a thick round nose, thick bushy eyebrows and jet black hair falling below her shoulder. She was dressed in a black and white salwar kameez, matching bangles, silver anklets and sported a red and silver bindi on her forehead. In her ears were two sets of ear-rings and she sported a tiny nose ring as well. Priya's father was a security guard and mother a home maker who got married at the age of thirteen or fourteen years. Thanks to the NGO Kumari Vikash Prakalp and the encouragement of her parents, Priya wants to do her Masters in Social Work (MSW) and if possible wants to join the Indian Police Service (IPS). She said that also she wants to do social work like her 'teachers' do at Kumari Vikash Prakalp. Within the family, her biggest supporter is her brother. In Priya's words, 'My brother's support is the biggest for me in the family. I tell him that now that your career is settled, I want my career also to be settled. He says that whatever support you need, let me know and I will always be there with you.'

I asked Priya whether she was determined to continue working even after her marriage. She said that this will be a precondition for her marriage. She is very practical about the necessity to work as well as her economic independence. 'After all the efforts I have put in, I would like to work. I will discuss this issue of working before marriage with my would be husband.Then I can take care of my expenses and also help my parents financially. Plus in today's world, one income is not sufficient.'

What about caste issues and inter-caste marriages? What Priya said in Aurangabad is very similar to what I heard in Patna, Bhavnagar and in other places. 'It is not directly done but wherever we go we have to disclose our caste. For example, I get a scholarship because of my caste. This I think is not fair. In my college I have a friend, she deserves a scholarship because of her financial condition. But she doesn't get a scholarship because she is from the open category.' Priya's views are so similar to Meghna's even though their social and family backgrounds cannot be more different. This once again reinforces the importance of education and how it shapes and moulds views and thoughts consistent with a modern and liberal world. Priya's thoughts also support my view that more than patronage and dole-outs, the poor and the underprivileged need equal opportunities, access to opportunities and level playing fields.

During marriage, however, there is no running away from caste. 'Marriages take place only after looking at the caste. Our thinking has not evolved so much where caste is ignored during marriage,' Priya said.

Will you be allowed inter-caste marriage? Priya laughed and said, 'Sir, we will face stiff opposition. There is very little chance that such a marriage will happen. If my brother finds a girl from his work life but from a different caste and who has the right culture, then there should not be a problem. Of course, we will have to work on our parents a bit because there is bound to be some initial resistance. They will agree. However, I have no objection to an inter-caste marriage. The biggest change is being driven by NGOs like these. Kako (her mentor at the NGO with which she is associated) goes and speaks to our parents then everybody listens. Older people do not like Kako's interference. But my parents like it.' Priya is lucky to have parents who agree with Kako.

Priya wants to do social work because she believes it is her duty to help others, given that others are helping her. She says this is part of her culture, her 'sanskar', her 'parampara'. These are words I heard often during my research. 'We have to do something for others after taking care of ourselves.' I asked Daksha why she doesn't want to work in a company and her choice of social work as her profession. She answered, 'I do not want to work in a big company and earn lots of money. Because to survive if we get enough food three times a day and get all that is most necessary then I do not want more. What will we do by earning more and more if we cannot help other children like me? *Main zyaada kuch cheez ki ummeed hi nahin rakhti.*'

Main zyaada kuch cheez ki ummeed hi nahin rakhti—I do not have expectations for too many big things. This sentence stayed with me for a long time after I had finished speaking to Daksha. Whenever I think about Daksha and other girls like her, I wonder whether even their small little dreams will be realized. I hope, nay I have faith that their dreams will be realized—*Main iski ummeed rakhta hoon.*

HIJAB, PC AUR MOBILE

Forbesgunge, Munger, Dimapur, Bhavnagar, Allahabad, Nashik are little worlds in their own right and far removed from each other, but it is quite evident that big changes are underway. There is a generation of girls and women out there who are challenging the norms of yesteryears, breaking the shackles that their mothers and grandmothers silently suffered; they are demanding their rights and following what their heads and hearts are saying. The change started sometime back but is accelerating and reaching a tipping point.

What are the change drivers? During the course of my research for this book, I tried to find the answers to this question. There is no gainsaying that a confluence of factors is driving the change or that behind this is the sacrifice of a generation or two, as this usually happens when such monumental social changes take place. As I met and interviewed girls and women in 2013, education stood out as the biggest driver of this change.

Over the last three decades, between 1981 and 2011, women's literacy in India increased from 29.8 per cent to 65.5 per cent.[40] In 1990, only 60 per cent of 21-year-old women were literate and in 2011 this figure had improved to 85 per cent.[41] The 2011 Census was a landmark one because for the first time out of the total number of literates added during the decade, females outnumbered

---

[40]'Female Literacy Rate in India',Dr C. Chandramouli, *Provisional Population Totals* (Paper 1 of 2011, India Series 1), Statement 20—Literacy rate in India 1951–2011.

[41]Ajay Shah, (2014), 'Labour Assets in 2054 India', *The Economic Times*, 13 March.

males. A reverse trend was noticed during 1991-2001, once again underscoring the fact that during difficult economic times it is the girls who are first pulled out of school.

One of the rare successes of various policy efforts and the efforts of NGOs is that by 2000-01, 96 per cent of children within the eligible official school-age population are enrolled in primary schools.[42] Between 1980-81 and 2000-01, the percentage of girls who were in school at the primary level (Standard I to V) increased from 64.1 per cent to 85.9 per cent (85.5 per cent in 1990-91).[43] As is evident in the last three decades the sharpest increase in enrolment happened over 1980-90 and then over 2001-12.

In urban India, women's literacy levels increased from 58.1 per cent to 79.9 per cent over the last three decades.[44] In rural India women's literacy levels improved from 21.4 per cent to 58.8 per cent[45] in the last three decades. Absolute statistics for urban India are expectedly better than the all India average. Rural India is not far behind in terms of decadal improvement although there is still a long way to go.

The national trend of improving literacy is also reflected in rural areas among the 11-14 year old cohort. However, in the age group of 11-14 years in rural India, 6 per cent of the girls were not in school while the comparable number for boys was lower at 4.8 per cent.[46] While on the face of it these numbers may be discouraging,

---

[42]http://infochangeindia.org/education/statistics/gross-enrolment-ratios-in-primary-and-upper-primary-schools.html.

[43]Ibid.

[44]Female Literacy Rate in Urban India,Census of India, (2011), Chapter VI, Statement No. VI. 1—Literacy Rate in India and Kerala by Sex and Residence—1961-2011, http://www.censusindia.gov.in/2011-prov-results/paper2-vol2/data_files/kerala/Chapter_VI.pdf.

[45]Census of India, (2011), 'Female Literacy Rate in Rural India', Chapter VI, Statement No. VI. 1—Literacy Rate in India and Kerala by Sex and Residence—1961-2011, available at: http://www.censusindia.gov.in/2011-prov-results/paper2-vol2/data_files/kerala/Chapter_VI.pdf.

[46]Pratham, (2012), *Annual Status of Education Report (Rural)*—ASER 2012.

in 2006, 10.3 per cent of the girls in the 11-14 years age group were out of school and the comparable number for boys was 7.5 per cent.[47] Clearly even in a short period of five years, between 2006 and 2011 the enrolment of girls and boys is converging even in rural areas.

What is clearly evident is that on an average girls and boys are spending more number of years in school now than they were even a decade back. An unintended consequence of this is that the age of entry into the labour force is getting delayed, which is good and also many of these youngsters do not want to do traditional unskilled jobs any longer. The net result is the apparent labour market paradox. We have 13 million youngsters entering into the workforce every year and almost at every level labour availability is not adequate and relevant skilling is sorely lacking. As a result there is high pressure on wages across the board both in urban and rural India. Since 2009 nominal rural agricultural wages in India have been growing in excess of 15 per cent annually. The real rural wage growth was over 7.5 per cent between 2008-13 as compared to between 0.5-0.6 per cent per annum between 2000-08. This was also due to two other reasons: first, MNREGA[48] pushed up minimum wages and to some extent discouraged workers to take up other jobs. Second, there was a massive demand for workers in the construction sector and naturally the wage rates increased.

Education is, and will be, the single biggest change driver for girls and women over the next decade and more. Education empowers women by giving them a voice, opening up the windows to the world, making them aware of their rights, encouraging them to demand them, making them aware of avenues for remedy and very importantly giving them choices. Education also helps in

---

[47]Ibid.

[48]MNREGA—Mahatma Gandhi National Rural Emplyment Guarantee Act, a flagship programme of the UPA government that guaranteed 100 days of minimum employment to one able bodied member of every rural family living below the poverty line.

shaping more progressive attitudes and behaviour, although as we will see later in this book, such attitudinal and behavioural changes cannot be taken for granted. Nothing is more empowering and liberating when people have choices as access to choices truly empowers a person, although some people at times do end up taking the wrong decisions.

According to the World Development Report (2012), education investment along with that in health for women is special in three ways:

> First, educated women pass on the benefits of higher education to their children. As we will see even uneducated or semi-literate women are ensuring that their children get better educated. Children born to more educated mothers are less likely to die in infancy and more likely to have higher birth weights and be immunized. In Taiwan, the increase in schooling associated with education reform of 1968 saved almost 1 infant life for every 1,000 birth, reducing infant mortality by about 11 per cent. In Pakistan, even a single year of maternal education leads to children studying an additional hour at home and to higher test scores.[49]

Chandra's mother was barely literate and therefore, did not see much merit in her daughters being educated, although the family could well afford to even after the death of Chandra's father. But Chandra who was literate saw the merit in her daughters being educated. Rachita, Chandra's daughter, got married when she was only nineteen. By then or shortly thereafter Chandra had started standing up for her rights and the rights of her children within the larger family.

I spoke to Chandra's younger daughter, Sanchita, who lives and works in Sweden with her only daughter. Her house is double-storeyed with a small garden in the front, and towards the back the lawn merges with the woods. On bright summer days, birds come on to the porch to take a bath and drink water. Sanchita was tall,

---

[49]The World Bank, (2012), *World Development Report 2012: Gender Equality and Development.*

fair skinned and slightly overweight, with thinning hair. She wore high power prescription glasses with a trendy frame. The first proposal for marriage came when she was seventeen or eighteen, very similar to the age when her elder sister had got married. Sanchita recollected, 'The proposal came directly from the boy to my mother. Thankfully my mother said first I had to finish my graduation and be independent.' In another era, the proposal would have been welcomed as the boy was studying in one of the elite engineering institutes, IIT.

Sanchita went on to complete her graduation and then moved to Mumbai (then Bombay), in 1991. In Mumbai, Sanchita enrolled in an eighteen-month course at NIIT and her life changed. Mumbai and NIIT liberated her. This was a time when India had just started opening up its economy and suddenly the job market was booming. This was the period when thousands of students all over the country were enrolling in courses in information technology from institutes set up by NIIT and Aptech, two of the largest companies in this space; body shopping outfits were sending them to USA on projects. A few years later the Y2K boom resulted in demand for software professionals going through the roof. And for once India was ready to supply the world's requirement of software professionals.

The world knows of Indian giants like Infosys, Wipro and TCS which forced the likes of IBM and Accenture to start setting up offshore development centres in India. These corporates also provided unprecedented opportunities to a generation of youngsters like Sanchita who did not make it to one of the elite colleges or institutes in India like the IITs or AIIMS or IIMs. Sanchita started her career with a Tata group company, and then over the years moved from one multinational to another till she landed in Sweden and now works for one of the global telecom giants. Years later she completed her MBA from Gothenburg University in Sweden and is now working in a leadership role in project finance with responsibilities for a few regions like Northern Europe and Central Asia. Sanchita has a successful corporate career while single handedly bringing up her daughter. Economic independence and a gender friendly country gave her the courage to walk away from a bad marriage. But the steps towards a career of her own were not easy when in her extended family no girl or woman had worked outside their homes before.

Her mother's support, education, changes in society in the late twentieth century and India's economic reforms started under the stewardship of then Prime Minister P V Narasimha Rao changed Sanchita's life. As I realized during my interviews, these are necessary conditions but are not always sufficient. Over and above or maybe along with them, the presence of a role model or support system within the family or society is very important.

In Sanchita's words, 'I graduated from a girl's college in Kolkata in 1991. That year was the turning point in my life. After my exams, we went to Mumbai to spend my vacations at my brother's place. Since the vacations were for few months, my brother proposed that I should do something constructive during my stay. It was with his encouragement that I joined NIIT in Mumbai. The duration of the course was one and half years—after much discussion, disagreements and lots of encouragement from my brother, it was decided that I would stay back in Mumbai to complete the course. I would say that the foundation of my career was laid there. I had the most wonderful period of my life in Mumbai; the stay in Mumbai built a lot of character in me and made me quite an independent and strong woman. I used to stay at Mumbai with my brother and his friends and never felt I was being judged as a girl.'

Growing up in an India full of gender biases Sanchita needed a lot of luck, grit, determination and support, in her case to a certain limited extent, from her brother to get where she is now. She told me, 'When I look at the mirror, I see myself as both a prisoner of birth in certain aspects (certain inhibitions inculcated due to gender biased ideas from my childhood) and also a prisoner of circumstances. But when I see my daughter growing up in a free society, I see her as a free personality without any shades of being a prisoner of circumstances.'

In Indian society even today role models for young girls and some extra support are very essential and this is not just for the not so privileged. Meghna, the student from Cathedral School, Mumbai, told me about the support that the girls in her school receive from their principal. Her main role model is her father who has done very well professionally even as though he had to go through a very difficult period at a very early stage in his career because his mother was seriously ill.

The support that the girls in school receive from their principal is helping them get ahead in life and bring greater focus to their academics and careers. This is important because every student in the school may not have a role model at home like Meghna does. Meghna told me, 'In our school, our principal is a feminist and she is pushing the girls to go for every event and do well. She also gives talks in the assembly on women's empowerment. She highlights the girls' achievements. She has got physics, chemistry and biology prizes for girls. If the boys do well in a football match, it's great but if the girls do well, it's like out of the world. Do the guys resent this? Yes, they do. They say it is sexist, which it is and I totally agree. The issue is that she is trying to equalize the status of girls and boys. Once it equalizes, this will stop.'

I cannot emphasize often enough that irrespective of the socio-economic strata that the children come from, it is important to have some additional support and right role models. Most of the times there is a role model inside the home, and we also have role models from outside, primarily from schools or NGOs. Sometimes it is the same person, as in the case of Saira from Mumbai. Her aunt who works in a NGO ensured that Saira's education went in the right direction and thus, she escaped studying in a religious school in a slum.

Salva's role model is outside her home. Salva in Hyderabad trained to be a commercial pilot and had just obtained her commercial pilot license (CPL) when I met her. She is the first Muslim girl from Hyderabad to get a CPL thanks to her determination, hard work and a lot of support from her benefactor, Zaheeruddin Ali Khan, the proprietor and editor of *Siasat*, an Urdu daily published from Hyderabad. Without Zaheeruddin's encouragement and financial support, a baker's daughter would never have become a pilot. And of course there was her mother's support. When she was in Class X, her mother sold some of her jewellery to fund Salva's studies.

When I met Zaheeruddin and Salva at *Siasat's* office in Hyderabad in April 2013, I learnt that there were eleven other Muslim girls in the city training to become commercial pilots. Their ambitions were fuelled after reading Salva's story in the media and their families also supported them. Salva unbeknownst to herself has become a role model for Muslim girls in the city. When I met Salva, she was dressed in a smart pilot's uniform. As she was leaving, in one swift movement with practiced ease she wore a hijab on top of her uniform, covering herself from head to toe. The transformation from a modern aspiring pilot to a traditional Muslim girl was complete in less than a minute. It is tough being a girl in India, but Salva is also signalling the giant strides that girls like her have taken.

It would be difficult to appreciate how big a step this is for girls like Salva and the community they come from for people who are not familiar with the old city of Hyderabad. Muslims comprise over 40 per cent of the city's population and in the 1980s and 1990s the city unfortunately gained notoriety as young teenaged Muslim girls, often from impoverished backgrounds, were married off to wealthy sheikhs from the Middle East for small sums of money. Twelve and thirteen-year-old girls were forcefully married off to sixty and seventy year old men.

This was very well captured in the Hindi film *Bazaar*, which not only won critical and popular acclaim, but also became well known for its lilting and haunting musical score. Thankfully one does not hear about such incidents anymore. Media outrage, the spread of education and awareness, economic growth and opportunities, the work of NGOs and the philanthropy of families like the proprietors of *Siasat* and the emergence of Hyderabad as an IT centre, all helped to stem the rot that had spoilt and destroyed the lives of a generation of young girls. Girls like Salva are also playing a significant part in this change by serving as right role models. I asked Zaheeruddin what impact the education of girls was having on families and society. He said, 'They are challenging all the older norms. When a mother gets educated, then no child will remain illiterate.'

The decision to educate a girl child or for that matter young children has been aided to a certain extent by the government's efforts and campaigns to get children to school and also by programmes like the mid-day meal scheme. There is also the law of unintended consequences at work here. Slowly families have realized that getting a girl educated means less dowry, as we heard from Tanvi. I heard the same thing again and again during my travels through 2013. Manisha told me, 'Families have also realized over a period of time that education is very important even for marriage and finding a good groom. Without education, it will be difficult to get a groom. So freedom for girls is an unintended consequence of education to get a good groom. You sent a girl to study and then the side effects happened.' The side effects that Manisha mentioned are having boyfriends, deciding to take their own decisions and also taking fate in their own hands. It is like letting the genie out of the bottle and then losing all control over it.

Two social changes have also played a big role—the nuclearization of families and urbanization. The nuclearization of families is very important when one considers that in most traditional Indian households it is the larger family, primarily from the husband or father's side, which is involved in every major decision making for better or for worse.

In Priyanka's case (from Munger, Bihar), it was the extended family which influenced major decisions and since her father was younger than his brothers his writ rarely ran in the family. So how did things change for Priyanka or even for Tanvi? Priyanka's family was a nuclear family in the sense that they lived separately though in the vicinity of their extended family members. So while the 'family council' had a say and influence, the sisters could stand up for their rights. This would not have happened if they had been living under the same roof. In Tanvi's case her father was a practising doctor in a town, Forbesgunge, while the extended family lived in the village. Her mother, therefore, had an influence over family decisions and it helped that her father was well educated. Therefore, instead of getting tutored at home as many of her cousins did, Tanvi went to a proper school.

It is anecdotally evident that joint families are breaking down and nuclearization of families is on the rise. Even when families in small towns or rural areas stay in one house or complex, often for all practical purposes there is nuclearization with separate kitchens and separate floors. Census 2011 data supports this. Households with nine persons or more in family size declined by 4.7 per cent in the last decade. This decline was faster in rural areas at 5 per cent while it was 3.9 per cent in urban areas.[50] Households with 6–8 persons declined by 3.2 per cent, with the decline in rural areas being 2.6 per cent and in urban areas 3.8 per cent. Households with 3–5 persons showed the sharpest increase of 6.3 per cent, with rural growing at 5.7 per cent and urban at 6.4 per cent. Extended families' influence on decisions will also continue to reduce and this by itself will reduce patriarchal dominance in decision making.

I met nineteen-year-old Reena Chouhan at her home in Bhavnagar shortly before meeting Daksha. It was a fifteen-minute ride by an auto-rickshaw from the Shaishav offices. I got off the auto near a small temple and then started my walk into the narrow lanes and by-lanes of the slum where Reena lived. The tree outside the temple had discoloured kites stuck in its branches, a reminder of the famous kite festival held in January during Sankranti[51] which is a major tourist draw in Gujarat.

Off the main road, suddenly the landscape changed—the narrow

---

[50]http://www.devinfolive.info/censusinfodashboard/.

[51]Makar Sankranti is one of the most auspicious days for Hindus and is celebrated in almost all parts of the country in myriad cultural forms with great devotion, fervour and gaiety in January. While it is based on the lunar calendar, it is also a harvest festival. In many parts of India it is celebrated by flying colourful kites.

road was made of gravel and stones while low hanging electric wires, crisscrossing each other were visible all over the place, as were open drains. The houses in the locality were all single storied with tiled roofs and brightly painted walls. It was afternoon and young people, particularly boys, could be seen in the streets in small groups, some perched on motorbikes that have become ubiquitous all over India. I crossed the courtyard to enter Reena's house through a narrow and low door. Her mother was stitching a bright multi-coloured quilt, the kind that Gujarat is well-known for.

The room where we sat was largely bare except for utensils. The walls were adorned with a calendar and pictures of sundry gods and goddesses. The roof leaked and this was obvious from a strategically placed plastic bucket in the middle of the room. Surprisingly and incongruously the floor was tiled. Reena's mother, Geeta behn, does multiple jobs to make both ends meet and didn't look a year above thirty-five. Her slim build would be the envy of many affluent urban women and she showed no signs of having reared three children. She wanted to send one of her daughters to fetch some Coca Cola for me and I had to literally plead with her not to. We settled for lime water made at home since she would not let a first time visitor go without having anything in her house.

Reena's father, Ashok bhai, paints houses and depends on daily work to earn his livelihood. Reena is the oldest of three children and is in the second year of her three-year undergraduate course. Her brother is the youngest in the family and studies in Class VIII. Reena was encouraged to study by her mother. In her words, 'My mother never studied; in her time, people did not educate girls. Therefore, she can't read or write. I have taught her how to sign her name. She still doesn't have a bank account. But she worked her whole life in other peoples' houses (bungalows) as a domestic help to ensure that I studied. And that's how I have studied so far. She continuously encouraged me even when I did not do well. From her I get the encouragement to move ahead in life. I failed in English in Class X and left my studies. But my mother said that I had to work hard and try again and give the exams. I left studies for a year and then restarted with encouragement from my mother and the people at Shaishav. I sat for my exam again and cleared it.'

Thanks to Shaishav and the youth festivals it sends the children to, Reena is surprisingly well travelled within the country especially for someone coming from an economically challenged background. Reena also got an opportunity to visit the US but her uncle (father's elder brother) whom she calls dada scuttled the plans. Five other girls went to America but Reena did not because she thought some paper work could not be completed in time. However, it was her dada who had put a spanner in the works. Reena told me, 'Dada told my father not to let me travel abroad. My parents are not educated and dada helps with things like documentation. One month later I learnt that it was dada who had stopped me from going. I will certainly let my daughter go, if such an opportunity arises, and will not listen to any objections from my family. I will be the one to take the decision in her case.'

Not just for her daughter, if Reena gets a second opportunity, her dada will no longer be able to influence the decision. As I got up to leave, I could not resist asking about the floor tiles in a house where the roof obviously leaked. Reena told me that the tiles came for free (from her maternal grandmother) and her mother laid them. Her mother is a cook, home maker, seamstress and a mason as well. When people like her start coming into the mainstream, as has started happening now, the impact will be nothing less than revolutionary.

Nuclearization of families is closely linked to the phenomenon of urbanization. In India there has been a tendency to romanticize village life and all that it means. This has been reinforced in contemporary India primarily by politicians and also by many NGOs, which find it easy to quote Mahatma Gandhi, the father of the nation, who once said that India lived in its villages. India lives in its villages but it doesn't need to continue living there with all the ills as well as deleterious social norms and practices.

B R Ambedkar, independent India's first law minister and the chairperson of the Constitution Drafting Committee, said about villages and panchayats, 'A population which is hidebound by caste; a population which is infected by ancient prejudices; a population which flouts equality of status and is dominated by notions of gradations in life; a population which thinks that some are high and some are low—can it be expected to have the right notions even to discharge bare justice? Sir, I deny that proposition, and I submit that it is not proper to expect us to submit our life, and our liberty, and our property to the hands of these panchas.'[52]

Ambedkar believed and rightly so that villages were cesspools of communalism, gender injustice, casteism and the resultant cruelty. I remember a trip to Rajasthan a few years back when I, along with one of my then colleagues Anshu Govil, travelled to a village to see the check dams built by Magsaysay Award winner Rajendra Singh, also known as the waterman of India.[53] The driver, belonging to the Rajput clan, started throwing his weight around once we reached the village and went about ordering people to fetch water for us to drink and even asked whether the well that the water was coming from was used by upper or lower caste people. I was amazed and I asked him how he made these distinctions when he was drinking tea in a roadside tea stall in Jaipur. He answered, 'Saheb, this is a village and here things happen like this only. In the city who bothers or cares about caste?'

What is true about caste is also true about gender justice to a large extent. Noted columnist Swaminathan Anklesaria Aiyar writes:

In Punjab and Haryana, village councils called khap panchayats act as de facto courts settling rural disputes on everything from land and cattle to matrimony and murder. They break every rule and law on human rights. Their decisions range from banning women from wearing western clothing and using mobile phones to supporting child marriage and sanctioning the lynching of young couples in so-called 'honour killings'. These killings typically

[52]Speech at Bombay Legislative Council when it debated enhanced powers for panchas through a Village Panchayats Bill.

[53]http://sociovigil.in/rajendra-singh-waterman-of-rajasthan/.

happen when the young girl and boy are from different
communities, but also when the youngsters belong to the same
Hindu gotra. Let nobody think this occurs only in the barbaric
north...Tamil Nadu is supposedly much more civilized than
Haryana. But in 2012, Vanniyars (members of an intermediate
caste) burned the houses of 268 dalits after a dalit boy eloped
with a Vanniyar girl.[54]

Urbanization because of pressures of space and also given the
difficulties in uprooting entire families from villages, results in the
breakdown of joint families at a rapid pace. This is as true of rural
families as of large urban households, which are increasingly breaking
down into smaller units. As more and more families become smaller
units, the decision making unit is also becoming smaller and women
and children have a greater say in decisions in the household.
Secondly, urbanization breaks down the village social structure
based on caste hierarchies and the new urban social structure is
primarily based on shared economic interests and to a lesser extent
on shared geographical or state identities.

There are many ills of unplanned and unregulated urbanization,
including increase in stress levels as traditional support structures
vanish and increase in the migration of young single males may
result in greater violence and crime, particularly if job opportunities
and the ability to support a family in towns and cities are lacking.
But it clearly also drives better gender sensitivity and empowers
women to question traditional social mores and empowers them to
have more control over their lives and future and the lives and
futures of their children and their families. Urbanization leads to
improved productivity in even poor households because of simple
changes like women not having to go out to collect firewood or
fetch water from kilometres away, although they may still have to
wake up at 4 a.m. to collect water which comes only for half an hour
in the slums in a city like Mumbai. Urbanization also drives better
access to resources and infrastructure like schools and colleges.

---

[54]http://blogs.timesofindia.indiatimes.com/Swaminomics/entry/ambedkar-vs-
gandhi-the-risks-of-village-empowerment.

Over the last three decades, urbanization in India increased from 23.3 per cent to 31.2 per cent,[55] an annual pace of nearly 1 per cent. During the same period, family sizes declined from 5.5 persons per household[56] to just over four per household.[57] It is true that there are various factors at play when we look at reduction in family sizes and reduction in fertility, but urbanization is a key factor.

I met Shafiq, a taxi driver in Mumbai one afternoon as I was driving to a meeting at Four Seasons Hotel in the middle of the city. In his late twenties, Shafiq hails from Uttar Pradesh. His extended family in the village has about 200 members. His immediate family— his father's brothers and sisters and his first cousins number over sixty. Shafiq has been married for six years and has one child. His wife and child live with him in Mumbai and he candidly said that if he was living in his village, by now he would have had five or six children. In Mumbai he cannot afford that and he wants his three-year-old daughter to go to a decent school.

And then—and this surprised, amused and educated me in equal measure—he said that in villages good quality condoms are not available. In Mumbai he got good quality condoms—Rs 125 for a pack of ten he informed me—and well, it just feels as good as not wearing one! Moreover, in the village, the young couple would face social and family pressure to have more children. The poor and the lower middle class and the choices they make! Sitting from my perch I would think that sanitation, a bigger house, more nutritious food would be Shafiq's priorities but his priority is spending on

---

[55]Urbanization in India: Office of the Registrar General, India; Table 1.8: Trend in Urbanization—India; Selected Socio-Economic Statistics India (2011).

[56]Household Size in 1981: Census 2001; Statement-1: Number of households, population, average household size and growth by residence 1971–2001; http://censusindia.gov.in/Data_Products/Data_Highlights/Data_Highlights_link/data_highlights_hh1_2_3.pdf

[57]Household Size in 2011: *New Estimates of India's Middle Class*—Christian Meyer, Nancy Birdsall; Center for Global Development; http://www.cgdev.org/doc/2013_MiddleClassIndia_TechnicalNote_CGDNote.pdf.

great quality condoms, as per his own admission, and his daughter's education. The choices that the poor make and what drives these decisions is best discussed in the book *Poor Economics* by Abhijit Banerjee and Esther Duflo, professors of economics at Massachusetts Institute of Technology (MIT), Cambridge. After reading the book and getting to know about the various characters it discusses, I should have been less surprised by the choices Shafiq was making, but I have to admit I still was.

Urbanization has both intended and unintended consequences. Smaller or nuclear families are not necessarily intended, but are a consequence of lack of space as also of expenses given the cost of living, particularly of renting space. On the other hand, living in towns and cities gives more, and often better quality, information to individuals. This is due to higher media penetration, more social awareness and access to NGOs. Urbanization also provides access to educational institutions in terms of numbers, in terms of proximity to place of living and in terms of quality, infrastructure and teacher attendance.

As a proxy it is interesting to see the enrolment of students in primary classes in different types of schools and the differences between genders. The District Information System of Education (DISE) statistics published in 2012 showed that the percentage of students going to private schools increased to 29.8 per cent in 2011 from 24 per cent in 2002. ASER 2012 (Rural) said:

> The trend is unmistakable. Private school enrolment in rural India is increasing at about 10 per cent every year or about 3 percentage points per year. In the election year of 2014, about 41 per cent of all of India's primary age children will be in private schools, and by the time 2019 elections come around, private sector will be the clear major formal education provider in India.[58]

Seventy-six per cent of total enrolments in classes I to V were in government schools, including schools run by local bodies. When

---

[58]Annual Status of Education Report (Rural) 2012 Provisional, 17 January 2013, p. 4.

we look at gender differences, nearly 78 per cent girls went to government schools while 75 per cent boys went to government schools.[59] A greater proportion of boys going to private schools were due to the perception and beliefs that private schools provide better education and therefore, better prospects. The trends were similar in rural India as well.

Let us take a look at the differences in enrolment by type of school from classes I to V in urban and rural areas. In 2002, 87 per cent of rural students were going to government schools while the corresponding numbers for urban areas was a mere 43 per cent.[60] Clearly urban students had better access to private schools and in metro cities like Mumbai there are enough anecdotes to indicate how municipal schools are empty even as there is a queue to get into private schools, sometimes even of dubious quality, by paying usurious fees. ASER 2012 (Rural) says:

> It is time to start looking at private schooling more carefully and understand problems of urban education planning as also to regulate private schooling without taking away the essential strengths of the private school. Government funded and regulated, but not controlled, private schools—like the aided or 'charter schools'—replacing government-run schools seems to be the way of the future.[61]

The Municipal Corporation of Greater Mumbai (MCGM) has started experimenting with the public private partnership (PPP) model by handing over some schools to NGOs like Akanksha, Aseema and Muktangan.

Since there is commitment of money from the families when it comes to private schooling, clearly even today more investments are being made on boys. Therefore, it is not surprising to see that in

---

[59]NCERT, (2002), Seventh All India School Education Survey.

[60]Ibid.

[61]Annual Status of Education Report (Rural) 2012 Provisional, 17 January 2013, p. 5.

urban areas 40.4 per cent of the boys go to government schools as against 45 per cent girls.[62] For rural areas, the corresponding numbers are 85.4 per cent and 88.1 per cent for boys and girls respectively.[63] If rural India starts getting anywhere close to urban amenities then the trend of more private schools will only increase as more private schools will be set up and access to these schools will become easier. Even in a state like Maharashtra where infrastructure is very good, in village Bhoirepathar, district Ahmedanagar, I was told that 30 per cent girls drop out after Class X because the junior college is in the city and public transport is unreliable. Along with that the not so subtle gender bias evident in statistics—more boys attending private schools as compared to girls—will also hopefully end.

ASER 2012 (Rural) notes:

> In the early days of this third millennium, shanty 'affordable' schools started coming up in rural and urban areas. Gradually investors have done their math and gauged the demand for education. It appears that big 'international' schools are coming up in rural areas that bus children from distant villages for economic viability. This model will probably start to dominate rural landscapes as India's wealth increases. On the urban side, the Municipal Corporation of Greater Mumbai came up with a proposal to hand over management of at least some of its schools to private education providers and a few other governments seem to be considering similar approaches. Such ideas known as PPP are opposed on purely ideological grounds by some; while schools run by governments in many states (especially in urban areas) are emptying out.
>
> The best example of this may be Tamil Nadu, which is now 48 per cent urbanized according to Census 2011. DISE reports that in 2010-11, 59.4 per cent of all (urban and rural) children in Std I-V attended private schools in Tamil Nadu. Only a third of these were in aided private schools. ASER 2010 estimated that the

---

[62]NCERT, (2002), Seventh All India School Education Survey.

[63]Ibid.

rural private enrolment in Std I-V in the same state was around 28.5 per cent, and is up to 34.8 per cent in 2012. A simple back of the envelope estimation says that anywhere between 80 and 100 per cent children in Std I-V in urban Tamil Nadu are in private schools and less than a fifth of these are government aided.[64]

Urbanization in many ways is the great equalizer as it gives access to physical infrastructure like schools and also to information. Urbanization is a natural outcome of growth and development. In India, urbanization has not been done in a planned and controlled manner as has been done in China. The rate of urbanization in India was about 0.8 per cent per annum[65] in the last five years and from 2005 to 2010, the urban population grew at a rate 2.58 per cent annually. Given the lack of concomitant investment in urban infrastructure and facilities, there has been rapid growth in slum population, stress on urban facilities, deterioration in the quality of life and increasing law and order problems.

However, in recent years access to urban facilities and amenities grew rapidly thanks to the road development programme undertaken by the NDA[66] government under the then Prime Minister Atal Bihari Vajpayee. The NDA government undertook two flagship road building programmes—the National Highways Development Programme (NHDP), which had two main programmes to start with, a golden quadrilateral (GQ) and a north-south-east-west (NSEW) corridor, and the Pradhanmantri Gram Sadak Yojana (PMGSY), which envisaged linking rural dwellings with a population of over 250 with motorable roads.

Notwithstanding time delays, the GQ and NSEW programmes

[64]Annual Status of Education Report (Rural) 2012 Provisional, 17 January 2013, p. 4.

[65]World Urbanization Prospects, the 2011 Revision and 2014.

[66]The National Democratic Alliance was a BJP led coalition and the first non-Congress government to last its full term of five years, first from 1998-99 and then from 1999-2004.

were substantially completed. Although subsequent development plans floundered after the UPA[67] government came to power, the PMGSY programme continued to see significant progress even under the UPA government. Under the PMGSY 366,788 kms of roads had been constructed and upgraded connecting 89,071 inhabitations by all-weather roads over 2000–01 and up to December 2012 at a total cost of Rs 96,676 crores (about US$18bn at Rs 55 for US$1).[68] As road development progresses, the trend of rural India getting access to urban amenities will only accelerate. In fact the rise of Census towns[69] is testimony to this.

The road development programmes have changed the lives of rural families and increased and diversified their income options. Some of the benefits have been documented in research papers and I, too, have witnessed anecdotal evidence of incomes going up by ten to fifty times. What has also happened is that road development has made schools and colleges accessible to both boys and girls and made it safer to travel, which is especially important for girls in small towns and rural areas. According to Pradeep Lokhande of Rural Relations of Pune, the access to primary schools is presently within a radius of 1.5 kms as against over 7 kms in the mid-1990s.

It is not just schools and colleges, but beyond that too there have been employment opportunities opening up where there were none. Research has shown that the national highways development programme has resulted in a:

> [...] distinct structural shift in the rural economy in terms of an increase in non-farm activities, higher workforce participation, an increase in school enrolment and better literacy levels. There

---

[67]United Progressive Alliance is a Congress led coalition, which won the election in 2004 and 2009.

[68]Ministry of Rural Development, 'Annual Report 2012–13', available at: www.rural.nic.in.

[69]Census towns are defined as inhabitations with more than 5,000 people with at least 75 per cent of the male working population engaged in non-agricultural activities and a minimum population density of 400 persons per square kilometre.

is a noticeable increase in female participation in the workforce as also the school enrolment of girls. These beneficial changes help in the empowerment of women [...] this is a clear indication of improvement in job opportunities and access to markets, schools and other services.[70]

It is also changing the pattern of migration in the country. For the ten years ending 2007–08, poverty-induced migration had become a less important component of mobility over time as is evident from the decline in rural-rural (RR) migration. There is no evidence of strong distress factors behind rural-urban (RU) migration, driving the migrants out of their place of origin or keeping them in distress in the labour market even after the migration. Migrant workers' dependence on rural agriculture came down between 1999–2000 and 2007–08. Data on migrant and non-migrant workers in rural areas also points to lesser dependence on agriculture.[71] If temporary distress induced migration reduces, more children, particularly girls, will remain in schools for longer.

Easier travel has made it possible for many girls now to go to nearby towns and cities to study and take up employment opportunities. I met Vidya Hande, twenty-six, at a Dr Reddy's Laboratories Foundation (DRF) centre in Hyderabad in 2013. The security guard outside the building was wearing ill-fitting grey clothes and had a wooden baton in his hand. He directed us to the DRF office with a bored look. Security guards have been in great demand all over India in commercial buildings, factories and residential homes and this segment has created the most jobs along with the construction sector over the last decade. If the latter is the symbol of strong growth in the country, the former is the symbol of the failure of the government to provide safety and law and order. It

---

[70]Socio-Economic Impact of National Highway on Rural Population, (2011), Asian Institute of Transport Development.

[71]Amitabh Kundu and Lopamudra Ray Saraswati, (2012), 'Migration and Exclusionary Urbanization in India', *Economic and Political Weekly* XLVII (26–27): 219–27.

does not require much training or education or skills to become a security guard, and if you have a gun license, which usually retired armed forces and police personnel have, then you could be assured of a significantly higher salary than your baton wielding colleagues.

The ground floor of the building had a rice 'supermarket' and we had never seen a store with such wide varieties of rice. In a most unlikely place we stumbled upon the diversity that this country is all about, whether it is about food, clothes, religion or social practices. Similarly at times the most unlikely of tastes in two vastly different parts of the country fascinate me immensely. In the morning when we had driven into the city from the airport, our attention had been caught by a building that resembled a fish. I had seen a building between Chandigarh and Ludhiana in Punjab which had a pink coloured concrete airplane on its roof. While the airplane demonstrated the taste and wealth of the owner, the fish it seems was the work of some not so imaginative bureaucrat in the fisheries department of Andhra Pradesh.

Tina, my co-researcher on this trip, and I climbed the narrow dark steps to reach the centre located on the first floor. Most of the other offices in this building were of stockbrokers and wore a deserted look with their signboards desperately in need of a fresh coat of paint. This run-down look was not surprising since for the last nearly five years the benchmark Sensex had been flat and investors had lost a lot of money in stocks betting on the potential economic growth in the country, which had rapidly unravelled since the great financial crisis of 2008 and more so after 2010 when various alleged scams during the UPA regime came to public knowledge. By 2012 the stock broking industry was laying off people with frightening regularity as business dwindled. Retail investors stayed away from the markets and instead preferred to invest in gold, the perennial favourite, and real estate in an environment of low growth and high inflation.

I digress. We were shown into a room adjacent to cramped security-cum-reception desk. The walls of the centre had posters and flow charts with daily activities about the foundation's various courses and listed the names of the corporate sponsors or clients for whom a specific course had been designed. It was a busy time of the day and a couple of classes were on.

Vidya had recently started working in a BSNL[72] call centre. Dark in appearance, she wore a white necklace and was dressed in a gold and mauve coloured salwar kameez with a matching dupatta. She had a tiny nose ring, commonly worn by women in this part of the country, and was carrying a purple purse matching her dress. She was constantly coughing during our conversation and as we learnt she was asthmatic. The lab was right next to a busy road and our conversation was frequently interrupted by loud horns of public buses and trucks going past.

Vidya hails from a village in Nanded, Maharashtra and lived there with her parents and two siblings. Her eldest brother joined the army after studying up to Class X and at the time of our meeting was posted in Jammu & Kashmir. Her father, an army personnel, had moved to his ancestral village after his retirement but over a period of time he had lost most of his land and property to his other family members. It came to a stage when Vidya's parents could not afford the education of all the three siblings. This was when Vidya decided to move out and fend for herself.

She had friends in Hyderabad, the city where she had lived in till she was seventeen since her father was posted in the Army Centre in Secunderabad and they encouraged her to come there and start working. In her words, 'When I came here, I first went to Lifestyle[73] in Begumpet to work as a tele-caller. But since I had no experience in any job, I could not understand anything and at the end of the first day I was very worried about what I would do. I was quite tense because I had left my village to come here. Then a friend of Vijay Sir (an instructor at DRF) told me about Dr Reddy's

[72]Bharat Sanchar Nigam Limited, a public sector unit that provides landline and mobile telephony services all over India, except in New Delhi and Mumbai.

[73]'Lifestyle' is a chain of department stores set up by a Dubai based NRI family that has interests in retailing in the Middle East.

Foundation and the training they offer. The same day I came here, enrolled myself and paid the fees of Rs 2,400.'

About fifteen years back it would have been unimaginable that Vidya would be able to get out of her village and travel to Hyderabad on her own to search for a job, even though the distance between Nanded and Hyderabad is a mere 300 kms. The road, the resultant connectivity and ease of communication have clearly helped; bus services are more frequent and there is safety in numbers. In fact the latest Census threw up a very interesting statistic. Census towns—towns that have a population of more than 5,000 with 75 per cent of the adult males being engaged in income generating activities other than agriculture—declined by 341 between 1991 and 2001,[74] and most policy makers that I had met then said that intermediate towns that served as bridges between rural India and larger towns had lost their raison d'être.

However, over the last decade, between 2001 and 2011, the number of Census towns increased by 2,532,[75] the highest ever increase reported in any decade since independence. What is the reason for this sudden spurt in Census towns? I do not have exact answers and bureaucrats, independent economists and analysts that I spoke to did not have any convincing answers either. Hence, I can only speculate and my own sense is that the road development work since 2002 rejuvenated Census towns and other small towns.

These agglomerations and towns have seen a spurt in economic activity and economic opportunities, whether related to sales, repair and servicing of electronic equipment and consumer durables or outlets selling mobile phones and DVDs. Good roads have meant more road travel and some of these towns have dealerships and service centres for two and four wheelers. Ravish Kumar, a senior

---

[74]Census, (2001), available at: http://censusindia.gov.in/Census_Data_2001/ Census_Newsletters/Newsletter_Links/eci_3.htm.

[75]'New "census" towns showcase new India', *Live Mint & The Wall Street Journal*, available at: http://www.livemint.com/Politics/HQzcUy1meBiq2aeaS9dAZO/ New-census-towns-showcase-new-India.html.

and well respected journalist with NDTV India, in an investor conference in early 2014 mentioned that his village in Bihar had seen a spurt in stores selling readymade garments and the first sweet shop too had opened in his village. At one end if better infrastructure has helped in improving access to goods and services, it has also helped the population to diversify their incomes and reduce their dependence on agricultural income and hence, monsoons.

I had heard the same thing in Chhattisgarh a few years back. I had met Prayaag Joshi who runs a school, Imlee Mahua,[76] in a village called Balengapara, which is a Naxal infested area. The village didn't have any electricity, running water or phone connections and the villagers were subsistence farmers belonging to the Gond tribe. The school then had less than ten students and now has about sixty students. Prayaag told me that thanks to better road connectivity, readymade clothes and packed spices were now available in the village. When Prayaag had first started working in the village most of the children would not wear clothes, but with time, things had changed. Multiply this with 600,000 villages in the country and a revolution seems to be taking place. Roads have made it easy to distribute different products and services in rural India.

Roads have rapidly shrunk the distance between urban and rural India but they are not the only drivers of connectivity. There are others that are as important and these are mobile phones, internet and media, particularly television. About fifteen years back Vidya would not have been able to keep in touch with her friends after moving back to her village. Letters can take a very long time, are unreliable and simply lack the convenience of a phone. Imagine what would have happened to Vidya then. She would by now be working in someone's house as a maid or would have been married off or most likely both. The only obstacle to an early marriage was that her father did not have the cash to pay for her marriage.

---

[76]Imlee Mahua—for more details on the school and Prayaag Joshi's work, please visit the website www.imleemahuaa.org.

Mobile phones have been truly liberating and empowering. In an urban setting, a street vendor or a small businessman offering services like that of an electrician, plumber or chemist has been able to multiply his earnings many times as he has become easily accessible to his customers, his response time has reduced dramatically and as a result the whole nation has got a productivity bump up. I remember meeting a farmer en route to Mathura from Delhi a few years back. Sitting in his home just off the main highway to Mathura, he told me how he called his wife from the fields when he was ready to have his lunch and his wife got him piping hot food—better food, a happier farmer and a wife who didn't have to get up at the break of dawn to prepare lunch. If the pump in the field or the tractor broke down, he simply called up the mechanic in the nearest town on his cell phone and usually help was at hand within a couple of hours. A decade back this simple task would have taken a couple of days and the equipment would have lain idle for at least three or four days.

Mobile phones have also increased economic opportunities for women in villages and smaller towns and cities. This is especially relevant when most jobs are being created in the informal sector. Mobile phones along with the use of information technology are empowering the disenfranchised, more particularly women in different parts of the country in another very significant manner. They are bringing banking to their doorsteps. It is estimated that over 50 per cent adult Indians do not have a bank account and are thus, outside the purview of the formal banking system. Their savings are often kept in jars and tins meant for groceries, if they indeed have any savings. These people are more often than not at the mercy of usurious moneylenders. Both men and women are affected but women are worse impacted. This story plays out across urban and rural areas.

For the formal banking system, getting such people into its fold is commercially not a viable or a wise decision. For one, it is very expensive to reach out to this segment of the population, especially in remote rural areas, and it does not have enough wealth to justify the time, efforts and costs involved in making them a part of the banking system and then keeping them within the folds of the formal banking system. From time to time the government and the Reserve Bank of India (RBI) have made some efforts and thus public sector banks have been forced to open rural branches. But the managers and officials there have no incentive to bank the unbanked and often treat their prospective customers with disdain and also harass them at times. The problem is compounded for women who cannot even travel to a bank branch without being escorted by a male member from the family. Illiteracy makes their situation worse. Priyanka from Munger told me of the harassment her father faced when he wanted to open a bank account in her name.

It is here that microfinance institutions, coupled with mobile phones and technology, are providing affordable banking solutions. According to one news report, 'Information technology and the innovative use of the ubiquitous mobile phone are bringing banking to the doorsteps of people living below the poverty line in states like Uttar Pradesh and Bihar. In the process, poor women are now being increasingly brought into the banking fold. They are able to economically empower themselves by opening their own savings accounts, access micro-credit schemes and start small businesses of their own.'[77]

According to Mukul Jaiswal, Managing Director, Cashpor Micro Credit, a not-for-profit microfinance institution based in Varanasi, 'Mobile phones have helped reach out to those village women who would have never thought that they could engage with a bank. It has become a game changer considering the socio-economic barriers and cultural norms that prevent them from engaging with formal banking services.'[78] This is not only about empowering rural women. Disadvantaged girls and women in urban areas are also benefitting from these developments. Additionally some NGOs are working to

---

[77]http://indiatogether.org/how-mobile-phones-help-poor-women-economy#s thash.ffTO4ucq.dpuf.

[78]Ibid.

improve the financial literacy of women. One such organization is the American Indian Foundation (AIF), which has two mobile phone applications for improving the financial literacy of young girls. This is exactly the kind of empowerment that Nandan Nilekani, as the chairperson of UIDAI, was visualizing and targeting.

It is difficult to imagine the kind of empowerment that mobile phones are bringing to girls and women both in urban and rural areas. It has given them a tool not only to be in touch with near and dear ones without depending on a male member of the household but also brought the world closer to them. Santosh Desai, CEO of Future Brands and regular columnist in *The Times of India*, told me to watch out for conservative religious leaders and society elders opposing or raising their voices against mobile phones because their opposition will be reserved for things that are empowering people, specifically women and liberating them from age-old shackles. Jeans and mobile phones fall into this bracket. Empowerment comes from the ability to exercise choice when there are multiple options. The backlash that we see from khap panchayats or family patriarchs is also a move to deny girls and women choices that will lead to their empowerment. Such choice is often denied in the name of the safety and well being of women; it's played out, for instance, when women are pulled out of schools since otherwise they will have to travel long distances.

Television and internet are also playing a large role in changing power equations. Information is available literally at everyone's finger tips at the press of a button. Today nearly 117 million households[79] in India have a television set, up from 61 million households in 2001.[80] The number of households that have access

---

[79]Census, (2011), CensusInfo India (2011), available at: http://www.devinfo.org/indiacensus2011/libraries/aspx/Home.aspx?refer_url=catalog&jsonAreas Topics= {%22apn%22:%2235%22,%22i%22:%22Availability%20of%20assets:%20Television%20-%20Households%22,%22i_n%22:%22144%22,%22a%22:%22India%22,%22a_n%22:%221%22}

[80]Census, (2001), available at: http://censusindia.gov.in/Census_And_You/availability_of_eminities_and_assets.aspx.

to televisions is obviously more. In the last nearly four years, I have not seen any village without a Tata Sky or Zee or Videocon or Airtel dish antenna atop a few houses. In slums in urban areas almost every household has access to cable television.

Television viewing is bringing the world inside the living rooms and bedrooms of people and shrinking the knowledge gap between rich India and poor India and between urban India and rural India like nothing has before. It is also empowering women by telling them about their rights in society, about birth control measures, about pregnancy, about relationships and most importantly about how society is changing.

I asked a village elder in Sehor, Madhya Pradesh, about the impact of television sets in almost every household in the village. He said that earlier they watched Krishi Darshan on Doordarshan, a programme targeting farmers on the state owned television channel. After the advent of cable TV, he said the men could hardly lay their hands on the remote. Now after watching serials and movies, the boys and the girls get into a relationship and run away (*chora chori bhaag jaate hain*).

I had a similar conversation with a group of villagers in Warora, Maharashtra, when I had gone to visit Baba Amte's ashram. There a panchayat leader told me that divorce rates in the villages in the region were going up. I asked him whether it was the men who were driving this and his answer stumped me. He said that even women had started deciding to end marriages if something was not working out as they had learnt from watching TV soap operas that divorce was a way of life for women elsewhere. The taboo associated with divorce and separation was suddenly no longer there. While I have no data on this, I will not be surprised if this empowerment where women are able to take decisions about their future in their own hands leads to better gender equations all over the country and less domestic violence.

I asked Manisha in Delhi about the influence of television on changes in society. She said, 'Exposure coming from TV is important. Wearing jeans is of course influenced by TV. TV also tells you about fashion. In Allahabad I had no idea about waxing; I had never visited a parlour. When I left Allahabad I was twenty-one. When I went to Bombay I was exposed to these things for the first time in the hostel I was staying in (Manisha studied at the SNDT Women's University). I have to say that whatever I am today I give a lot of credit to that city, Bombay. May be that spark of rebellion was inside me, but the release, the canvas and the ground for it was provided by the city.'

The small television set is having such a large impact on the lives of people that the clerics, priests and khap panchayats will not be able to take television sets out of homes however much they may want to. They will also not be able to take mobile phones out of the hands of girls and women.

There are over 800 million mobile phone connections in India today. At the end of 2013, there were 205 million internet users in India, making India the third largest base of internet users in the world. Adding 4 million internet users every month, India will overtake USA to become the second largest internet user market by end of 2014. The fascinating part is that while some of us are rueing the lack of high speed broadband as a constraint to internet and e-commerce, about 65 per cent of internet users in the country are accessing the net through their mobile devices. Every one of the 4 million new internet users is accessing the internet through mobile phones. How will village elders, khap panchayats, clerics, and control freak husbands, boyfriends, brothers and fathers ever control what information girls and women have access to?

According to the World Development Report 2012, a globally inter-connected world and the spread of information and communication technologies have resulted in more jobs and stronger connections to markets for women in many countries, thus increasing the economic opportunities accessible to them. Further, given global awareness about issues around gender equality and women's rights, continued gender inequality and women's oppression can hurt a country's international standing and economy. For example, the increase in violence against women in India impacted tourist inflows into the country. The report says that 'greater access to information has allowed many in developing countries to learn about life and mores in other parts of the world, including those pertaining to the role of women, possibly affecting attitudes and behaviours.'

In a country where girls cannot express themselves or publicly vent their feelings in a manner similar to boys and men, internet and social media have been a boon. It is very difficult for many of us to imagine this, given the world we live in. Tanvi finished her medical studies in 2005. How have the attitudes of young girls changed since then? Do the boys in her college behave differently now? During Tanvi's time eve-teasing was rampant on the medical college campus. Even as girls entered a class, the boys—even their own batch mates—would comment on their looks, their clothes and pass sexist comments and innuendos.

I believe this is a result of the restrictions placed by society and the resultant social mores that frown upon free mixing of boys and girls; children grow up segregated in the name of Indian culture and tradition. 'We were so afraid of going to classes,' Tanvi remembered over a decade later. Girls like Tanvi were constantly under scrutiny because of their gender. Rumours would spread throughout the campus if a girl was seen talking to a professor. A girl's personality and character were judged by the kind of clothes she wore.

When and how did things start changing? Tanvi told me about how girls in her batch stood up against a practice in their campus, which had probably been going on for years. In her words, 'Let me tell you...may be the change started in our time. In our first year we had to study anatomy, physiology and biochemistry. In every batch the boys made a list of the first year girls—it is very funny and not funny. You know in anatomy the body is divided into different parts like head, abdomen, upper limb, lower limbs, pelvis, thorax etc. Each part of the anatomy of first year girls was given a score—given marks—by the boys. And the list was made into posters and placed all over the institute including on the notice boards. A boy from our class, Niazi, had this list of all the girls with scores and when I asked him about it, he said it was nothing. I didn't know about this "tradition" then and the next day the posters were all over the institute.'

'There was a meeting in the girls' hostel and some girls suggested that we should formally lodge a complaint. This time the posters had a list of first year students, five girls from each of the other batches and even the names of some of the female professors. Actually instead of real names of the girls, some very silly acronyms were used. The posters were all over the institute—in classrooms, on notice boards and on the institute's walls. I said that I had seen the list in Niazi's hand the day before it went public. Five-six girls were very agitated. In the morning we went and caught hold of Niazi and thrashed him and locked him up in the canteen. We said unless the administration took some action we will not release him. The boys attacked us and we went and filed a complaint against them in the nearest police station. The boys also filed a complaint against us for character assassination. The administration had to step in and it started requesting us to take back the complaint. Classes were suspended for a few days. After that year the tradition of posters and giving scores to the girls on the campus stopped.'

The girls today in PMCH and possibly across campuses in the country have overcome the fear that they felt even a decade back. There is a new found confidence; some may even say aggression. Girls are expressing, declaring and discussing their desires, their love, and their crushes more openly. It is part of the revolution where girls are no longer the suppressed and the oppressed. As Tanvi told me, 'Things have changed in Patna. On a Facebook page called PMCH Confessions many girl students post their crushes on some boys in the college.'

What led to the change?

'I think the change is due to the fact that in our time there were 30 per cent girls in our batch while now there are 60 per cent girls in every batch. There were very few girls who were the centre of all attention, now the reverse has happened. Girls have crushes on boys now.'

It is not just about the ratio of girls to boys, although the numbers must surely have helped. I went to the PMCH Confessions page on Facebook and like a voyeur started reading some of the messages. A boy had posted: 'We have seen a huge transition of era...from base phones to smart phones, from DDs (demand drafts) to net banking money transfer from our home to us...from rare talking between boys and girls and that too between same phylum [sic] to now girls proposing boys... From only salwar suit to most notorious symbol or signal of girls: "JEANS".' A ha! So jeans are still a notorious symbol. Jeans have become a symbol of feminism and modernism, and by wearing jeans, a break from traditions, girls announce their independence and show their confidence. The girls are changing and also proposing to boys, but many of the boys are not changing.

What the girls cannot do in public, they are expressing in the virtual world and very soon they will express it in the real world as well. Early signs can be seen in the relationship surveys done by magazines like *India Today* where women are suddenly more vocal about their needs, choices and desires than say a decade back. They are finding their voice and this is part of the change.

Of course everyone does not think that the impact of TV, internet and mobile phones is positive, as is obvious from what the old farmer in Sehor said. Like any tool, the impact is a mixed bag. When I asked Supriya of Vidya & Child about the impact of TV and mobiles, Supriya broke into a guffaw. Then she said, 'If you ask me, it is only bad. Because I think—you know what is happening and it is not just about these kids; it is everywhere. The sense of responsibility is not something that we are able to make a child understand. It is more important for many to spend on an expensive mobile than to spend on education; it is also a good way to spend time—chatting on mobile, Facebook all through your mobile. The fact is that the amount of money being actually spent is significant. We have to state it quite categorically to some of the students and their families that they belong to a background where they cannot spend money on this and on education. They do not have the wherewithal to spend on both so they have to decide what to spend their limited resources on. Education is not taking a backseat but some additional money that could have been spent on education is not being spent. Similarly an extra hour that could have been spent studying is being spent on phones.'

But the good thing according to Supriya is that there is no lack of accessibility. 'As far as gadgets are concerned there is no lack of accessibility—they know where to get them, where to get them cheap and where to get them repaired!' These tools of empowerment are liberating not only in terms of information accessibility and hence, challenging traditional power equations, but also economically. For many girls and women the first step to economic independence and high self-esteem comes from an opportunity to earn some money by working or setting up a small business from home. Information back and forth with customers comes over the phone. This serves as a huge confidence boost and a body blow to male dominance in a patriarchal society.

The boom in the telecom and IT sector has also helped in other ways as well. Research in Bangladesh[81] shows that poor women are more receptive to information on family planning when they receive it in the privacy of their homes, without having to step out to a community or healthcare centre. It is difficult for us to fathom, particularly for a man, why a woman would find it difficult to step out of home. But once again mobile phones are helping various agencies in reaching out to girls and women in the confines of their homes, which is also leading to better health among other things. Since girls and women more often than not face more restrictions in their movements outside home and have more competing demands on their time due to household chores, access to mobile phones helps them more at the margins to access opportunities and information; 41 per cent of women in different and diverse countries like Bolivia, Egypt, India and Kenya assert that their incomes and

---

[81]Abhijit V Banerjee and Esther Duflo, *Poor Economics: A Radical Thinking of the Way to Fight Global Poverty.*

access to economic opportunities increased after owning a mobile phone.[82]

According to a news report:[83]

Across 250 villages in Maharashtra, pregnant women are feeling a little less confused. They have someone telling them how to take care of themselves this week. A friend, if you like. They receive this counsel through voice messages on the mobile phone. They receive this counsel where they wish to receive it, even in the privacy of their homes. This is relevant in a state where only 43 per cent of women have freedom to travel alone outside. These messages may spur them to change certain behaviours to benefit them and their babies. This is also a state where 1 million new-born babies die every year.

The messages they are receiving are part of mMitra, a mobile health project that uses voice messages to provide rural women information on antenatal care. Developed by Mumbai-based NGO Arman, the project is hoping to change the way women access knowledge during pregnancy and post-partum, and their behaviour as a result...Women in many places will be able to enrol and receive the messages on their own phones. This is because of the success of mobile phones in rural India. Many women have phones or their husbands do and they can access them at a particular time in the day.

The challenge in rural areas is also the lack of sufficient economic opportunities; not enough jobs are being generated in rural and semi-urban areas. In 2011, I had visited Soda village in Rajasthan to meet Chhavi Rajawat, the woman sarpanch equipped with an MBA, who had left a job with Airtel in Delhi to work in her ancestral village where her grandfather was once the sarpanch. Chhavi was petite, and fair complexioned. She was dressed in an

---

[82]The World Bank, (2012), *World Development Report 2012, Gender Equality and Development.*

[83]'Mobile friends for healthy mothers', by Anindita Sengupta, available at: http://infochangeindia.org/public-health/features/mobile-friends-for-healthy-mothers.html.

ethnic embroidered bright coloured kurta and designer jeans. I met Chhavi at her ancestral house and even as we talked I helped her draw a pattern on a piece of cloth that would later be embroidered by one of the village women. Chhavi was trying to bring some additional income generating opportunities to the village women by using her contacts in Jaipur. But this was not scalable and the opportunity could vanish the day Chhavi ceased to be a sarpanch or moved back to her city life. Maybe technology and e-commerce will give many artisans access to a larger market—similar to what roads have done, except on a much larger scale.

Sectors like IT and financial services have generated hundreds of thousands of jobs over the last decade or two. Today 30 per cent of the employees in the software industry are women.[84] The millions of jobs created by the IT, telecom and financial services sectors have opened up opportunities for girls and women like no other sector previously did. Between 2001 and 2011, the percentage of women employees in Infosys went up from 17.2 per cent to 34.4 per cent. This even as the number of employees increased from a mere 9,831 to a whopping 160,405. Between 2011 and 2014, at the entry level the percentage of female applicants has gone up from 41 per cent to 45 per cent in Infosys. In TCS, India's largest IT services company, out of 263,637 employees, 32 per cent of the workforce was women as of 31 December 2012.[85] The percentage had increased marginally to 32.4 per cent by 31 March 2013;[86] 20-25 per cent employees in banks and financial institutions were also women. Similarly in the organized and modern format of retailing, 60 per cent of the employees on the shop floor are women. Organized or modern format retail along with the hospitality industry and services like

---

[84]Y L R Moorthi, Subhadip Roy and Anita Pansari, 'The changing roles portrayed by women in Indian advertisements: A longitudinal analysis', Working Paper No 446. January 2014, Indian Institute of Management, Bangalore.

[85]http://www.tcs.com/SiteCollectionDocuments/Investors/Presentations/TCS_PressRelease_IFRS_USD_Q3_13.pdf.

[86]Tata Consultancy Services, (2013), *Corporate Sustainability Report.*

beauticians, e-commerce will be among the biggest employment creators over the medium term.

Parents are also comfortable with their children working in these sectors and this is especially true for girls. Zaheeruddin of *Siasat* informed me that 18-22 per cent of the workforce in BPOs in Hyderabad was Muslim and a significant percentage of the workforce was girls. Job opportunities that arose due to the mushrooming of call centres or BPOs, according to one research, led to an increase in the number of children enrolled in schools by 5.7 per cent in India and all the change was accounted for by English medium schools.[87]

Technology has helped in creating job and employment opportunities. But this revolution is not over yet. Only 25 per cent women aged fifteen and 20 per cent women at the age of thirty have a mobile phone while the comparable numbers for men are 70 per cent and 80 per cent respectively.[88] During my research I also found that a majority of the girls coming from low income or lower middle income strata that I spoke to did not have mobile phones.

As I end this chapter on change drivers, I return to the city of Hyderabad. In the old city of Hyderabad known for its conservative ways, child brides and religious riots, a huge social change is underway which is not always very visible to an outsider. This change that I witnessed in Hyderabad is happening all over the country. As Tina and I took a quick round of the *Siasat* office after a long day of very interesting conversations, the image that stuck with me was that of a young girl conducting computer classes. Why was this image so unusual? It was unusual because the girl was wearing a *hijab* with her eyes barely visible, 98 per cent of the students in the class were young boys, possibly of her own age, and in front of her was a PC with a mobile phone near her fingertips. While the boys turned to gawk at the visitors, their young lecturer didn't.

---

[87]The World Bank, (2012), *World Development Report 2012: Gender Equality and Development.*

[88]Ajay Shah, (2014), 'Labour Assets in 2054 India', *The Economic Times*, 13 March.

YEH CHUP NAHIN RAHENGE—THEY WILL NOT KEEP QUIET

Even as the position of girls and women in society is changing for the better, ever so often their position and status is harmed by derogatory statements made by people in public life, most notably political leaders. Sample the following:[89]

'Dented-painted women protesters in Delhi went to discotheques and then turned up at India Gate to express outrage.'

—Congress MP and President Pranab Mukherjee's son Abhijit Mukherjee on the Delhi protests after the rape and death of Nirbhaya.

'I don't have to listen to you. It's been four days since you have entered politics and you already think you are a great political analyst, till yesterday you were dancing on television and today you have become a politician.'

This sounds even more vulgar in Hindi, '*Char din hue hain aur aap rajnitik vishleshak bani firti hain. Aap toh TV pe thumke lagati thi, aaj chunavi vishleshak ban gayi. Aap ke sanskar bahut acche hai. Kya character hai aapka.*'

—Sanjay Nirupam, Congress MP making derogatory remarks against BJP leader and TV actress Smriti Irani during a television debate (Sanjay Nirupam lost the elections in 2014 and Smriti Irani is now the Minister of Human Resource Development).

---

[89]All the quotes have been taken from various media articles (primarily from *The Times of India* and CNN-IBN). The positions mentioned of the people quoted were what they were when the statements were made.

'New victories and new weddings both have their own importance. As time passes, the joy of the victory fades, just like a wife becomes old and loses her charm as time passes.'

—Sriprakash Jaiswal, Congress MP and Union Coal Minister, comparing a woman to a cricket match victory celebration on hearing the news of India's victory over Pakistan in an ICC World Twenty20 match.

'Just because India achieved freedom at midnight does not mean that women can venture out after dark. They should ensure that they do not board buses with few passengers. The woman should have thought twice before boarding the suspicious private bus that night. Though the incident was condemnable, she should also have behaved keeping in mind the situation. Although it [Delhi gang-rape] was a minor incident, Soniaji made it a point to meet the protesters when they called on her.'

—Botsa Satyanarayana, Andhra Pradesh Congress chief reacting to the gang-rape of a 23-year-old student in Delhi.

'There is no need to give phones to women and children. It distracts them and is useless. Why do women need phones? If you have given phones to them, take them back. Without mobiles which important work are they missing out on? My mother and sister never had mobiles, did they die?'

—Rajpal Saini, BSP MLA while addressing a gathering in UP.

'We should learn from the past, especially in Mughal era, people used to marry their girls to save them from Mughal atrocities and currently a similar situation is arising in the state. I think that's the reason khap has taken such a decision and I support it.'

—Om Prakash Chautala, ex-Chief Minister of Haryana supporting the bizarre suggestion by a khap panchayat in Haryana that girls should be married off early to prevent rapes.

'In earlier times, hormones became active at a later age. Now due to our diets and so on, hormones are becoming active sooner. That is reason why khaps said that when girls are 15–16, they should be married. This will prevent rapes to a large extent.'

—Jitender Chhattar, a member of the system of social administrative apparatus (khap panchayat) in Haryana's Jind district.

'There is only one phrase for this and that is "moral limit"; there is a Lakshman rekha [a line] for every person, when that is crossed then the demon-king Raavan will abduct Goddess Sita.'
—Kailash Vijayvargiya, a BJP minister in the Madhya Pradesh government.

'We ask, Didimoni, what is your fee? How much will you take for getting raped?'
—Anisur Rahman, elected member of a legislative assembly in West Bengal, addressing the question to Mamata Banerjee, the Chief Minister of West Bengal.

'That was a different case altogether. That was not at all a rape case. It was a misunderstanding between two parties involved in professional dealings. Between the lady and her client.'
—Kakoli Ghose Dastidar, a female lawmaker from the political party Trinamool Congress.

'The intention of this demand [girls should be banned from wearing skirts to school] is to keep girl students away from men's lustful gazes and for their comfort in hot and cold weather conditions. It is not a Talibani type of thinking or restriction on girls' freedom or right but a concern for their safety.'
—Banwari Lal Singhal, an elected member of the legislative assembly in the northern state of Rajasthan.

'Eve-teasing is a very old thing. It has been going on for ages. One of the reasons behind the increase in incidents of eve-teasing is short dresses and short skirts worn by women. This in turn instigates young men.'
—Bengali actor and Trinamool Congress legislator Chiranjeet aka Dipak Chakraborty.

As these quotes show a section of the political, religious and social leadership is insensitive and still lives in a world of weird morality where the safety of a girl is her problem and more often than not her behaviour or her dress or something else is blamed for the violence against her. Guilty men are committing crimes against women because they have been tempted or they are men after all. Objectification of women is rampant and they are looked down upon and disparaging comments are passed on working women.

The solution that many of these religious and political leaders suggest is confining women to homes, controlling the way they dress and taking away their mobile phones and their freedom. Is this important enough for me to mention here? I believe so because these law makers influence society and they have an influence on the way in which the law enforcement and legal machinery behaves. Their thoughts and beliefs must be practiced in their own homes. Change has to start there and such mindsets have to change. Naming and shaming them may be one way of driving change, changing the way a patriarchal society treats its women folk and reducing, if not eliminating, gender based discrimination.

More than three decades later Rachita still vividly remembered the subtle and not so subtle discrimination that she faced in her house while growing up or the signals that would come once in a while in her direction that a boy was preferred as a child in their household. She had no problems even after all these decades in recalling incidents from her childhood. 'Two incidents come to mind. An atlas was bought for my studies when I was in Class V. Baba put a cover and put my name on it. My younger brother was in Class I then and Ma created a ruckus in the house as to why my brother's name was also not put on the cover. It somehow upset me a lot at that age and it is something I still remember. A second incident happened when we were visiting my maashi (mother's sister) in Jabalpur. My uncle put some perfume on my younger brother and I also asked for it. My uncle just flew into a rage. Looking back now all these were trivial incidents, but at that age they left an impression on me that girls are unwanted and undesirable.'

The so-called trivial incidents clearly left a deep impression and impacted the psyche of Rachita and her actions and reactions later on in life and also shaped her personality. Later on in her married life and living in a joint family, the young bride would be the last one to eat her meal after everyone had finished, sometimes well past midnight and then she had to be up at the crack of dawn to start the new day's chores. Needless to say she cooked every meal for the extended joint family. Rachita was not alone. Millions of girls face similar hardships all across the country and some with disastrous consequences.

Then they face discrimination as well. Sometimes the discrimination is subtle—the best or the choicest piece of chicken or mutton or fish is given to the son, husband, father or son-in-law in the family, but almost never ever to a female member of the household. At other times the discrimination is more overt—a girl is sent to a government school while the son goes to a better private school; the son gets a mobile phone, but the daughter is denied one; or the girl, not the boy, is pulled out of school during times of financial difficulty

After marriage Rachita did think of taking up a job. But she gave up the idea because her family would have got neglected. Would her husband have supported her if she had taken up a job? 'My husband was supportive, but there was opposition from others in the joint family. My husband would not have been able to stand up to his mother and oppose her.' What has changed in India now is that many girls in Rachita's position would decide very differently. If the husbands do not stand up to their mothers and extended families, the wives will still go ahead. Thankfully some husbands are also standing up.

I asked the same question about discrimination to her sister Sanchita, who is younger to her by ten years. 'Yes, I also faced discrimination at home and if I am honest, gender discrimination was mainly done by my mother and sarcastic comments came from my father. But one incident remains quite vivid in my mind even today and frankly I am not able to find an explanation for it till today. I was in Class V, if I remember correctly. We did not have a television at home, and since my brother had finished his Class X final exams, my mother would take him to watch TV in one of our family friend's house most of the evenings so that he did not mix with the local boys and lose his focus on his studies.'

'But then I was supposed to be alone at home and study. And I used to be terribly scared of staying back alone (after dark) but never for once would she listen to me about why I didn't want to stay alone; what was the reason behind my being afraid. I still remember one day when I became quite adamant and I told her I was not going to stay alone and I also came out following my mother and brother. There was a busy main road which had to be crossed to go to this family friend's house. What hurt me the most is that not for a moment did my mother worry or bother to look behind when I was all alone crossing the road with all vehicles passing by me. That day I actually felt like an orphan.'

Sanchita's mother's attention on her son paid off and he went to one of the IITs. While this happened too late to change Rachita's life, in a small way it helped change Sanchita's future. Sanchita went to live with her brother in Bombay after her graduation and then wrote her own destiny by sheer grit, determination and hard work. The girl who felt like an orphan took charge of her destiny. Apart from her brother being a role model for her, a changing India helped open up opportunities. Sanchita made sure that she was never ever made to feel like an orphan again and also that that her daughter would grow up to be a truly independent and empowered woman.

This is neither the place and nor am I qualified to discuss why many times women turn out to be the worst enemies of girls and other women. Or how did Indian society become so regressive in its attitude towards girls and women? I have read that in the Vedic age women occupied prominent positions in religious and social life and when it came to religion they had a position equal to that enjoyed by men. In the post-Vedic period, women lost equality when it came to religion and later they were not even eligible for Vedic studies and religious rites. Among Hindu gods, women occupy the pride of position and represent strength, power, wisdom and learning and wealth. But in real life it is a different story.

Women's empowerment in the last nearly 200 years had been reduced to symbolism and they became more and more disenfranchised, sometimes in the name of religion, sometimes in the name of social customs and sometimes in the name of preserving their own or their family's honour. It is paradoxical that in a country where there are many goddesses and power and valour are more often than not represented by a goddess rather than a god, women are treated so poorly in society even in modern times. This is also a country which has seen some very powerful women politicians, including Indira Gandhi, the second woman in the world to become the Prime Minister of a country. Of Indira Gandhi it was said that she was the only man in her cabinet, much like Margaret Thatcher. And yet the lot of women did not improve.

Violence against women has almost assumed endemic proportions whether at home or outside. Dowry deaths, torture for dowry and rapes have shown no signs of abatement or so it seems. In 2009, the number of rape cases reported in India was a staggering 21,397.[90] This means that nearly sixty girls and women were being raped on an average every day and 2.5 rapes were taking place every hour. This figure had increased to 24,923 by 2012, or 2.85 rapes every hour; 25 per cent of the rape victims were under eighteen years of age and 9 per cent under fourteen years of age.[91] In 2009, the number of dowry deaths reported was 8,383 while 89,546 cases of torture were also reported.[92]

As in many other countries, violence and exploitation of girls is often perpetrated by someone known to them—father, boyfriend, cousin, neighbour, brother-in-law, husband, father-in-law...the list is endless. In 2010, a Ministry of Home report on crimes against women noted that in rape cases in India, in 97.3 per cent of the cases (21,566) offenders were known to the victims. The report said, 'Parents/close family members were involved in 1.3 per cent (288 out of 21,566) of these cases, neighbours were involved in 36.2

[90]Government of India, Ministry of Home, available at: http://mha.nic.in.

[91]Indira Jaising, *Mapping Violence Against Women*, 13 March 2012.

[92]Government of India, Ministry of Home, available at: http://mha.nic.in.

per cent cases (7,816 out of 21,566) and relatives were involved in 6.2 per cent (1,344 out of 21,566) cases.'

Social conditioning and economic dependence mean that women often tolerate beatings and violence and many a times rationalize that they probably deserve it. Studies have found that childhood experience of abuse and violence is associated with perpetration of abuse and violence in later life.[93] It is not surprising that 47 per cent of women in India believe that beatings by husband are justified. This is a matter of pure conditioning and wrong role models while growing up. The conditioning works for both men and women. In a talk that I once attended, boxer Mike Tyson admitted that he had been violent in many of his relationships with women and he felt it was because he saw his mother being abused as a child and thought this is the way things were.

When it comes to violence and physical abuse of women, India is not very different from many other countries. A study conducted across a few developing countries—India was not one of the countries included in the study—found that 35.2 per cent of the women interviewed had experienced physical violence at least once and 11 per cent were experiencing violence during the study, 27 per cent of the women had faced sexual violence (rape) and a staggering 43 per cent had faced physical and/or sexual violence.[94] In the same study 10-62 per cent of the men interviewed reported that they had raped a girl or woman in their lifetime and rape of an intimate partner was more common than non-partner rape in all the countries except in Papua New Guinea.

Statistics from the developed world are not very different and per capita rape is significantly higher in countries like Sweden and USA than in India. Yogesh Upadhyay, an alumnus of IIT Bombay

[93]'Why Do Some Men Use Violence Against Women And How Can We Prevent It?' Quantitative findings from the United Nations multi-country study on men and violence in Asia and the Pacific, UNDP, UNFPA, UN Women, and UNV, September 2003.

[94]Ibid.

and IIM Kolkata, started the initiative AskHowIndia just ahead of the 2014 general elections to improve the level of discourse during the elections to focus on issues and solutions rather than personalities and general slanging matches. One of the questions that AskHowIndia raised is, 'How can women in India be safer?' given the number of rapes reported by women in India per 100,000 people at 1.7 is significantly lower than in countries like USA (30.2) and France (17.4).[95] In 2012, in India two per 100,000 Indians were raped while the number for USA was 13 times higher and for Sweden it was 35 times higher.[96]

Clearly there is a case of severe under-reporting but what is also equally clear is that there is an increasing trend of rapes being reported. But cold statistics cannot hide the fact that India is a gender unfriendly country. Not surprisingly India ranked 129 out of 187 countries in the Gender Inequality Index.[97]

While awareness about these issues is growing, India is different from the developed economies in one significant manner. The Indian society even today has very limited sympathy for girls and women and the system of law and justice is more often than not stacked up against them. Not only can a case which goes to court often take decades to reach its logical end, but in between witnesses and victims can be threatened and further subjected to violence, and the police often refuses to register such crimes. The victim is frequently blamed for having brought the problem on herself either by the way she dresses or by her behaviour or being out in the company of men or boys. The victim is often made to feel guilty rather than the other way round and disclosures are discouraged even by the immediate family in order to protect family honour.

---

[95]http://www.slideshare.net/AskHowIndia/womens-security.

[96]Carl Bialik, 'Statistics Shed Little Right on Rape Rates', available at: http://online.wsj.com/news/articles/SB10001424127887324324404579043623106927570. The statistics do not reveal the different definitions of rape in different countries. For example, as per Swedish law, the Swedish police record each instance of sexual violence in every case as a separate incident.

[97]Indira Jaising, *Mapping Violence Against Women.*

In another shocking incident in the northern state of Uttar Pradesh, the mother of a rape victim was mercilessly beaten by the rapists for not withdrawing the rape complaint filed in the local police station.[98] Further a victim of sexual violence can be subjected to interrogation and investigations that discourage most victims from going public. Often in the name of family honour, threatened victims are forced to keep quiet by the immediate family. The culture is one where shame and perceived family honour forces the victim to feel guilty and the perpetrator often suffers no punishment or guilt; silence is preferred to the hassle of going through the police and courtrooms to get legal redress.

Is India changing or is it still regressive? Is violence against women rising or is it that there is more reporting and better disclosure now? There are no easy answers but these questions assailed me even as I was about to start my research in early 2013. These thoughts were primarily triggered by the brutal rape and death of Nirbhaya on the streets of Delhi. Rape and other forms of violence are not uncommon and Delhi has earned the moniker of being the rape capital of India. This is the same city where a leader of the Congress Party was arrested for trying to burn his wife in the tandoor (earthen oven) in a government owned hotel after killing her and a few years back a young model was shot dead for refusing to serve alcohol to a person after the bar had closed.

Nevertheless Nirbhaya's case shocked Delhi and the nation. This was not only due to the brutality and violence associated with the crime, but also because of the young age of one of the rapists and the fact that the rape took place in a bus that had no license but pretended to be picking up passengers. Plus people were angry with brazen corruption and the slowing economy. Their anger spilled over on to the city's streets and Delhi came to a grinding halt. The government belatedly promised a lot but going by subsequent events has delivered little on its promises.

---

[98]'Mother of India rape victim beaten for refusing to withdraw complaint', available at: http://www.cbc.ca/news/world/mother-of-india-rape-victim-beaten-for-refusing-to-withdraw-complaint-1.2659188.

In another shocking incident in January 2014 in West Bengal, a couple was found guilty of falling in love. The panchayat ordered the 20-year-old girl to pay a fine of Rs 25,000 for falling in love with a boy from another village and when the girl could not pay up, the panchayat ordered that she be raped by thirteen men.[99]

In March 2013, one Friday evening, I was going to meet Manisha from Delhi at her residence. Her house is close to a large mosque where every Friday the faithful gather to offer namaaz and a local market selling all kinds of wares springs up on the footpath to cater to the crowd that assembles at the mosque. The temporary shops are in addition to an already thriving bazaar that exists there. Between the crowd and the shops, it is very difficult to walk without bumping into others.

As I walked towards Manisha's house, a girl was walking in front of me and even as my attention was focused on finding Manisha's residence, a young boy, barely in his teens, coming from the opposite direction brushed his hands against the girl's breasts; may be not brushed as much as hit. A Delhi girl probably has her antennas up and she immediately turned with a vicious snarl and her lips mouthed a profanity even as she raised her hand. But the boy had vanished into the crowd. The brazenness of the young boy in a crowded marketplace shocked and unnerved me.

Later that same night in March 2013 I asked Sohini, in whose house I was staying in Gurgaon, whether things had changed since the Delhi rape case in December. Sohini has been a career NGO professional for over two decades and now works as Director of Fund Raising with Breakthrough in New Delhi. Sohini had a round friendly face and was dressed ethnically in a dark coloured cotton salwar kameez, a matching bindi on her forehead and large silver danglers in her ears. She is not very optimistic about things changing. After the Delhi rape case, some of her colleagues were

[99]http://www.dailymail.co.uk/news/article-2544450/Kangaroo-court-orders-Indian-woman-gang-raped-13-men-having-relationship-man-village-judges-carrying-punishment.html.

conducting an exercise in Miranda House, an elite college in Delhi, where a student narrated a recent experience. When in a Delhi Metro train she protested against the lewd behaviour of a boy in the compartment, the boy turned and asked the girl if she had forgotten so soon what had happened on the night of December 16 (the night when Nirbhaya and her friend were lured into a bus and then both were beaten and the girl was raped). That this incident was being used in broad daylight to intimidate a girl who dared to protest against eve teasing is scary, despairing and disappointing.

In general, Mumbai has been seen as a safe city for girls and women and I for one believe that by and large the western part of the country is much better and safer than the east and north. But how much safer? There was a rude awakening for Mumbaikars in August 2013 when a young journalist intern visited a deserted textile mill in the heart of Mumbai with a male colleague on an assignment and was gang raped; once again one of the rapists was a juvenile. As this case made progress, a nineteen-year-old girl working in a call centre came forward and disclosed that she had also been raped by the same people in the same place. Three of the five rapists were repeat offenders.

Twenty-year-old Anita Badarappa stays in a slum in Worli. Anita's father works as kadiya (mason working on construction sites) and her mother works as a household help in three homes. Early on in my research I asked Anita, whose parents are reluctant to let her work far away from their house, whether she had heard of the Delhi rape case. She said yes and said as a result her parents were very worried about her working hours. I had then asked her whether she believed an incident like what happened in Delhi could take place in Mumbai. She had no hesitation in saying yes, she believed that even Mumbai can witness such crimes. After the August incident I was left wondering how prescient Anita was. Girls do have a sixth sense.

Some girls that I met were very angry. I asked Daksha about the Delhi rape case when I met her in Bhavnagar. She told me, 'What happened in Delhi also happens in Bhavnagar. In Bharatnagar, a small girl was going to school and a sadhu picked her up and took her away. Another girl was raped by five people. We get the news from friends and from TV. When my father sees all this, he tells me not to stay out of the house till late. I feel very angry then because these people do what they want to and then there are threats and restrictions on the lives of girls like us. After a lot of hard work and struggle we win the confidence (vishwas) of our parents to step out of the house, but after seeing all this, we lose the faith of our parents. If I had my way I would have beaten to death these rapists. Such rapists should be hanged till death. Or they should be handed over to the public...'

Meghna, during our meeting, was adamant that she wanted to complete her studies abroad and come back to India and work. I asked her about her choice of cities and incidents of eve teasing. Her choice would be Mumbai or Bengaluru. One city that she is sure she is not going to live in is Delhi. In her words, 'I think it is a scary place. One of my best friends is from Delhi and when she goes to her grandparents' house, she cannot step out wearing anything that is above her knees. Guys whistle at you on the roads. It is something beyond me and absolutely disgusting. My friend hates going to Delhi. She doesn't step out of the house unless it is completely completely necessary. Her reaction is more extreme than I would have had.'

She continued, 'In my school, Cathedral, when we have football matches, we have to pass by Siddharth College to reach the ground and the guys there whistle at you. It is the only place we have experienced such behaviour in Mumbai. It is a rule that we cannot go out of school in shorts irrespective of the length. So we have to wear our school uniform over our football dress when we step out, which is really inconvenient. I know that the principal is doing this for our safety. After sometime I guess you just get accustomed to it and don't bother about it.' Even in parts of Mumbai girls have to learn to dress in a particular way so that they do not attract unwarranted and unwanted attention. For their own safety, they are told, otherwise they will attract the wrong kind of attention.

Like girls, boys also get conditioned and probably the role models around them tell them that such behaviour is acceptable. May be some of the cat-calling and whistling is harmless, maybe most girls get used to it and learn to ignore it, but it is also equally possible that some of these boys transgress boundaries and norms of civilized behaviour later on; the bar on what is acceptable keeps getting lowered.

Will this country ever change? I still cringe when I recall an incident in IIT, Kharagpur. During my stay there, the chairman of the board of governors was Russi Mody, the charismatic managing director of Tata Steel or Tisco, as it was then known. In one of the open house sessions in the institute's auditorium, most probably in 1986 or 1987, a girl student two batches junior to us went up to the podium and said that incidents of eve teasing had gone up in the campus and asked what Russi Mody, the chairman of the governing board, proposed to do about it. Hushed silence descended on the auditorium full of young boys and very few girls.

Russi Mody in his inimitable style told a story, which went something like this: 'Last Saturday after watching a play at NCPA in Mumbai I was walking along Marine Drive with three (or maybe two) very beautiful ladies when some boys whistled at them. After we had crossed them, I said to the women that they had enjoyed the whistles, hadn't they? And all the women said that they had enjoyed it.' Predictably this brought the house down. The girl stood blushing on the stage and then resumed her seat.

I now wonder how a very well respected corporate leader could say something like this. I understand that the times were different and political correctness and gender sensitivity had different norms then. But I now feel ashamed of myself to think that I enjoyed Russi Mody's story immensely and with my other friends heartily shouted and clapped. At the same time my admiration for that girl grew tremendously—she had the courage to go up and ask such a question and even after the answer she got, she retained her composure and confidence.

Today no Russi Mody can tell a story like this and get away with it. Times have changed. Even in the countryside, things are changing for the better. For one, many girls are willing to speak up and take matters in their own hands, whether it is Daksha in Bhavnagar or the girls in Patna Medical College and Hospital (PMCH).

Or take this incident from Allahabad that Manisha told me about when I met her. 'There are huge changes. When I was in Allahabad—I left in 2001 and I am thirty-two now—I had never ever worn jeans. In the university campus in Allahabad—in the arts faculty—you could not see a girl in jeans; wearing a salwar kameez without a dupatta was unthinkable and no one did that. But today when I go to the campus, girls are freely moving around wearing jeans. In spite of that, incidents of eve teasing are rampant (*chedkhani aur badtamizi abhi bhi hoti hai*). But there was this girl who was harassed by a guy. One day she accosted the eve teaser and pushed his bike on the road and it fell down. Petrol started leaking and she took a matchbox from an observer and set the bike on fire. She was so fed up with the daily harassment that she had reached the end of her patience.' While narrating this Manisha broke into laughter, obviously relishing the memory of the incident.

Is anything changing at all? I asked Daksha about discrimination and dowry. 'In my area/locality, both boys and girls want to study. But because of the conditions at home, many are not able to complete their studies. What I have seen is that when boys insist then the families allow them to study. The girls are taken out of schools far more easily. The girls do not have it easy. They are told that there is no use of studying since they are going to get married and go to their in-laws' place and also money has to be saved for their dowry. However, dowry demands have come down and in our area there is not much of a tradition of giving dowry, but there is peer pressure.'

The struggles of girls to study and get educated are not only the problems of those from economically challenged sections of society, or those from small towns or belonging to any particular religion or caste. Manisha told me about her cousin sister's story in Mumbai. 'In my own family I have seen my maternal uncle's daughter—my cousin—get married at eighteen. She was studying in Mithibhai College in Vile Parle and fell in love with a boy. They are all based in Mumbai. Her parents could not accept this. This cousin had passed her pre-medical tests (PMT) and was going to study MBBS and become a doctor. But her parents were scared that in the hostel she would continue to go around with the boy. The objection was that the boy was not a Brahmin. That was the biggest problem. So she was married off. My sister did not or would not resist.'

The maternal uncle in question is a high court lawyer in Mumbai and the family is clearly well-off and educated. Manisha continued, 'My uncle often says that he has reached the conclusion that girls should not be educated. Why? Because today after getting educated girls are coming to the court and asking for a share of paternal property, they are asking for a divorce. This is unthinkable. He says, "Arre, you ask for jewellery, I will give it to you, you ask for a saree, I will give it to you. But you are asking for property and divorce!" He really gets angry with the girls of today.'

Her uncle's views have been shaped by the way he was brought up and what he was told. According to Manisha, 'My grandmother used to tell us that girls should be like water, as in whichever vessel you pour it in, it will take the shape of the vessel. Girls should adjust. They used to adjust themselves and mould themselves according to the whims and desires of their husbands and in-laws, irrespective of whether he was good or bad.' If boys grow up hearing such things, their worldview will be no different or will take ages to change, if it ever does. Not only do girls need the right role models, boys need the right role models too.

Encouragingly, Narendra Modi raised the issue of the change needed on how boys are brought up during his Independence Day speech on 15 August 2014. He said:

> Today from this platform, I want to ask those parents, I want to ask every parent that you have a daughter of ten or twelve years age, you are always on the alert, every now and then you keep on asking where are you going, when would you come back, inform

immediately after you reach...but has any parent ever dared to ask their son as to where he is going, why he is going out, who his friends are. After all, a rapist is also somebody's son. He also has parents. As parents, have we ever asked our son as to what he is doing and where he is going. If every parent decides to impose as many restrictions on the sons as have been imposed on our daughters, try to do this with your sons, try to ask such questions of them...the law will take its own course, strict action will be taken, but as a member of the society, as parents, we also have some responsibilities.[100]

Hopefully a social movement will start to change the behaviour and conditioning of boys and men.

Manisha's uncle may get angry when girls are demanding their rights but he will not be able to do much about it. As we have seen, the gen-next girls are standing up for themselves. Manisha's uncle's youngest daughter is growing up. And Manisha believes that her uncle's third daughter will change her father's attitude and he will not be able to have his way with his youngest daughter. 'That is my sense,' says Manisha firmly.

While Manisha's uncle may rant and rile against girls who demand a share in paternal property, which is guaranteed by law, some boys are changing and once again it has little to do with education or affluence. Mehul is one such boy. Mehul walked into the Shaishav office in Bhavnagar when I was having a chat with Daksha. She introduced him as her brother.

Mehul was a very confident boy with a slight swagger. He was tall, languid, slim with jet black hair, always smiling, quite good in English and there was an air of quiet confidence around him that belied his age. He was wearing a shirt with Madras checks and jeans. As we spoke I realized that Mehul's life experiences made him much wiser beyond his physical age. There was easy camaraderie between Daksha and Mehul, the comfort levels very

---

[100]Narendra Modi addressed the nation in Hindi. Excerpts from his speech on 15 August 2014 have been taken from an English news website.

visible as one completed the half-finished sentences of the other. Mehul was working as a part time electrician in Bhavnagar. His father is an alcoholic and even ran a hooch shop in the not too distant past. Mehul has been primarily brought up by his mother and not surprisingly he also started drinking and smoking at a young age, but has now given them up. Thanks to Shaishav and of course, his mother.

I asked Mehul what was changing. 'The educated girls know how to lead their lives and are living their lives openly, as per their wishes. Those who are not educated and stay at home they do not know much about outside life. I am happy with this progress. I do not know what my friends think because I never ask them. We do not speak about girls.'

'What kind of girl will you marry,' I asked. Daksha broke into peals of laughter and said that he had already found a girl for himself. Mehul said, 'Yes, I have found my girl. She is in the Arts College. She is studying BA. We met in a marriage hall when we went there to attend someone else's marriage. My parents have no objection. The girl's parents may have some objection because I am yet to find a decent job.' Daksha piped in and informed me that their caste is also different. There was some pride in Daksha's voice that Mehul was going ahead with this relationship.

I was given a quick lesson in caste dynamics by Mehul and Daksha. Usually the boy's parents have no objection to caste issues. Most of the objections come from the girl's parents. If the girl runs away and gets married, then the girl's family would kill her. Both Daksha and Mehul agreed on this and there was no shock or outrage in their voices as they said it. I could not detect even the slightest tremor in their voices. I guess if one has grown up hearing stories of honour killings and the like, one is no longer affected by them in the same way as an outsider is. They said that when a girl runs away, it is seen as if her honour and her family's honour have been sullied. There is no such stigma on the boy or his family! Daksha said that if her brother had married his girlfriend, her father would have grudgingly accepted the relationship. But if she did the same thing, she would be killed. And even as she said this she was laughing as if this was the most normal thing to be expected. I hoped she was joking, but something told me that she was dead serious.

Mehul studied only up to Class XII and then went to work in Pune. He came back. I am not too sure if he came back for his mother or because he did not like his life in Pune or because of his girlfriend. Most likely it was because of his girlfriend since he gave up a job with good future prospects in a city with lots of opportunities, especially when compared to Bhavnagar. Mehul continued his story, 'I learnt a lot in Pune. Everywhere I saw the same thing. A woman was earning and her husband was enjoying the fruits of her labour. After marriage every woman goes through trouble. Beating of wives is very common. The man spends all his earnings on alcohol. But a woman always thinks of her child and feeds the child and herself. A woman never keeps her child hungry. I will never let that happen to my wife. I do not want my wife to work; but if she wants, then she can work. It's her will. I do not want her to face difficulties and that's why I do not want her to work.'

In his limited experience Mehul stumbled upon a truth which economists have taken a lot of research and data collection to arrive at. As we neared the end of our conversation, Daksha said, '*Bhagwan sabko aisi hi buddhi de* (May god bestow the same intelligence and way of thinking to everyone).' Yes, that would be nice, wouldn't it?

Mehul is going to break two big barriers when he gets married—caste and the fact that his wife will be more educated than him. Both have prevailed for generations. While I believe that caste barriers in urban areas are becoming less important and often disappearing in our day to day lives, when it comes to marriage there is no getting away from it. Or this seems true in a majority of the cases. My favourite barometer for this is the weekend matrimonial adverts in newspapers in any town or city. Pages after pages are arranged according to caste affiliations and then there is usually a very small set of advertisements under the head 'Cosmopolitan'. These advertisements tell a story of their own. In recent years the number of pages for such advertisements has drastically reduced. Before we rejoice, I have to tell you that the advertisements have migrated online—a sign of changing times. But disappointingly most people still specify caste, religious and even sub-caste preferences of the life partner they are looking for.

Along with caste, sub-caste and religious rigidities, there is a clear preference for fair complexioned girls when it comes to the marriage market. This obsession with fair complexion continues if the soaring sales of Fair & Lovely, a best-selling product from Hindustan Unilever (HUL), are any indicator. But it is not a one way obsession. Men also want to be fair. On realizing that men are also users of Fair & Lovely, Emami, a domestic FMCG player, launched Fair & Handsome a few years back and the brand ambassador for the product is Shah Rukh Khan, the present Hindi film heartthrob. Guess what? Even the sales of Fair & Handsome went soaring. Since its launch in FY06, Fair & Handsome grew from a Rs 320 million to an over Rs 1.5 billion brand in FY13, an annual growth rate of 25 per cent. Now HUL has launched a variant of Fair & Lovely targeting men.

While Mehul is open to marrying a girl who is more educated than him, what about the girls? I had asked Meghna about marriage and relationships and she had told me that she would not like to get married before she was twenty-six or twenty-seven years and would like to have two children. Would it be acceptable if her husband was less academically qualified than her? Meghna said, 'It depends if he is smart enough...I mean he should be as educated as I am. If he is more educated than me then it is not an issue. But I would prefer that we both have the same level of education.'

I found Meghna's answers fascinating. This was a girl from an affluent background, with her academic goals set very straight and very strong academic credentials. However, generations of conditioning takes time to change and even Meghna finds it difficult to think of a life partner who is less qualified than her. A survey with over 25,000 young respondents conducted by a marriage portal found that 69 per cent of women would like to marry someone who is more educated than them and 26 per cent wanted a life partner with similar education.[101] Mehul's girlfriend is one of a tiny minority in that she has agreed to marry a boy who is less qualified than her—maybe her choices of boys who are understanding and enlightened is severely limited; or maybe she is madly in love.

Priya in Aurangabad had similar views although her overall ambitions and dreams were more modest as compared to Meghna's and consistent with her background and environment. On educational qualifications and background of her husband, Priya told me, 'My husband should be at least as much qualified as I am. He should be more educated than me ideally. Education changes our way of thinking. He should be interested in music and have no objection to my taking part in music sessions or performance or training. I would also like him to do household work along with me. I wouldn't want him to do the lion's share of the work. He should also manage the children if I am busy with my work. This much I will expect from him.'

Meghna and Priya's answers are not surprising when even in a developed country like USA these issues matter and are still being debated. Sheryl Sandberg wrote:

> Making gender matters even worse, men's success is viewed not just in absolute terms, but often in comparison to their wives. The image of a happy couple still includes a husband who is professionally more successful than his wife. If the reverse occurs, it's perceived as threatening to the marriage...More and more men will have to do the same (brush off comments when the wife is more successful), since almost 30 per cent of US working wives and 18 per cent of British working wives now earn more than their husbands.[102]

[101]Madhavi Rajadhyaksha, (2013), 'Mr Right Not Good Enough', *The Times of India*, 9 April.

[102]Sheryl Sandberg, *Lean In: Women, Work and the Will to Lead*, p. 115.

What applies to levels of success applies equally to issues like educational qualifications and sharing of household chores.

Meghna and Priya are not alone when it comes to subconscious conditioned responses. When I spoke to Priyanka in Patna, the girl who had bravely fought various odds, I asked her whether she would like her husband to share household chores with her. She replied, 'Of course, I expect that he will help me in my household chores. But if both of us come back from work and are tired, I will never ask him to get me a glass of water.'

Never? Why? 'No, my heart will never allow me to do that and these are some things that I have learnt as a part of my culture. I cannot order him but I can request him to work with me. Or he may be sensitive enough and offer me a glass of water. But I would like him to help me with cooking and rearing our children.'

I asked Priyanka about marriage outside her caste since caste equations are a big deal in Bihar unlike say the rest of eastern India. 'I would not like to go down a path that hurts the sentiments of my family. If I insist on an inter-caste marriage, then all the objections that were raised for our education will come true,' she said.

But when you stood up against your uncles, even then the family was hurt. So what is right and what is wrong? I asked her. 'I think inter-caste marriage is not correct as it does hurt the family. It also fortifies all the arguments about why girls should not be educated. But my getting ahead in life by educating myself doesn't hurt anyone. I do not want to hurt my parents by anything that I do. But personally I have no issues with inter-caste marriages.'

I was bowled over by Priyanka's responses. She had a very clear idea about what is wrong and what is not and she had rationalized it also. She is not against inter-caste marriages but she will not go in for one not only because of respect for the traditional values inculcated in her but more importantly because she does not want to prove her detractors right. Sunita in Noida is also mindful that anything she does should not be used as an argument in favour of not educating girls. At the same time in Noida, Sunita's mother has advised her, 'If you like someone, do let me know; don't run away and get married.' This is a big change in attitude in a country where bride burning does not shock people and honour killings are reported even today, but inter-caste or inter-religious marriages shock and hurt people.

RJ Jiya, a radio jockey in Patna, prefers to be known by her professional name. After being educated in Mussoorie and Delhi, RJ Jiya came back to Patna to work so that she could live with her parents. What were her views on inter-caste marriage? Would her parents be fine? 'There will be a bit of disappointment but it will be accepted. Even I won't like to disappoint my parents. But I think there is no problem, none at all. In the atmosphere and environment where I have lived, if I love somebody and if I want to spend my entire life with someone, then it is my decision and I will try and convince my parents about it. This may sound clichéd but I truly think I will do this.'

RJ Jiya does not rule out an inter-caste marriage but she would rather not disappoint her parents. Even Tanvi never thought of an inter-caste marriage because she was sure her father would boycott her forever if she opted for one. Are Priyanka, Tanvi and RJ Jiya right or are they wrong? There are no easy answers. Everyone cannot revolt and fight on every issue of disagreement and sometimes with larger goals in mind, small sacrifices have to be made. The girls are picking and choosing the battles that they want to fight. Priyanka made that choice and she has found a partner who has not asked for a single rupee in dowry. For those who have not lived in the system it is difficult to imagine how much of a change this is in a country where even elite and educated men and their families routinely demand usurious dowry, and marriages often breakdown because of such demands.

What I find interesting is that the conditioning—husband should be more qualified or husband cannot serve a glass of water to his wife—works across socio-economic strata and will take a long time to work its way out of the system. Probably it is changing in a small way in the homes of highly successful professional women and it certainly is changing in many urban households that I see around me. I can see this change in developed economies where house-husbands are slightly more common and are also becoming an acceptable part of the social landscape. India is still a long way from this scenario and it would be naive to expect that such changes will happen in a span of just five or ten years.

A change that is already visible though is that in many cases women professionals are more visible and the spotlight is firmly on them, whereas the husbands are less known and less celebrated. Think of Chanda Kochhar, Naina Lal Kidwai, Shikha Sharma, Arundhati Bhattacharya, Kaku Nakhate, Leena Nair, Visakha Mulye, Lalita Gupte, Avani Davda, Usha Thorat to name just a few.

Abhimaan, a Hindi film released in 1973, dealt with the issues that a couple face when the wife is more talented than the husband in the same profession and the spotlight moves away from the husband and gets firmly focused on the wife. In a development where real life imitated reel life, Jaya Bachchan (nee Bhaduri), the heroine of the film, after winning the *Filmfare* Best Actress Award went on to marry Amitabh Bachchan, then a struggling actor who later became the biggest star of Hindi films. Jaya gave up her career and devoted her energy and time in bringing up their two children. Today in India it is easy to find women who have had more successful and/or visible professional careers than their husbands and then there are many, certainly a larger proportion than the first group, who also give up budding careers. At the same time, 78 per cent of female graduates choose not to participate in the job market[103] and enter the workforce. This 'social dropout' is mostly explained by the fact that these women want to complete their education till the graduate level for social reasons like better marriage prospects, while some others are not allowed to work by their husbands or in-laws.

At least among some professionals the dropouts are partly due to conscious choices that women make based on their priorities of family and household or other interests but even then it is a loss to

---

[103]ICICI Group, *Women in Leadership*. Human Resource Research Desk, 2014.

the economy and the country. Better support systems, better crèches and greater flexibility and understanding at the workplace would help keep a larger proportion of women working even as they raise their children and take care of their families. In her book *Lean In*, Sheryl Sandberg cites the example of how a more considerate parking lot closer to her office in Google helped her when she was pregnant. She writes, 'To this day, I'm embarrassed that I didn't realize that pregnant women needed reserved parking until I experienced my own aching feet.'[104]

In this context I have to mention ICICI Bank once again. It has become a factory for churning out women leaders in the financial services sector. In interview after interview, successful women professionals from the ICICI Group have spoken about how there exists a truly meritorious culture where women are neither given extra privileges nor are they discriminated against.

Chanda Kochhar, the present managing director and CEO of ICICI Bank, in a recent interview[105] said that when her three-month maternity leave got extended to six months, it made headlines in business newspapers. It was a rare event but ICICI was already showing how an organization could be gender friendly and retain exceptional talent. Now maternity leave in ICICI Bank is for six months and young women routinely extend it without making it to the front pages of newspapers. In the same interview Chanda Kochhar also said, 'It is important to clearly convey that they are purely merit-oriented and women are rewarded on the basis of their performance.'

Apart from maternity leave, ICICI Bank provides thirty-six days of 'paid childcare leave' each year for mothers and single fathers till the child attains the age of two. Further, 'fertility leave' of 180 days is available for employees seeking to undergo fertility treatment. For adoption, thirty-six days of paid leave is available each year for

---

[104]Sheryl Sandberg, *Lean In: Women, Work and the Will to Lead*, p. 4.

[105]http://www.business-standard.com/article/companies/workplaces-face-supply-side-constraints-of-women-professionals-icici-bank-report-114041101143_1.html.

women employees as well as single fathers who adopt a child. It is time for other organizations to learn from what ICICI Bank has done.

Women accounted for 25–30 per cent of ICICI Bank's workforce in the last few years. In frontline sales and customer facing roles, women are about 30 per cent of the bank's workforce and make up 17 per cent of its top leadership positions.[106] But company policies alone cannot help; the nature of jobs available is also changing. For example, the profile of junior management employees at ICICI Bank has undergone a transformation over the last three years with 75 per cent of these being sales oriented as compared to only 33 per cent in 2010[107] and many women do not want to take up sales jobs.

As I interviewed girls across the country I was happy to hear about more of them being educated. At the same time I heard again and again about the unintended consequences of education. Time and again I was told that education is helping in reducing dowry demands. And here I was thinking only of jobs and empowerment when I started my research. One reason why many parents are willing to educate their daughters is because the demand for dowry is either reduced or better still there is no demand.

I asked RJ Jiya in Patna about dowry. She said that it was prevalent in society. Before marriages are solemnized these things did come up. But during her sister's marriage, which was an arranged one, the question of dowry did not arise since both of them were against it. Maybe it helped that RJ Jiya's sister was well educated. Maybe some boys and men have changed.

This is what I heard across the country. Salva in Hyderabad said, 'When parents look for a marriage proposal, all boys who are well educated want a girl who is also well educated. Every parent dreams the best from life for their children. Because of this thinking, attitudes are changing. If a girl is not well educated, then the boy's family asks for dowry, even though she maybe beautiful. If not

---

[106]ICICI Group, *Women in Leadership*. Human Resource Research Desk, 2014.
[107]Ibid.

dowry in cash and jewellery, then there will be demands like we want a car or a bike. If a girl is also educated, then such demands are not there or are certainly reduced. That is a big driver why parents are getting the girl child educated.' Tanvi from Bihar had also told me that education of girls is being driven by expectations of good marriages and less or no dowry.

Mustafa Pervez, Director, Foundation for Effective Learning Techniques, returned to India after thirteen years in Saudi Arabia where he worked with Dr Steven Covey's company. In Hyderabad he is adopting the lessons learnt there to try and change children's future. What are the change drivers for the families, I asked him? 'Parents are the big change drivers; they want their girls to get educated. What parents want is a good husband for the girl and the criteria to get a good husband is good education. The first thing that is asked today is about educational qualifications, then beauty and then dowry. Like it or not, dowry is still there, but education is taking the number one spot.'

Why do boys want more educated girls? 'The mindsets of boys are also changing. More than 50 per cent of the boys have changed their mindset. They want their wives to work because two incomes are necessary. They agree that one income is not enough. The other half which don't want their wives to work still want an educated girl because their mental wavelengths will be the same and also she will be a good mentor to their children.'

Salva, the trainee pilot I met in Hyderabad, agreed to get married to the person selected by her parents with Zaheeruddin's blessings. A year after my first meeting with Salva, I met Zaheeruddin again in Hyderabad—first at his office and then over a sumptuous dinner at his home. As the dinner drew to a close, I asked him about Salva. He informed me that Salva's nikaah had been performed. But the story did have a positive ending—although Salva did not get a pilot's job, given the ongoing recession, she is working in the aircraft maintenance department with a private company. Maybe as the airline industry starts growing again, new entrants like Air Asia and Tata-SIA will hopefully give an opportunity to Salva and her husband will not stop her.

Even as I heard these positive stories, once in a while I also came across stories that were depressing although always full of hope. These are from a world that we are mostly far removed from. This is especially true when it comes to Muslim girls and women. According to the Sachar Committee report,[108] 'Muslims have not been able to respond to the challenge of improving their educational status...the mean years of schooling of Muslims is the lowest (about three years four months).' The report further notes that 25 per cent of Muslim children in the 6–14 year age group have either never attended school or have dropped out and the educational attainment of Muslim women in rural areas is lower than those of SC/ST women. India cannot progress if nearly 15 per cent of its population is left behind. As we saw with Saira and will see with Tehseem, many Muslim children even in cities like Mumbai and Hyderabad attend religious schools even when there is access to proper schools.

To find out if things are changing within the Muslim community, I met Farzana Badruzzman in Hyderabad. A middle aged portly lady, I met her along with a few girls she helps educate at her home. *Siasat*, an influential Urdu daily published from the city, described her in one article as, 'Farzana Badruzzman is a God-fearing lady who is always concerned about imparting education to financially weak Muslim students. Mother of three sons and a daughter, Mrs. Farzana belongs to an affluent and educated family. Farzana Badruzzman who stays in a flat in Famous Apartment at Khairiatabad lives with her son, while her other children, who are all engineers, stay abroad.'[109]

I asked Farzana whether Muslim girls were getting more educated and challenging established social norms. 'I have seen these girls— their mothers are inspiring them to study. They think for a better

---

[108]Government of India, (2006), 'Social, Economic and Educational Status of the Muslim Community in India', A Report, Prime Minister's High Level Committee, November.

[109]http://www.siasat.com/english/news/generous-woman-who-sponsored-education-15-children.

life education is necessary. The men in the family continue to be against education. Their logic is—what's the use? We will have to spend for dowry. And education will delay the marriage. Within middle class families the marriage age has now been pushed back to twenty-five or twenty-six; they are imitating the upper middle class. The poor in turn are imitating the middle class. The middle class is becoming the new role model.' Role models are important whether in an individual's life or within society as a whole.

At Farzana's house, as a long day turned into night, I along with Tina also met Tehseem, a very pretty 15-year-old. She was probably the prettiest girl I met during the course of my research in 2013. Tehseem had big sparkling eyes and was very fair, an asset in a country obsessed with light skin. The black dress with a black leopard print head scarf with large red roses that she was wearing accentuated her skin tone and ethereal beauty. She was not very comfortable with English and mostly spoke in chaste Hindi. But Tehseem was very smart and worldly wise. As I heard her story I thought her eyes looked sad or maybe it was my imagination. Clinging on to her salwar was a very young boy, Ilyas, her brother, who looked apprehensive or scared—I couldn't make out. Accompanying her was also her younger sister, Zehnab, who is also very pretty and confident. Tina twice commented that Zehnab will soon have a career in modelling.

To come back to Tehseem's story. Tehseem was studying in sixth grade in Rehmania Ideal School. Before that she had not been to a formal school as her family could not afford to send her to school. '*Ghar ke halaat achche nahin the,*' she told us. 'Our economic condition was not such that I could afford to go to school.' So her education before this was in an Urdu school (she has done the Aleem course). With Farzana's support she has secured admission in a proper school and next year she is going to get a double promotion because of her performance.

If not for Farzana, Tehseem in all likelihood would have been married by now and may have even become a mother. 'There were other problems as well. We hardly had any resources to run the household (*ghar hi bahut mushkil se chalta hai*). In fact my mother wanted to marry me off. Madam (Farzana) made my mother understand and she has promised support for my education,' Tehseem said.

What about your father, we asked her? Her father divorced her mother and that is when they moved to Hyderabad from Mumbai. When she arrived in Hyderabad with her three children, Tehseem's mother did not have any source of income and not even a proper room to live in. In Tehseem's words, 'My father never worked, he stayed at home. We lived in Mumbra (a predominantly Muslim suburb of Mumbai). My father was not working and he also indulged in violence at home (*maram peeti bahut karte the*). He didn't want daughters (*unhe bachchiyan pasand nahin thee*); so even though my mother did not want a divorce, my father divorced her. Even my uncle used to beat us. Once I was injured because he kicked me in the stomach and I am still being treated for that. The beatings used to be by hand, feet, belt etc. We came here because there were some relatives here (grandfather's brother), but they told us they couldn't help or keep us.'

Listening to Tehseem's story without moist eyes and a lump in the throat was difficult. Words cannot be an anodyne for what she has gone through, experienced and seen in the last fifteen years. Farzana found them through a NGO. She found a job for Tehseem's mother in a mall in Hyderabad as a housekeeper and got Tehseem admitted to a regular school. Farzana says, 'I am teaching Tehseem personally and have taken this up as a challenge. I have to ensure that her English language skills improve and become good. Otherwise she has very good communication skills. Society is made by the middle class (not me, Aristotle said this). Now among the middle class, before marriage the first thing the boy's family asks is whether the girl has studied or not. But they are not encouraged to work because if they become financially independent they will demand their rights and their share in everything.' I am convinced that it will be the inevitable next step and no one can stop it.

Farzana says that Muslims need a jihad for education. And then another jihad to make sure that the girls start working and stay working. There is no gainsaying that the need for a jihad for education maybe more urgent in the Muslim community, although they are not the only ones. Even in well-educated and well-off Hindu families, parents do not want to give certain rights to their daughters.

Tehseem has just got into a regular school and she is dreaming of becoming a doctor. What Tehseem experienced would have broken the spirit of most people, but not hers and also not of millions of young girls and women in India for whom discrimination, violence, a daily struggle to get educated and to survive is the norm. As I met these confident young girls throughout the country, I felt optimistic and vindicated at my choice of subject for this book. But there are two questions or issues that keep worrying me whenever I think of Daksha, Salva, Priyanka, Tehseem and all the other girls like them. First, while ambition is good, some of them do have unrealistic ambitions or hope. It is not audacious hope but the basic grounding is not strong or good enough to realize the ambitions that some of these girls have.

Anita's sister, Jyoti, is one such girl. Along with Anita Badarappa, I had also met her sister. In spite of having completed her high school, it was surprising that Jyoti was not very articulate even in Hindi and she had virtually no idea about the opportunities in front of her, although she wants to become a Chartered Accountant since one of her teachers has told her that it's a good career to pursue. We met them when the schools and colleges were closed for summer vacations. Jyoti did not help in any household chores, slept late in the night because she listened to music on her cell phone and got up late in the morning, after the entire household had left for their respective jobs. Certainly not the right attitude for an aspiring chartered accountant.

Geetanjali Krishna in her column 'People Like Them' in *Business Standard* writes about another such girl, Anita, who has studied up to Class X. She writes:

I realised that this girl [Anita] who had supposedly studied and passed nine grade, could barely string together a lucid sentence in English [...] Anita's mother says, 'She wants a mobile phone, lipstick and a job in a call centre—but she can't even draft a leave application to submit to her school [...] A family I know needs a nursemaid for their newborn and are offering good money, but ma'am here doesn't want to do such work.' Anita says, 'I haven't spent so many years in school to become a nursemaid, have I?'[110]

A little bit of education and training and some not so sound advice means that many of these girls are dreaming or aspiring well beyond their capabilities and means. When reality hits them, sooner or later, it will hit them hard and some of them may not recover. Even when their ambitions are not unrealistic, some of these girls will find it difficult to break through the shackles that society has tied them with. Will their dreams crash once they meet the unyielding rocks of reality? I hope not and I have a feeling that even when they do, these girls will have added one more layer to the foundation that is driving this enormous change in the country.

The second and more serious issue or question is that these girls are super confident and are challenging established societal norms and power equations almost on a daily basis, but how will the men react? Will there be increased violence against women as men react to the inevitable decline in the powers of a patriarchal society and the dominance that they have had over womenfolk for generations?

Anecdotal evidence seems to suggest that the answer to the second question is yes. The pronouncements of khap panchayats, the edicts about girls not being allowed to carry mobile phones or wear jeans or short skirts are all signs of a patriarchal society striking back and trying to maintain status quo. Statements by political and religious leaders are an expected reaction of a segment that sees itself losing its privileges and powers. Difficult as it is to believe, a

---

[110]Schooling not schools, Geetanjali Krishna, April 5, 2013, Business Standard, http://www.business-standard.com/article/opinion/schooling-not-schools-113040500554_1.html

55-year-old woman was beaten to death by a mob in Aligarh because she allowed her college-going daughter to wear jeans and if this was not enough, the mob was led by a woman.[111] In all likelihood there are more reasons for what happened but it is still illustrative of the backlash that is being seen as women embrace modern roles and get out of their traditional ones.

I asked a few people whether they have seen any backlash against women with a rise in women's empowerment. Falgun at Shaishav said, 'Yes, there have been problems in families and some parents feel that we have caused trouble. But most parents want good for their girl children but were bowing down to pressure from society at large.'

Supriya from Vidya & Child in Noida had no doubts that some men are not changing. She told me, 'Absolutely not. In fact, I think it has become worse. I think the level of insecurity in men has increased. Mothers have become very strong and they are financially running many households. The husbands are succumbing to their insecurities which result in alcoholism, gambling and major problems at home and a lot of violence. Violence has increased.'

Manisha from Delhi had almost similar observations. 'This is happening, men are hitting back not only mentally but also physically. My dadi (grandmother) used to say that women get beaten only if they protest. She also used to say, "So what if your husband beats you, he also loves you. So don't protest, keep quiet, bear up to whatever he does..." But today's girls will not keep quiet.'

She added, 'In my time, girls used to be withdrawn, reserved and timid in public (*dari, sehmi, sar jhooka ke*)—*adarsh bhartiya nari* (an ideal Indian woman). But today the girls are different—they no longer conform to the older mores; they walk with their heads held high, they are not bothered whether they are carrying their dupattas or not. Today a girl is free of her body baggage and men are not yet ready to accept this. As a result men are becoming more violent and hostile.'

---

[111]http://indiatoday.intoday.in/story/aligarh-girl-and-mother-killed-for-wearing-jeans-pants-by-a-mob/1/279749.html.

Sohini of Breakthrough has primarily been working in the areas of children and women's issues and development, innovation and social entrepreneurship. We are sitting in her apartment in a skyrise located in a tony Gurgaon neighbourhood, which has one of those American names that one can see dotted across the city. The sitting room is tastefully decorated with paintings and book cases, reflecting the tastes of Sohini and her husband. She told me, 'I think the large number of women out there makes it difficult for men to accept that they are now vying for the same jobs and same education. One of the reasons for increase in crimes against women is because of increasing visibility of women. Society is also not ready for women who dress differently, have opinions, stay out late and frequent the same public spaces that men do. Men also need to come out of their attitude towards women—clubbing them into the mother-sister-wife-daughter category and not looking at them as equal human beings.'

Sohini is optimistic even though she is seeing an increase in violence against women. According to her, 'More domestic violence is being reported and it might also increase as women take on different roles. But in future I see a decrease in it when women reach a level where they will not be tolerant of violence anymore and where men have also learnt that zero-tolerance for domestic violence is the better route to go. Women have to learn to not be tolerant of violence—physical and psychological—or not take things lying down.' Basically the social conditioning has to change from early upbringing. Men may not be changing enough, men maybe reacting with increased violence, but the girls are no longer willing to keep quiet. Society is changing and men have no choice. The sooner they accept it, the better it will be for everyone.

LADKIYON KI PASAND: CHEH PACK—
GIRLS LOVE SIX PACKS

The changes that I have spoken about so far are getting reflected in advertisements, films and TV serials in the country. The best places to observe how much things are changing are small towns and cities, which are usually more traditional and conservative. What better city to start this journey than Hyderabad, a large but conservative city?

A once staid city known for its Mughal architecture, Charminar, Golconda Fort and Paradise biryani, Hyderabad is now known for the IT industry that grew here competing neck to neck with Bengaluru. As a result Hyderabad's name has changed from Curfewbad (due to recurring communal violence) to Cyberabad, a long term resident of the city told me. To cater to the young and affluent population, shopping malls, pubs and night clubs have started dotting the city, as have various training centres and institutes to turn young people overnight into 'world class programmers' in Java, Cobol, C++, or to teach one how to speak like an American.

The landscape of Jubilee Hills, the most sought after and plush residential and commercial area in Hyderabad, changed massively in the years since Chandrababu Naidu's thrust to attract the IT industry to Andhra Pradesh, and specifically to Hyderabad, started. Real estate rates zoomed and global giants like Microsoft, Google, JP Morgan and Goldman Sachs set up their campuses in this city employing tens of thousands of youngsters from all over the country. A swanky new internationally renowned business school also came up—Indian School of Business (ISB)—thanks once again to Chandrababu Naidu's efforts.

It was a bright morning in Hyderabad as I drove out of the Taj Krishna Hotel, where I had stayed overnight, to go for the day's meetings. Right opposite the hotel, at less than a five-minute walking distance, the GVK One Mall had come up. There was a huge advertisement covering a large part of one façade of the mall, which caught my eye. The glitzy advertisement read—'Girls love six packs'. I asked a client from Australia who was accompanying me, what product the tagline was talking about. Not surprisingly for an Australian, he said it must be a beer brand. I SMSed a few of my colleagues back in Mumbai with the same question. The answers were varied and ranged from beer to a fitness centre.

None of the answers hit the bull's eye. The advertisement was for Durex condoms. In conservative India where Victorian mores still dominate and more so in conservative Hyderabad, an advertisement for a multinational condom brand targeting young women would have been blasphemous a few years back. To me this symbolizes how much India has changed and how much it is changing every day. Advertisements and films are now telling us how much and how fast things are changing in India.

I remember telling this story to a newly arrived septuagenarian North American diplomat in Delhi as we sat at his well-appointed home, he sipping a glass of the red and I a cup of tea, in the middle of a typical summer afternoon. When I told him that this is what is changing in India, he said he completely agreed (with me). He said during his first week in India he spent significant time watching different Indian TV channels and the advertisements they were beaming. His preconceived image of a conservative India was blown to bits in no time when he saw advertisements for the morning after pill. The pill was being advertised as a choice for young girls who wanted to have some fun or had one night stands; it was not just about an accident. I always think of this conversation whenever I see an ad for an I-pill.

I do not want to trigger a debate on morality and moral values of what is good and what is not, but the advertisements reflect the changing face of more assertive and independent women who are in control of their choices and are no longer shy or holding back their desires and choices. According to Dr Kiran Coelho, Head of Gynaecology Department at Lilavati Hospital, 'I see at least ten new users of the pill every month with even teenage girls using it. It is being widely abused, with some women taking up to ten a month.'[112] The question that often comes to mind is whether this change is a very metro-centric urban phenomenon limited to an affluent educated social class or does it go beyond that.

To see or understand how much of this change and churn is all-pervasive one need not look beyond the annual surveys carried out by magazines like *India Today* and *Outlook* on sexual desires, fantasies and habits. The responses from small towns are surprisingly candid and bold. I perfectly understand that some responses maybe doctored to titillate readers, but the changes nevertheless are undeniable. From Ludhiana to Cochin, from Bhopal and Indore to Guwahati, girls and women know what they want and are not afraid to voice their needs and choices.

The sexual revolution that seems underway from these surveys is reflective of the revolution taking place in other areas in the lives of these girls and women. The surveys mentioned earlier are printed in their vernacular editions as well indicating their appeal across the countryside where most readers of vernacular editions reside. A decade back editions like these with suggestive pictures on the cover would have been burnt and most likely the offices of these publications would have been attacked and vandalized by some fringe group claiming to protect the 'Indian culture'. Introducing the 2013 survey, Aroon Poorie, editor-in-chief of the *India Today* group wrote, 'I believe the biggest change in the last two decades has been the greater liberation of women and assertion of their rights.'[113]

---

[112]http://indiatoday.intoday.in/story/quick-fix-pills-unwanted-pregnancies-teenage-girls/1/260843.html.

[113]http://indiatoday.intoday.in/story/from-the-editor-in-chief-india-today-sex-survey/1/328110.html.

In the mid-1990s, in 1995 to be precise, there was a print ad for Tuff shoes where the then leading models, Milind Soman and Madhu Sapre, who were also dating each other, posed in the buff with a python wrapped around them wearing only white Tuff sneakers. The ads had to be taken off as protests erupted even in cities like Bombay (yes, Mumbai was still Bombay then) and there were legal cases heaped against the models and the brand. It took fourteen long years for the legal cases against the then supermodels to be dismissed and frankly by then nobody gave a damn. Today's generation I am sure wonders what the fuss then was all about.

I witnessed the changes sweeping through when visiting Raipur, Chhattisgarh in 2009 and it convinced me that the changes I was witnessing were not just about metros and big cities. Raipur is the capital of Chhattisgarh with a population, as per Census 2011, of just under 800,000. I was there for a day to meet Prayaag Joshi of Imlee Mahua along with a few other meetings and in one of the main streets in a marketplace I saw a mannequin placed in the middle of the pavement in front of a garment store wearing a baby doll suit leaving very little to the imagination. Nobody was gawking at it.

Within a few weeks, I saw something similar in Rae Bareilly. In a narrow by-lane where it was difficult for even a scooter to enter, I was sitting in a shop-cum-warehouse with a local BJP leader discussing the forthcoming national elections of 2009 and right opposite was a shop selling sexy lingerie and night dresses, which were also openly displayed. In a society where in the 1990s buying a condom was a furtive affair with the chemist wrapping it in a newspaper before handing it over to you, clearly a revolution was underway. In 2012, I saw similar displays in a store window in the small town of Jalna, Maharashtra, which has a population of around 250,000 people.

Of course, there is no gainsaying that much of this merchandise caters largely to male fantasies but various online stores reveal that significant purchases of these products online are being done by girls and women and many of them are from small towns and cities.

This has as much to do with accessibility of products as much as it has to do with the anonymity offered by online stores. Saurabh Dadu, co-founder of strapsandstrings.com, was quoted in *Hindustan Times*, as saying, 'We ordered plenty of one-piece swimsuits in anticipation, but surprisingly, we've received most requests for bikinis.'[114]

To quote from a report on e-tailing in Zee News, 'Conversations with Manu Kumar Jain, co-founder and Managing Director of Jabong and Ganesh Subramanian, chief merchandising officer at Myntra revealed that almost one in two online purchases in the fashion and lifestyle segments are made by a woman, and that sales to women are increasing almost 25 per cent faster than sales to men...While convenience maybe the reason women in big cities shop online, e-tailers say it's likely that women in Tier II and Tier III cities (who are accounting for an increasing share of sales) shop online for the sheer variety of products that are not available in their local stores.'

'When it comes to intimates, the limited sizes available offline (J cups have never been available in India), the poor experiences provided by inadequate consultation, and the social discomfort of dealing with disapproving sales girls and even worse, sales men, seem to be driving women to opt for online purchases,' reveals Richa Kar, CEO of Zivame, India's first online lingerie store.'[115]

It is true that many products and services cater to urban sensibilities. But desire is not necessarily a privilege only of the urban, suave and English speaking elite. Further, as discussed in a previous chapter, thanks to media and hard infrastructure like roads, the urban-rural divide is rapidly vanishing. We now have a large chunk of 'rurban' population, which is aware and has access to products and services; its sensibilities are still largely rural in nature but are fast adopting urban ways of life.

---

[114]http://www.hindustantimes.com/lifestyle/fashion/india-s-first-luxury-lingerie-online-store/article1-631590.aspx.

[115]http://zeenews.india.com/entertainment/and-more/e-tail-trends-women-shopping-online-on-the-rise_139601.html.

The Times of India discussing Ronnie Screwvala's investment in
Zivame.com wrote, 'Globally, lingerie giant Victoria's Secret garners
over 27 per cent of its $5.5 billion from online sales.' The leading
domestic lingerie brands like Peri Peri and Enamor are taking cues
in a rapidly transitioning market. 'We started selling online just
twelve months ago, but 70 per cent of our sales are already through
multi-brand e-commerce channels. This amazed us. Good deals,
convenience and privacy are among the key reasons driving the
growth,' said Akshay Mahendran, managing director of Daiki
Brands, the Mumbai-based owner of Peri Peri and Biara. Kar
(Richa Kar, the founder of Zivame.com) said the latest funding
would be deployed to bolster technology backbone—to improve
personalization, recommendations and visual merchandising—as
well as marketing to get more tier II women to buy online. We are
preparing for the fast approaching inflection point. We want to
give a beautiful experience, making it impulsive and indulgent,' Kar
added. 'Lingerie is new chocolate,' she quipped.[116]

If lingerie is the new chocolate, then condoms are also another
variety of new chocolate, and I am not talking of flavoured condoms.
This is a country where condoms were rarely displayed openly by
pharmacists and when one bought a pack of condoms, the
pharmacist would wrap it in old newspapers and hand it over across
the counter. You would not think that in a country of over a billion
people and the land of Kamasutra, buying condoms would be a
furtive activity. This changed when the KS brand of condoms were
launched, which splashed bold, by the then standards of the day,
advertisements in magazines and on billboards—it was about
pleasure and not birth control alone.

If KS made a great leap, then the recent launch of Skore took
another giant leap that once again showed the changes that are
taking place in Indian society. In a series of ads, Skore tried to reach
out to the young with messages that were not moralistic but were

[116]http://timesofindia.indiatimes.com/business/india-business/Ronnie-backs-
lingerie-site-Zivame/articleshow/27202796.cms.

about pleasure, enjoyment and desires of not just men, but women as well. It was about being naughty, it was about a man being chased by many women not because he was just good looking, but because he could last longer. These ads ran at prime time across television channels and even during broadcast of cricket matches, when the viewership in India reaches its peak. The various tag lines in the ads were: 'What women look for in your wallet beside cash or card?', 'What flavours do you keep?', 'Not all marathons happen on track', 'Go Bananas', 'The colour of passion is no longer red', 'Ways to cut her down to sighs', 'Women love dots', 'It's a naughty world. Get ready' and so on and so forth. The ads were about new age women as much as they were about the changing mores of society, the new woman who is not shy of expressing her desires and demanding her pleasure.

While much of the communication that we see is related to sexual choices and desires, the churn and debate is taking place at different levels, be it about education, careers, sharing of household chores and rights and duties. Nowhere is this better reflected than in some of the advertisements that we see on television and in the print media these days.

Cynics will argue that there has not been much change in the way the media and advertisements portray women in India. At first glance it does seem so. Advertisements continue to routinely portray the role of women as home makers and care givers. Cooking breakfast for the extended family, worrying and taking care of the health of her children, her husband, and her in-laws even as she is making the tastiest meal by using some masala brand, another oil brand or simply making two-minute noodles, keeping the home clean, making sure that the children's and husband's clothes for school and office respectively are properly cleaned and ironed, all these are only a woman's job if you watch advertisements on Indian television.

She also prays for her children's and husband's well-being and as far as financial matters are concerned, she is more often than not either silly or a duffer. Her husband tells her how by investing in a particular brand of insurance or mutual fund, he the smart man, can now pay for the latest holiday or the mortgage for a bigger house or buy a new car. The husband goes to work, returns home tired, drives the car, goes to battle donning fatigues, buys insurance for the family, plans family holidays and plays outdoor sports with his children. And when he is not rushing out of home, he is relaxing by reading a newspaper or book. Needless to say, the husband almost exclusively drives cars and if advertisements are to be believed women generally do not drive cars in India, except in some isolated cases when the co-passengers are exclusively her female friends.

A woman is also the one who manages and balances the family budget, buys vegetables, shops for jewellery and clothes, sanitary napkins, skin fairness cream almost always dressed demurely in a saree or salwar kameez. And most of the time she is buying this for who else, but the men in her life unless it is exclusively a feminine product or pain relieving balm. She has to be fair, because her would-be husband and in-laws want her to be fair, her employers apparently also want the same. She buys jewellery because her husband wants her to or she wants to look good for her husband, she buys two-minute noodles because her son likes to eat them, she buys a brand of healthy cooking oil because she worries about her husband's lifestyle and his health. Well, you get the picture. The quintessential Indian woman or 'bhartiya naari' is a superwoman but only lives for others—mostly her male relations.

While all this is true, somewhere and for some time, there is another type of advertisement which has started appearing in the Indian media—not as often as one would have liked, not by too many brands, but it has firmly found a place. It all probably started with sanitary napkin ads that showed young college-going girls wanting to live life the way they want to in an active manner without being constrained during those few days every month.

At the risk of digressing for a minute, it is a reflection of a changing society that recently a low cost sanitary pad was launched by Arunachalam Muruganantham,[117] a man, because women from

---

[117]http://www.bbc.com/news/magazine-26260978.

economically challenged backgrounds end up using rags and pieces of cloth instead of proper sanitary pads and out of embarrassment end up staying at home missing school or work. Arunachalam is not shy of speaking about his venture and this too is a reflection of how society has changed.

There are more of the other kind of ads that show how much things are changing. An ad by Havells shows a husband adopting his wife's surname after marriage. The campaign was conceptualized by Lowe Lintas and was one of four in a series. This film— 'Registrar's Office'—shows a newly married couple at a marriage registrar's office, where the husband explains to the official that he will adopt his wife's surname. In an interview to an industry magazine, Amer Jaleel, national creative director, Lowe Lintas & Partners, clarified that 'instead of an attempt to change people's mindset, the campaign merely chronicles the change.'[118]

Ranjana, a close family friend, recently recounted her experience. When she got married over two decades ago, an arranged marriage into a family that had been close friends for two generations, her father-in-law told her that while she was free to choose whether she wanted to retain her paternal surname, he would be happy to see her change her surname. Ranjana changed her surname as it was not a big deal for her. Her twin sister, on the other hand, did not change her surname. It really doesn't matter to both of them. While this may not seem like a big deal to many, it is well worth remembering that within many communities in India girls not only have to take their husbands' surname, but often after marriage have to take a completely new name and their husbands name as their middle names. But Ranjana's husband would like to see their daughters retain their surname; that would make him happy, and he has told his daughters as much. It is a sign of changing times, as Amer Jaleel says.

This is not a chronological history of 'women in advertising' in India and hence, advertising buffs should ignore any chronological

---

[118]http://www.afaqs.com/news/story/36920_Havells-fans:-For-a-change.

bloomers that may have seeped into my writing in spite of my well intentioned efforts to avoid such errors. To come back to the emergence of a new kind of woman in advertisements—we now have daughters savvy enough to earn, save and invest to help their fathers buy bigger cars. The girl is still doing it for a man in her life, in this case her father, but there is a subtle change in her position of strength. Women are now with reasonable regularity portrayed as scientists, engineers or finance professionals. She is no longer necessarily married and can be a single woman with a career of her choice, not looking for the next fairness cream product either for her face or for her vagina. Yes, believe it or not, there has been such a product as well in Indian markets.

There are advertisements these days that show young girls and women who are open to having fun at their own terms. Whether it is taking her girlfriends to a picnic or giving a pillion ride to her brother or boyfriend on her scooty or pulling her boyfriend inside a cupboard for a quick tumble, it is all happening. And then there is also a girl in another campaign who steps in to take out a SUV or ambulance stuck in mud when the crowd gathered around, mostly boys and men, are just gawking. Advertising magazine, *Campaign India* in an article said, 'The Indian woman has moved from one who preferred pillion side-saddled on two-wheelers, to the one who likes manoeuvring the vehicle herself to the destination.'[119] Hero Motocorp used leading Hindi film actress Priyanka Chopra to promote its brand Pleasure with a tag line 'Why should boys have all the fun?'

A recent ad by telecom major Airtel generated a heated debate on whether it is progressive or in the end succumbs to gender stereotypes. The ad showed a woman who occupies the corner office giving instructions to a male subordinate, setting some stiff deadlines and then in the evening asking him about the progress as

---

[119]'All About: Marketing Scooters to Women, Raahil Chopra, Campaign India', 22 November 2012, available at: http://www.campaignindia.in/Article/323857,all-about-marketing-scooters-to-women.aspx.

she leaves for home, even as the man is bent on his desk completing his assignment. On her drive back home she asks her husband what he would like to eat for dinner. Once she reaches home she changes into something casual and starts whipping up a quick dinner for herself and her husband. Her husband as it turns out is none other than the subordinate in the office and she flirtatiously asks him to come home fast. It is once again a woman who is comfortable with her role in office and her role at home and clearly cooking is something that she enjoys and does it by choice and of her own volition.

Similarly there are the Fast Track advertisements which show young urban girls having one night stands or in a lesbian relationship and all these advertisements reflect the tremendous changes taking place in society in terms of what is acceptable, what is tolerated and what is not. Even a decade back, the Fast Track ads would have met with a howl of protest from the morality brigade with the mandatory stone throwing at some of its stores. Now people hardly care. In some respects, if one goes by the number of books or films that get banned, Indian society has become more intolerant because they seem to have hurt the sentiments of one obscure segment of society or the other. But in respect of relationships, rights of women and the choices that women can exercise, society has come a long way in the last ten or fifteen years.

One of these choices is with respect to virginity. Virginity is still treasured and cherished, but the long wait till the marital night to lose one's virginity is no longer there. Once again without getting into a debate on morality and influence of 'decadent western cultures', girls now are more assertive and willing to have fun on their own terms. Preserving virginity for her dream man or losing her virginity before marriage is not a big deal any more, as Manisha told me.

'Getting out of home, in particular moving to another city makes a lot of difference. More and more girls are doing this and are willing to live life on their own terms. At least in metros today I meet a lot of young girls who are twenty, twenty-one who are absolutely comfortable with the idea of pre-marital sex. The idea of virginity is antiquated,' Manisha added.

Is this across particular socio-economic strata? 'Mostly upper class, but among girls living alone in cities, it cuts across socio-economic brackets. At the same time I have to tell you something that is quite contradictory—things like hymenoplasty surgeries are emerging and becoming popular,' she said.

Manisha's answers are a true reflection of the youth today. In a youth survey done by the *Hindustan Times* (HT) in 2014, 61 per cent of the respondents were fine with the idea of pre-marital sex.[120] But in a country where the exact opposite of any statement is often true, the same study found that 63 per cent of the respondents wanted to marry a virgin. Double standards, hypocrisy or schizophrenia? Delhi-based psychiatrist Dr Sanjay Chugh says, 'While women are far more empowered today and ready to embrace their sexuality, the male mindset has hardly changed. The trope of the virginal bride still holds. Pre-marital sex and casual relationships have been de-stigmatized in youths' minds but they are afraid of being found out. The guilt is not about the act itself, but the fear of being discovered.'[121] Men are slower to change and this is a challenge, as I discuss later.

In a concession to tradition, therefore, hymenoplasty is booming in India. A search for 'hymenoplasty in India' on Google throws up 120,000 results in 0.16 seconds. In 2010 a report in *The Times of India*[122] quoted a 25-year-old girl saying, 'I didn't care about it but I come from a conservative family. I couldn't tell my parents that I am not a virgin. My parents have arranged my marriage. So I chose

---

[120]HT-MaRS Youth Survey 2014, available at: http://www.hindustantimes.com/ Specials/Coverage/YouthSurvey2014/Relationships.aspx.

[121]http://www.hindustantimes.com/specials/coverage/youthsurvey2014/ ys2014_sex_and_relationships/youth-and-relationships-are-they-broad-minded-or-bored/sp-article10-1250510.aspx.

[122]http://timesofindia.indiatimes.com/life-style/beauty/Women-going-under-knife-to-restore-virginity/articleshow/5715442.cms.

to get this surgery done.' In the same news report, a cosmetologist from Apollo Hospital had said that the demand for such surgeries was growing at 20-25 per cent per annum. Consider an ad for 18 Again, '...a vaginal rejuvenation & tightening gel [which] is redefining the term women empowerment...A remarkable product to empower the new age women.' While its claim is one of empowerment, 18 Again strongly reinforces the belief that virginity is one of the most prized possessions that a woman has. The slogan for the advertisement is 'Feel Like a Virgin Again'.

Advertisements are a reflection of the changing attitudes of society, which showcase changing women and men who are not changing. What they are also doing are changing the role models for girls. The impact that this has is difficult to measure or quantify, but there is a subliminal effect on how families perceive their daughters, daughters-in-law, wives or sisters or girlfriends. In the case of advertisements, I believe, it is real life that is leading the change and not vice versa.

In 2013, Tanishq, the No 1 jewellery brand in India from the house of Tatas, launched an advertisement which showed a woman dressing herself ahead of her marriage ceremony. There were a few things that were different about this ad. The woman getting married was dusky, was wearing a pastel coloured saree instead of the usual bright red and as the twist in the end shows, she has a young daughter, indicating that this is either her second marriage or maybe she is a single mother. This is quite revolutionary by industry standards, especially when it is a mainstream brand. While it is true that second marriages are quite common in India and do not make news, they are still not very frequently shown in mainstream media and thus, the advertisement was breaking a mould.

The advertisement was written about quite a bit in the media. When I put it on my status update on Facebook, the range of comments was interesting to say the least. While most praised Tanishq's efforts, some of my friends from the ad world pointed out that a decade back *Femina*, a women's magazine from the stable of *The Times of India*, had run a similar ad. Therefore, it seems that not much had changed in India if a similar ad was being talked about as breaking new grounds even after ten years.

But the fact that India has changed is evident from the amount of media space that the Tanishq advertisement got. Another advertisement or campaign that I must mention features Nandita Das, acclaimed actor and director. She featured in a campaign 'Dark is Beautiful' where she says 'Stay UNfair, stay beautiful' in what is essentially a campaign against fairness creams and the obsession with fair or light skin. It seems that a part of India has at last started speaking out against the fetish for fair skin.

Beyond advertisements, change can be tracked in mainstream media, particularly electronic media. At one level, media is the major change driver. At another level, the media also chronicles and reflects the changes that are taking place as we have seen with the relationship and sexual behaviour surveys. During my visits to small towns and cities, I invariably try to pick up a local newspaper, preferably one in the local language if I can read it. The number of advertisements targeted at girls and women exhorting them to have an education and career have burgeoned over the last few years. Then there are also the mandatory advertisements targeting women with beauty parlours, jewellery and clothes.

The most interesting section of the local newspapers is the pull out section, which address a different topic on select days of the week from education, career, relationships to real estate and personal finance. These pull outs are smaller and less sophisticated clones of the pull outs one finds in the newspapers in the metros and larger cities. But mind you, the content is similar. This has convinced me that the gender gap is narrowing both in large urban centres and also between large urban centres and smaller towns and cities. The fact that *Dainik Jagran* or *Amar Ujala* or *Punjab Kesari* or the FM radio stations in small towns and cities focus on these issues is a clear reflection of what the audience is demanding and consuming or is getting used to consuming.

Another reflection of the changing times is popular entertainment television. I am not a regular viewer of entertainment television, whether in Hindi or any regional language and most of my views or knowledge are shaped by what I read in newspapers and my discussions with people around me. My first memory of TV serials was when I went to study engineering and stayed in a hostel away from home for the first time in the summer of 1983. Our home was yet to get a television since my parents believed it would distract us from studies. As a result I had watched the 1983 Prudential Cup victory peeping through a window at a neighbour's place. After the midnight revelries on the street, I came home to a solid scolding from my parents.

One of my first memories of women in TV serials was that of Rajni, an intrepid woman played by Priya Tendulkar and directed by Basu Chatterjee in 1985. Rajni essentially took on injustice in Bombay and fought for it. The issues that she took up were what confront us on a daily basis like a taxi driver refusing passengers and lazy and indifferent government officials. The serial was a runaway hit. The other serial that I remember watching was Air Hostess, telecast in 1986, where the lead role was played by Kitu Gidwani and it portrayed the daily life of an air hostess.

Both the serials showed that television, even before the advent of cable TV, was reaching out to the masses with a very positive image of independent and capable women, very different from the lives of women which a lower or even middle class family was exposed to. Maybe this was due to the fact that producing TV serials was still not the mass factory that it became later or maybe it was a sign of the changing times since this was when the Indian economy had started tentatively opening up under Prime Minister Rajiv Gandhi. Maybe it reflected the optimism of the times under a young prime minister after India had successfully hosted the 1982 Asian Games. Maybe the serials were what they were because they were largely catering to an urban middle class and the affluent segment of society. There were really no masses then since TV had limited reach by today's standards.

It is therefore somewhat surprising to see the portrayal of women in TV serials becoming regressive as the twentieth century drew to an end. Opening up of the economy in 1991 under the leadership of P V Narasimha Rao, forced as it was by the foreign exchange payment crisis, changed India forever. But these are also changes that a part of India has still not come to grips with or is comfortable with due to ideological reasons. It changed Indian television and much else forever. About 117 million households out of the nearly 192 million households have access to television now. Today India has over 800 television channels in different languages; Doordarshan was the only broadcaster till the late 1980s.

An ever increasing number of channels and rising viewership meant that the demand for content increased manifold in the 1990s. The opening up of the economy also meant an influx of products, brands and services that needed to be marketed and sold to consumers across the country and not just to the educated, urban middle class and affluent people. And what better way to reach them than television? This brought in the money and the general entertainment genre just boomed.

As the economy opened up the media wanted to cater to what the people wanted rather than what an earlier generation thought the media's role should be. In print media the change was driven by *The Times of India*, which started seeing itself as being not in the news business but in the business of building and selling brands, a consumer marketing business. During this period the portrayal of women in television serials nosedived and ironically the person who can be credited with driving this was a woman herself—Ekta Kapoor. Daughter of a yesteryear's popular dancing hero of Hindi films, Ekta with her innate feel of the consumer pulse changed TV viewing in households forever with her prime time soap operas. It is to her credit that for many years it was not the channel or the stars that were important, but the content provider who attracted viewership and channels vied with each other for Ekta Kapoor's serials.

In one of those delightful paradoxes that life throws up, Ekta represents the new Indian woman—creative, confident, challenging old ways, breaking into what has primarily been a male bastion and emerging far more successful than her brother who had all the support of the family to launch his Hindi film career, and she is still single while well into her 30s. But in her most successful TV serials the portrayal of women has been seen as regressive. Instead of creating positive role models, her serials celebrate girls and women in traditional roles of mothers, daughters-in-law and mothers-in-law with their only interests being the various male members of the family, jewellery, clothes and they spend their time squabbling or scheming against each other. These women are invariably religious, traditional and the male members of their families are all by and large business tycoons with enormous wealth to squabble over and pass on to the next generation.

A research paper on the portrayal of women on television in India had this to say:

> The truth boils down to this that in the garb of presenting real condition of women in the Indian context and attempting to speak for these subalterns, these serials are just conforming to some of the deep-rooted commandments that control the social structure of India. Deliberate presentations and calculated deformations highlight once again that no matter what, free spirited women will always be labelled as transgressors; that's the notion society is entrenched with and that's the reality people will expect media to portray...The serials must stop categorizing Indian women either as the pitiable 'bahu' (daughter-in-law) or the interpellated 'saas' (mother-in-law) or maybe, the home-wrecking 'bahaar waali' (the other woman or mistress).
>
> It should tread beyond such divisive binaries and attempt to present a coherent and conducive picture of the 'real' women of today—inculcate in them the attempt to overcome stifles and join the mainstream of nation's progress.[123]

Even as India was moving towards modernity and small nuclear families, Ekta's serials were woven around large joint families

---

[123]Debanjoli Roy, (2012), 'Reality or Myth: Representation of women in TV serials in India', *Students' Research Global Media Journal, Indian Edition*3(1).

spanning generations. But clearly she knew what her audience wanted and they lapped up what her serial factory dished out. She became the biggest star of entertainment television without acting in a single TV serial. The most popular serial that she produced was *Kyunki Saas Bhi Kabhi Bahu Thi* (Because the mother-in-law was also a daughter-in-law once), which ran for many years and often made front page news at major turning points in the story.

During the ad breaks, fairness creams, hair oils, soft drinks etc. were aggressively marketed to the audience and the products' sales soared. The soap operas were so riveting that office going modern women across the country would rush home to watch these TV serials, maybe in relief that they did not have the lives of the women in the serials. For millions of others this was the life they led and they watched the serials, I guess, with delight. To gauge the influence that these serials have in real life one has to look no further than the festival of Karva Chauth. Thanks to serials like the ones Ekta Kapoor produced, Karva Chauth is now an all India festival, and has become a major marketing event around which husbands give expensive gifts to their partners. The serials have turned it into a community event marked by special deals in stores, malls and restaurants. And in one of those delightful twists and concessions to modernity, many husbands now fast in sympathy with their wives. So while maintaining a tradition, some men seem to be changing. They are joining their wives, something that would be unimaginable even a decade back.

Even as most serials continue to portray the image of an ideal woman, often referred to as the bhartiya naari, the storylines are weaving in sub-plots which indicate that society is opening up. The sub-plots are replete with extra-marital affairs, unwed mothers and pre-marital relationships. A few years back, these subjects were not discussed or spoken about openly in most segments of society, let alone being shown on TV channels which are beamed into hundreds of millions of homes. Taboos have broken down and it is a big step forward.

Of course, researchers wonder whether this trend is right or wrong and this debate will possibly never end. As per a research paper by Meenu Anand:[124]

> A serious question that the author wishes to raise is the justification for indulging in extra marital relationships as shown in many tele serials and the dilution of our moral standards. Are extra marital relationships that are casually shown on television hinting at the acceptance of such relationships by our society? Are we moving towards a society where fidelity is no more considered significant for a marriage? Are we blindly aping the western culture without imagining consequences of the impact of our present generation following similar trends? How justified is the third woman/man in a marital relationship? How correct or incorrect is it to be an unwed mother or to bear child of another man while still being married?
>
> The larger issue in question is the kind of role models that we want our young generation to emulate? Do we want to see our girls and women as idealistic, *pativratas* or do we accept the westernization of our traditional Indian values that stressed upon mutual trust, companionship, love and devotion in a relationship? Are we in any way through our television serials inculcating negative values of being unreliable, malicious and cunning in our relationships? Are we pressurizing our young generation especially women to match the flawless, larger than life, super human characters that are being portrayed on television?

The moral compass of the nation is changing and the advertisements and TV serials are showing this change. The moot question is whether real life is following reel life or vice versa. Most media personalities that I have interacted with over a period of time indicate that reel life is following real life and it is reflecting the changes that are taking place in society.

The other barometer of our society is films. There are very few things that unite a nation as diverse as India and they are, in my

---

[124]Meenu Anand, *Women in Television: Depiction and Distortions*. Foundation course, Human Rights, Gender & Environment, Women's Studies & Development Centre, University of Delhi, BA Programme II.

view, cricket, Hindi films and a feeling of nationhood that engulfs
us at times of crises. India has the largest film industry in the world
(by the number of films that it produces every year). Every year over
1,300 films are produced in India, whereas in USA, which boasts of
the largest movie industry in the world by revenue, just over 500
movies are produced every year. Just a nugget of information,
sandwiched between India and USA is Nigeria where nearly 900
films a year[125] are produced.

Given India's diversity there are movies produced in a number
of languages which reflect local tastes, cultures and predilections.
Given my limited degree of familiarity with only the Hindi film
industry, I limit this discussion to the Hindi film industry.
Aficionados of Tamil, Malayalam, Telugu and Bengali films will
protest at this one-dimensional discussion because Hindi films
certainly do not represent the entire Indian ethos, culture and
social beliefs. But the Hindi film industry is the largest and has the
greatest pan-Indian appeal.

How have the roles of women in Hindi films changed over the
years? To my untrained mind this is a far more difficult question to
answer since there is no one answer and I have not discerned any
powerful trend although some changes are distinctly visible. In the
1960s and 1970s, mainstream Hindi films had limited roles for
women and a majority of the roles that were essayed by women
could be categorized into a few stereotyped silos: the widowed
struggling and all sacrificing mother, the single mother wronged by
her husband or boyfriend, the vampish mother-in-law or step-
mother, the virginal heroine who waited to be wooed by the hero,
the hero's elder or younger sister, and the vamp or cabaret dancer
who was the gangster's moll. The women were mostly relegated to
small bit roles essentially to embellish the hero or the villain barring
very few exceptions. There were very few roles for real life women
but in a way the roles represented the way society saw the position
or role of women. Some of the roles were of very powerful women

[125]http://chartsbin.com/view/pu4.

like for example, the role essayed by Nargis Dutt as and in *Mother India*, a film that was released in 1957. But these were exceptions.

Probably the most popular Hindi film of all times is *Sholay*, which released in 1975 and broke all box office records. The two main women characters were essayed by Hema Malini, a chirpy and chatty young girl and Jaya Bhaduri, a young widow. Hema Malini's big intention in the film is to give up driving the tonga—a one horse drawn carriage—and get into a life of matrimonial bliss, for which she fasts every Tuesday. She is otherwise a very independent woman with a mind of her own but she wants to give up the 'hard work'. Jaya Bhaduri probably has a soft corner for one of the heroes and her father-in-law and father decide on her second marriage without even speaking to her once in the film! But in all fairness and without being too harsh on one of my all-time favourite films, both the characters were in some ways progressive, well etched and powerful. But the mandatory cabaret dance was performed by Helen, a vamp who had blonde hair.

However, the 1980s and the early part of 1990s brought in a wave of parallel or art house films based more on real life rather than reel life fantasies, with a significant number of the memorable female lead roles being essayed by Shabana Azmi, Smita Patil and Deepti Naval. This period also saw the middle of the road films that had powerful independent women characters being made. These also attained commercial success at the box office. *Arth* directed by Mahesh Bhatt and *Aakrosh* directed by Govind Nihalani were two such movies. The 1980s was also the first decade when the Indian economy tentatively started opening up before the real reforms started in 1991, and maybe it had some influence on the kind of films that were made during that period.

In the 1980s and 1990s a change that happened in mainstream Hindi films was that the roles of the heroine and the cabaret dancer almost vanished. The heroine was willing to shed her virginal image to engage in raunchy numbers and thus almost eliminated the need for a villain's moll. This is not to say that there were no movies in the 1970s or 1980s where the heroine appeared in what would then be considered a 'bold' scene like a cabaret number or a swim suit. But such scenes were rare. The opening up of the Indian economy, the overall growing confidence of the nation and influence of what was seen as being modern and contemporary led to the heroine shedding her shyness and doing 'bold' scenes like on-screen kissing, frequently appearing in swim suits, wooing the hero with a raunchy dance number or a slit skirt. There was no place for a cabaret dancer-cum-vamp like Helen any more. The strict silos of good and bad were no longer applicable.

But in my view these were mostly cosmetic changes. The roles were such that even the most popular heroines had hardly anything more than glamorous bit parts in mainstream Hindi films. Under the onslaught of commercial pressures, art house films all but vanished. However, in recent years the rise of the multiplex culture has made small budget or middle of the road films commercially viable. One can now see a small number of films with meaningful roles for women resembling real life rather than caricatures of their real selves. Even in mainstream films we now see single girls who are perfectly happy with their status and financial independence, we see a financially independent girl supporting her boyfriend as he starts a career, if need be even taking the lead in breaking up a relationship that is not working out and she is no longer saving her virginity for her marital night. It's her body and it's her choice.

Increasingly films are also revolving around a nuclear family rather than the big happy joint family of yesteryears. Once again one can see signs of a society that is changing in the different roles and they reflect the sense and sensibilities of present day India. The other mainstream cinema meanwhile continues to flourish. Like India, Hindi films, and I am reasonably sure this is true about Indian films, in general, exhibit the diversity that absorbs and encourages every kind.

When I was speaking to Manisha in Delhi, our discussions turned to films. She told me, 'I was watching Raj Kapoor's *Sangam*. Two friends fall in love with the same girl and one sacrifices his love for the other. But no one ever asked the girl what she wants or desires. Her views were not even considered. If today such a film is made, then there will be no audience; even the men will reject it. Even in *Naya Daur*, two friends decide who Vyjayantimala belongs to but no one asked Vyjayantimala. Look at today's movie *Wake Up, Sid*, where the girl asks the boy why he is not cleaning the house. These are making a lot of difference.' But why in movies alone, even in the great epic *Mahabharata*, Draupadi was never asked her views on having five husbands.

In the midst of finishing this chapter, I watched the movie *Queen* starring Kangana Ranaut in the title role. The movie embodies much of what I have written here; it is the story of a new age Indian woman who is self-confident, assertive and not shy about her identity. She was not always like this and circumstances forced her down a path of self-discovery, when she decided to go alone on her 'honeymoon' having been left high and dry at the altar by her fiancé. She has the time of her life, all with a little help from a bohemian girl of Indian origin living in Paris.

In the beginning Queen starts off as a person who is dominated by her fiancé and is willing to bend backwards to please him. But unlike the women of yesteryears, Queen has no desire to please anyone and lives life on her own terms, she is self-confident and happy in her world. Her fiancé even while studying and working in London remained rooted in conservative chauvinistic traditions, much like his counterparts in India.

As I came out of the movie theatre I was thinking that Queen, the heroine, is pretty much like India—what you see is what you get (WYSIWYG). She is unabashed about her origins and flowers into a confident young, single woman as she shakes out of her dependence on her fiancé. At the end of the movie, while the boy wants to come back into her life, she hands him the engagement ring and thanks him profusely because without his ditching her, she would never have discovered herself.

Whether it is print and electronic media or films, the new Indian woman is increasingly visible. At the same time what is also true is that there is an attempt to keep the ties to tradition and culture intact. The most appropriate word in Hindi that describes it is 'parampara'. We can see that in what Meghna, Priyanka and others had to say on different social issues. In an article for the news magazine *India Today*, film actress Priyanka Chopra wrote, 'Women of my generation have been raised to believe that men and women are equal. Men have to accept that...Young women in India are trying their best to find a happy mean between tradition and modernity...We cover our heads when we go to religious places, we stand up when our elders enter the room...but that doesn't mean we can't go out at night wearing whatever we wish to, or whenever we want to, with whoever we want to...Why can't we dent and paint if we want to? Or do thumkas on TV? Or go out at midnight? Or have a boyfriend?'[126]

Priyanka Chopra is talking about parampara, sanskriti and values making up the Indian women of today's generation. We see this in other chapters as well when I discuss Indian society and how it is responding to the rise of one half of the country which has been suppressed and subjugated for centuries even as it holds on to the traditions it wants to. Understanding parampara is important not only for understanding the changes and the ties that bind the new generation to the previous ones but also for understanding how to cater to the needs, desires and demands of this generation of rising women.

[126]India Today, (2013), 'No One Can Tell Us What to Do, Priyanka Chopra', 4 January, available at: http://indiatoday.intoday.in/story/priyanka-chopra-on-delhi-gangrape-case/1/240833.html.

JIDHAR ANDHERA HAI—THE DARK SIDE

'A foetus, suspected to be of a girl, was found in a nullah near Vijay Nagar slum area in Bhatta Basti on Friday. The police said that dogs had bitten it. The police are still clueless about who had dumped the foetus there.'[127] Many in India would have read this news item in *The Times of India* on 28 April 2013. Many more would have missed it as it was tucked away in one of the inside pages. After all in India an estimated 10 million female foetuses[128] had been aborted in the twenty years to 2006. *Lancelot's* researchers based in Canada and India estimated that 500,000 girls were being lost annually due to sex selective abortions. And this when under Indian law, gender determination tests are illegal.

News items like the one mentioned here do not send shock ripples in a society that is inured to such news. On 25 September 2011 another news item said that in Maharashtra alone 55,053 female foetuses were being aborted every year.[129] If this is correct, then the estimate of 500,000 sex selection abortions annually maybe an underestimate. Nobel Laureate Amartya Sen in his research estimated that 100 million girls had vanished in Asia,[130] of which

---

[127]'Fetus found in drain', available at: http://timesofindia.indiatimes.com/city/jaipur/Fetus-found-in-drain/articleshow/19760869.cms.

[128]http://news.bbc.co.uk/2/hi/south_asia/4592890.stm.

[129]http://www.dnaindia.com/mumbai/report-female-foeticide-toll-in-state-is-55053-per-year-1591312.

[130]'Number of Missing "Women"in Asia', available at: http://www.nybooks.com/articles/archives/1990/dec/20/more-than-100-million-women-are-missing/?page=1.

41.6 million were in India.[131] As a result of this the gender ratio in India has been lopsided for decades. Demographers have studied the likely impact of such a ratio, which among other things makes society more prone to violence. It also gives rise to increased trafficking and slavery of girls and women. According to one study, in 2011 alone 15,000 women were bought and sold as brides in India in areas where female foeticide had led to a low number of women for every hundred males.[132]

During my travels in 2009 I saw the first signs of gender sensitization in states like Haryana, Punjab and Rajasthan. There were two meetings in 2009 which I will never be able to forget. One was as depressing as the other was hopeful. I relate the hopeful story here. I met Premchand, a 28-year-old farmer in his two-room tenement at the edge of agricultural fields. Between the field and the house was his brood of eighteen water buffaloes, accumulated over years of hard work. This was on the outskirts of Chandigarh, just off the main Delhi highway where the sprawling and ever expanding city is slowly engulfing the nearby fields. The house was pucca but the walls were not plastered and the floor was uneven. The room where we sat was dark and tiny, had a large cot, a small colour television, on the wall a few calendars featuring Bollywood stars and a coloured framed photograph of Premchand with his wife and baby daughter.

When I met him, Premchand's daughter was six months old and he constantly referred to her as Gudiya (doll), a name often used affectionately for a girl child along with Rajkumari (princess). Premchand told me, 'I want her to study in a private school and study as much as possible. I understand the value of education and I want her to do well. This is the only way to ensure her future. I will try my best for her, but she will become what is in her destiny. I

[131]'Number of "Missing" Women in India: Sen's Estimate based on the actual sex ratio is Sub-Saharan Africa', available at: https://csde.washington.edu/~scurran/files/readings/April28/recommended/MissingWomen.pdf.

[132]http://nss.becs.ac.in/?p=41.

have started saving for her in fixed deposits at HDFC—something that other members of my family don't know.'

Premchand's story deserves special mention because the gender ratio in India is skewed. The traditional preference for a male child has given rise to the ugly and barbaric phenomenon of female foeticide and infanticide. The problem is exacerbated by the lack of empowerment and voice for the women concerned and within the families the elderly women often support such decisions and actions. The problem of a skewed gender ratio is particularly acute in the northern states and Haryana is among the states with the worst ratios. As per Census 2011, the gender ratio in Haryana was 877 while that in Delhi was even lower at 866.[133] In the child population in the age group of 0-6 years, the ratio for Haryana in 2011 was worse at 830, although this was an improvement from 819 in 2001.

Census 2011 data shows that the overall gender ratio in India was 940 females per 1,000 males, and was one of the worst in any country in the world.[134] Among the larger Asian countries, the ratio in China was 926 females per 1,000 males, in Indonesia it was 988 and in South Korea it was 1,000.[135] The ratio in India was 946 females per 1,000 males in 1951, when the first Census was conducted in independent India. Notwithstanding various campaigns by the government and NGOs to save the girl child, the gender ratio has remained skewed. Although the ratio improved marginally from what it was a decade back (933), it still is of grave concern. Further the gender ratio among 0-6 years was 914 in 2011 and had declined from 927 in 2001, indicating that over the next two decades India's gender ratio is set to worsen in the 20-26 years age bracket.

---

[133]Census of 2011: Provisional Population Totals.

[134]https://www.unfpa.org/gender/docs/Sex_Ratio_by_Country_in_2013.pdf.

[135]Gender Ratios in China and Indonesia: Dr C. Chandramouli, *Provisional Population Totals* (Paper 1 of 2011, India Series 1), Gender Ratios in South Korea, available at: http://www.theodora.com/wfbcurrent/korea_south/korea_south_people.html (2013 Estimate).

The first question that crops up is why the gender ratio is so poor and incidents of female foeticide so high in India? The second question that comes to mind is whether anything is changing for the better, given better education, deeper media reach, empowerment, economic growth and overall rise in prosperity levels? As I think of the first question, I am reminded of what Tehseem told me in Hyderabad—*unhe bachchiyan pasand nahin thee* (He—my father—didn't want daughters). Why is that so? Why don't families want daughters?

As I discussed these issues, the over-riding reason seemed to be economic in nature. Daughters are seen as a burden on the family since traditionally the bride's family has to bear all marriage expenses and there is a widespread tradition of paying dowry, which is usually a huge strain financially on most families. And for all that 'trouble' a daughter is not seen as economically productive since after marriage she will live at her husband's home.

A son on the other hand is seen as an economically productive resource who will earn money for the family and also in most cases bring in a fat dowry irrespective of his qualities, qualifications or achievements. It is presumed that he will not be a financial burden on the family and will take care of his parents in their old age, although increasingly, at least in urban settings, it is the daughters who take better care of their ageing parents. Then there is the issue of property, especially where land in rural India is concerned. If a daughter is to be given her share of the property, then land will get out of one family's hand to another over generations.

If these are the reasons for female foeticide, then regions, states and cultures that have higher incidence of dowry, are less prosperous and rural regions should see worse gender ratios. This is where the numbers get interesting and surprising. Chandigarh, the National Capital Territory (NCT) of Delhi, Haryana, Jammu & Kashmir (J&K), Punjab, Bihar, Gujarat, Maharashtra and Rajasthan are the worst states in terms of gender ratio.[136] Chandigarh, Delhi and

---

[136]Daman & Diu, Dadra, Nagar & Haveli, and Andaman & Nicobar are also among the worst, but have population less than 500,000 and hence, are not mentioned.

Gujarat are predominantly urban agglomerations, and barring J&K, Bihar and Rajasthan, the states listed are among the most prosperous and developed ones. In J&K, both the Kashmir (predominantly Muslims) and Jammu regions (predominantly Hindus) have witnessed a precipitous decline in the gender ratio. This is surprising since terrorism and war would normally mean that more men die and the gender ratios get skewed in favour of women.

The states that fit into the stereotype of high illiteracy, low per capita income and being less developed are Rajasthan and Bihar and maybe Haryana, which is prosperous but seen as socially regressive. Gujarat socially is in many ways what most would call modern or progressive where a girl is allowed to visit and stay in the house of her fiancé and vice versa once their marriages are fixed, live-in relations and remarriages are well accepted and large number of girls and women work outside their homes. While these are perfectly normal in most parts of the world, they are quite unusual in the Indian context. But these union territories and states have a high prevalence of dowry demand.

I asked a friend from Gujarat about the poor gender ratio in the state since it seems to be otherwise socially progressive. Apparently Gujaratis also want a male child more than they want a girl child. Access to better medical facilities makes sex selective abortions easier and thus the practice is in all likelihood more prevalent among the affluent segments of the population. However, according to the same friend from Gujarat, incidents of female foeticide will be very low in certain communities like Rabari and Bharwad. According to him, the desire for a male child stems from the desire to keep the family lineage alive, to ensure that the wealth remains in the family and the belief that after death one can reach heaven only if the funeral pyre is lit by a male child.

Data on the states having the best gender ratios is not very surprising. The best states, as per the 2011 Census were Kerala, Tamil Nadu, Andhra Pradesh, Chhattisgarh, Manipur, Meghalaya, Odisha and Mizoram. These states, barring Andhra Pradesh, are characterized by either high literacy and development levels (Kerala, Tamil Nadu) or are matriarchal societies (like the north-eastern states) or have high incidence of tribal population (Chhattisgarh and Odisha), which do not hate the girl child. Tribals in general have a more equal outlook towards their women, quite possibly lack the knowledge that prenatal tests can be done and also lack access to medical centres for the termination of pregnancies.

Madhya Pradesh's ratio is closer to Rajasthan's rather than to Chhattisgarh's, a state that was carved out from the larger Madhya Pradesh. Kerala has historically had high levels of literacy and human development indicators (HDIs); women have enjoyed property rights in the state for long and have played a prominent role in society. Both Andhra Pradesh and Tamil Nadu have had very good implementation records of the government's social schemes across sectors and this probably gets reflected in the decent gender ratio as well, notwithstanding the fact that the practice of dowry is as prevalent in these states as it is in any other state.

A lazy explanation would be that the scourge of female infanticide is limited to the Hindi heartland or the cow belt of India. If this were the case what is the explanation for the poor ratio in a large and developed state like Maharashtra and regular news items of female foeticide even in cities like Mumbai? An April 2014 report in *Hindustan Times* said:

> Abortions in Mumbai went up by nearly 10 per cent in 2013–14, making it the highest in the past seven years, according to recent municipal health data. The data collected from private and public hospitals by the Brihanmumbai Municipal Corporation's (BMC) health department showed that 30,117 abortions were recorded in the same year. Even as BMC officials attributed the increase in abortions to better reporting, data showed that the number of abortions performed in the second trimester of pregnancy (when the sex of the foetus can be detected) had increased by 11 per cent compared with the abortions in the first trimester (up to 12 weeks), which rose by 9 per cent.[137]

---

[137]'Alarming rise of abortions in Mumbai', available at: http://www.hindustantimes.com/india-news/mumbai/more-than-30-000-abortions-in-mumbai-last-year/article1-1213006.aspx.

I then looked at the data on the gender ratio among 0–6 year olds. This is after all what the future demographics will look like. The ratio became worse even in the last decade, moving from 927 to 914 (girls per 1,000 boys). Among the worst states in gender ratio among the 0-6 year olds were Haryana, Punjab, J&K, Delhi, Rajasthan, Maharashtra, Gujarat and Uttar Pradesh. The only silver lining is that barring Maharashtra and Rajasthan, the ratio is showing improving trends over the last decade in all the other above states. Bihar at 933 is a state that surprised me with the gender ratio within the 0–6 year age group. While in the last decade there was a marginal deterioration in the gender ratio in the 0-6 years age group in Bihar (942 in 2001 and 933 in 2011), when compared to the gender ratio within the overall population (916), Bihar's gender ratio among 0–6 year olds is significantly better.

I asked a few friends from Bihar and Punjab about the gender ratio, especially in the 0–6 year age group. They gave multiple explanations. In Bihar and from my Bihari friends I consistently heard that a girl child is not discriminated against in Bihari households. Anu Lall, a Haryanvi and an entrepreneur based in Delhi, told me, 'I have always thought that culturally Bihar is not averse to having women, as much as Punjabis or North Indians abhor their women. It's a curse to have a girl child in the north, in Bihar it's probably just a little bad luck.' It is also possible that since traditionally Bihar has been a centre of learning and culture, while a lot has degenerated in the state, it is still not barbaric in its treatment of the girl child and women. The other explanation that I heard was that due to lack of prosperity, many in Bihar do not have access to gender determination and abortion clinics or they cannot afford them. Back to the prosperity angle, unfortunately.

Possibly there are other mundane explanations for the slightly better ratio in Bihar than what I would have expected given the scourge of dowry in the state. The large-scale migration of workers from Bihar to Punjab and Haryana pushes up the male ratio in these states and makes the ratio optically better. When people from Punjab migrate out of Punjab, they migrate with entire families, but mostly male members migrate from Bihar; the females are left behind. This is not a new phenomenon. There are traditional folk songs in Bihar asking the lover who has gone to Punjab to get earrings and gifts when he comes back. But this still does not explain the fact that in Bihar the gender ratio in the 0–6 year cohort is much better than the overall gender ratio.

This takes me back to the second question that I asked at the beginning of this chapter—is anything changing and what has the impact of education, prosperity and development been in curbing this barbaric practice? Or do education, prosperity and development in a perverse manner encourage female foeticide in India, as data from some of the states seems to suggest? According to Anuja Gulati, the state coordinator for the United Nations Population Fund Agency (UNPFA), 'The data shows that sex selective abortions are on the rise. This is particularly true about the districts which have a good literacy rate and come under rich and affluent population.'[138] Why is this so?

In 2009 I met a lawyer, Baljit Dosanjh, in Jalandhar the day after I had met Premchand, a small farmer on the outskirts of Chandigarh. He gave me a quick lesson in female foeticide and its links to prosperous families. As I sat in the office of his modern vegetable store, *Veggie Wonders*, he told me that female foeticide 'is the biggest problem of Punjab; the second is drugs. The real sex ratio would be six girls for every ten boys. I have travelled across the state and it is appalling—and more so among the affluent.' The nip in the early February air felt chillier.

The richer families can afford to get gender determination tests done easily, which a poor family cannot afford. Apparently there are gender determination home kits available outside of India, which most prosperous families in Punjab have access to given that every family has relations living in the UK, USA or Canada, and it is easy for the women in such families to be flown to Bangkok for

---

[138]'Data on sex-selective abortions', available at: http://www.dnaindia.com/mumbai/report-female-foeticide-toll-in-state-is-55053-per-year-1591312.

gender selective abortions if they cannot have them done in India. I was horrified when I heard Baljit but as I looked at the statistics for this study, it seemed that he was speaking the harsh truth. Education, prosperity and development that we normally celebrate for empowering people and giving them choices and access to goods and services obviously have a darker side to it. If prosperity is one of the key reasons, then the gender ratio in rural India should be better than that in urban India. Thankfully the Indian Census data does provide us with this break up. Consistent with the theory mentioned earlier, in every large state, barring Tamil Nadu, the gender ratio is worse in urban areas than it is in rural areas and even in Tamil Nadu, the ratio is almost the same in urban and rural areas. The ratios in rural areas are worse in Delhi, Chandigarh and the north-eastern states, but the rural areas of Delhi and Chandigarh would largely have access to most urban amenities.

I had naively believed that education, characterized by better literacy levels and development, defined by better infrastructure, would have helped in improving the gender ratio. Punjab, Haryana, Gujarat, Delhi and Chandigarh have high literacy ratios (above the all India literacy levels) and still suffer from adverse gender ratios. I also compared the road network as a proxy for development and compared it to infant mortality, a key human development indicator (HDI), in the respective states. For the road network I used the roads built under the Pradhan Mantri Gram Sadak Yojana (PMGSY), started by the NDA government under Atal Bihari Vajpayee, which saw good progress subsequently under the UPA government as well. Uttar Pradesh, Bihar, Rajasthan and Madhya Pradesh have poor connectivity, a poor gender ratio and high infant mortality. But Haryana stands out in terms of relatively high infant mortality and poor gender ratio but it has good connectivity. This may signify poor access to proper maternity centres and lack of encouragement to the population to go in for institutional births, a state failure.

As this discussion shows, the practice of female foeticide is deeply ingrained in some parts of the country and unfortunately urbanization, literacy and development have not had a significant impact in changing social behaviour. In fact in a perverse way they have made sex selection and gender specific abortions easily accessible. Only interventions by the government and social organizations over a long period of time can change social beliefs and we have a long way to go.

Or maybe the reality of life will force some changes. The falling gender ratio means men are finding it difficult to find brides and maybe this will drive the desirable changes. The Satrol khap panchayat in Hisar, Haryana, recently changed a 600-year old tradition to permit inter-caste marriages and also allowed marriages within forty-two villages under its jurisdiction, which till now was banned.[139] According to a news report,[140] 'The khap, however, continued to ban inter-caste marriages in the same and bordering villages and same-gotra marriages.' In Bir Pipli, another village in the Kurukshetra district in Haryana, residents have decided to end the system of ghoonghat, a custom which forces married women to cover their head and often even their faces with the end of the saree.[141]

Some changes are not desirable, and are also a big concern. The falling gender ratio has also resulted in brides being bought from the poorer parts of India like West Bengal, Bihar and Assam and sold to richer states like Haryana. Trafficking has increased as per news reports. To quote a news report from *Jagran*:

> Driven by the low sex ratio in Haryana, the wannabe grooms in the state are going for bride-hunting to other states. Some of these brides have even been imported from non-Hindi states. The young brides belonging to a completely different culture,

---

[139] http://indianexpress.com/article/india/india-others/haryana-khap-panchayat-allows-inter-caste-marriages/.

[140] Ibid.

[141] 'Haryana village sheds purdah', available at: http://timesofindia.indiatimes.com/home/lok-sabha-elections-2014/news/Haryana-village-sheds-purdah/articleshow/34453963.cms.

language are trying hard to come to terms with the tradition of their in-laws place in Haryana. Several young men are passing their prime waiting for a prospective bride. Understanding the difficulties in finding brides for their boys, villagers are no more objecting to matrimonial alliance with the girls from other states, language and culture. Bride-starved Haryana is now looking up to Assam, West Bengal, Tripura, Chhattisgarh and even Kerala. In Bhiwani district, several young girls from Tripura and Assam married to Haryana men are adjusting in the alien world.[142]

In 2013, 24,749 children and women in the age group between fifteen and thirty years were kidnapped and sold for marriages across the country.[143] Sometimes such brides are sold multiple times and are treated like bonded labourers. According to social scientist Prem Choudhury, 'They tend to look down upon these women and don't give them their real status. There are instances when they are even resold to defray the cost. So several change hands very rapidly and they are exploited not only labour-wise but also sexually.'[144] It is of limited consolation that India is not the only country which is faced with the scourge of female foeticide, trafficking in women and also extreme violence against them.

However Baljit Dosanjh was not without hope: 'People have to realize that daughters are better than sons. They are more caring and take care of their parents in their old age.' One person who has realized this is Swaran Saini's father. 'I have three sons,' he once told his daughter, referring to his two daughters and one son. In 2009, 25-year-old Swaran was working in Ginger Hotel, the Tata Group's budget chain, in Ludhiana in Punjab after having studied

---

[142]http://post.jagran.com/bridestarved-haryana-imports-girls-from-other-states-1306299352.

[143]Human trafficking caters to demand for brides, Ashwaq Masoodi, 3 September 2014, available at: http://www.livemint.com/Politics/7cSn08nD9gvIEAbZcQrP7I/Human-trafficking-caters-to-demand-for-brides.html

[144]http://ibnlive.in.com/news/cheaper-to-buy-bride-than-raise-daughter/60766-3.html.

hotel management in Kerala. On one side of National Highway 1, which runs through Ludhiana from Delhi to Atari (near Amritsar) are half-constructed malls; on the other are green fields with yellow mustard flowers rippling in a gentle breeze. What has been Swaran's most expensive purchase since she started work, I asked her? 'A Scorpio car that we sisters bought for my father—and we didn't take any loan,' Swaran said proudly. And what was she saving for now? 'I want to send my parents on a world tour,' she said.

Baljit is right about daughters. The sooner more people realize it, the better it will be. It would be a proud day when Swaran's father no longer refers to his daughters as his sons.

Development, opportunities and wealth have brought out another trend in society that is disturbing. The moral compass seems to have changed. For a good life and for earning money and getting ahead, both men and women are willing to compromise, sometimes with disastrous and tragic consequences. On 5 August 2012, Geetika Sharma, a 23-year-old former air hostess with MDLR Airlines who was then working with Emirates, committed suicide. In her suicide note she blamed Gopal Kanda, founder of MDLR and also the home minister in the then Congress government in Haryana, for her decision to end her life. Gopal Kanda absconded for some time after Geetika's suicide but was later arrested.

As details started coming out it could be seen that Gopal Kanda fit the stereotype of the corrupt politician whose business dealings were mostly clouded in secrecy and much of them were also probably illegal. He had money power and from news reports it also seemed that he had taken a fancy to Geetika and they certainly had some kind of a relationship, which Geetika was keen to end but Gopal was pressurizing her to continue. What also seemed obvious from the various news reports was that Geetika had got into a relationship with full knowledge and she did not seem to come from a financially challenged background where she could have been compelled to compromise or which could have made her vulnerable to being sexually exploited. There are pictures in the public domain of Gopal Kanda holidaying with Geetika and her parents.

According to Kanda he sponsored Geetika for a MBA course and she was made the director of a Trust that ran an international school in Sirsa, Haryana. According to additional public prosecutor Rajiv Mohan, 'In January 2011, Geetika joined the company as a director without any shareholding in the company. One of the service conditions was that she would report to the MD every day in the evening hours.'[145] These are certainly not normal service conditions and seem straight out of a C-grade Hindi film. Was it ambition and greed that went horribly wrong or was there more to this tragic story? I have no idea.

Geetika's story is not an exception. Nearly a year before Geetika's suicide, an attractive midwife in Rajasthan vanished. She was later found murdered. Her death rocked the Ashok Gehlot led Congress government in Rajasthan. To quote a news report in *India Today*, 'Bhanwri Devi may have signed her own death warrant the moment she dared to blackmail one of Rajasthan's most powerful politicians. For more than a year, political circles, both in Jodhpur and Jaipur, had been whispering about a sex CD that starred Mahipal Maderna, then a Cabinet minister, wearing nothing but his wrist watch, caught in a compromising position with Bhanwri. She was clearly aware of the danger such a CD posed...On September 1, Bhanwri, the 36-year-old nurse, paramour of at least one former Cabinet minister and another Congress MLA, was abducted.'[146]

Where did Bhanwri come from and was she aware of the danger she was flirting with? The same news report[147] further said:

> The youngest of seven children, Bhanwri was born into poverty. Her parents were daily wage workers at the Aditya Thread Mill in Kishangarh, 25 km east of Ajmer. She studied in a government school till Class VIII when she was married at the age fourteen to

---

[145]https://in.news.yahoo.com/facts-about-the-geetika-sharma-suicide-case.html.

[146]'Moll who wrecked the government', available at: http://indiatoday.intoday.in/story/bhanwari-devi-scandal-video-cd-mahipal-maderna-ashok-gehlot-rajasthan/1/160604.html.

[147]Ibid.

Amar Chand, a senior secondary student from the rural Baraunda district. It was her father-in-law, a government health worker, who encouraged her to become a nurse. The young Bhanwri was posted in Jaislamer town in 1999 as an auxiliary nurse and midwife. It was here that she first tasted the power of monetary freedom. Earning Rs 8,000 a month, she spent her money on studio-photographs and roamed the city and its parks, hand in hand with her husband. It was perhaps then that she decided that she wanted more. For herself and her family.

She wanted to send her son Sahil to a decent college in nearby Bhilwara town, and to educate her two daughters Ashwini and Suhani so that they didn't have to live her kind of life. She wanted L'Oreal creams and aloe vera gels. She bought her husband a white Maruti Swift in 2009 so that he could operate a taxi service. In 2011, she bought him an Indigo. She was making what she could with what life had given her. But now her family sees it differently. 'Bhanwri was greedy and ambitious,' says elder brother Kishore Rajnut.

Bhanwri may have been greedy and may have wanted a good lifestyle but she also spent a lot of the money she earned to secure her husband's livelihood sources and also for her children's education. There is nothing wrong with being ambitious but it is of concern if morals are being compromised in chasing dreams and greed is the overpowering and overwhelming driver of behaviour because along the way this will certainly result in countless other tragedies like Geetika and Bhanwri. For some girls Geetika and Bhanwri may become role models, especially in a society where there are not too many role models available, aspirations are running sky high and not too many jobs are being generated to secure these aspirations.

I asked a question to many of the people I interviewed about moral compromises being acceptable as a means to achieving ends and an affluent lifestyle. Supriya of Vidya & Child said, 'They are willing to make compromises to achieve their materialistic aspirations. But that is as true of my generation as well compared to my parents or grandparents' generation. There is this whole need

to take shortcuts; to achieve something quickly.' There must be a
lot of truth in what Supriya said. Compromises and shortcuts to
achieve materialistic ends is nothing new. But has the willingness to
do this increased?

At least Manisha from Delhi certainly thought so, 'This is
another side of the coin. I know many girls in Delhi University
(DU) and Jawaharlal Nehru University (JNU) who are, you can say,
engaged in prostitution. They come from good families and all
their expenses are paid for their normal lives by their parents. But
they want to buy expensive stuff, chill out, go to bars and parties.
And for all that you need money and they are willing to do anything
for money. They are engaged in prostitution and I personally know
such girls. I have not experienced this in small towns. This impact is
also part of TV's influence. On TV you do not see anyone poor,
everyone is well off and everything is within reach. Everyone is on
an ambition trip, aspiring...it is not bad but somewhere you have to
realize that everyone will not get everything. This system is based on
inequality and disparity.'

In Bengaluru Deepika seemed to agree with Manisha's views.
'Umm...In college I have come across a few girls, who for pocket
money would do things. I have seen this in both Bengaluru and
Chennai. Just to dress up, have a good time...do they carry it into
their work life? In some instances yes, because it is a case of having
a mindset.' Habits die hard.

Sohini echoed Supriya's views, '(Women are) as ambitious as
today's men and will compromise as much as men do to achieve
their goals. Morality is not a question here, the ecosystem encourages
practices which you might not consider kosher, but that is the
practice among men and women. You have to do what it takes to
stay in the game, otherwise you might not even survive here. It
depends on whether you as a person will do it differently or join the
gang!' Women are no different from men. If the opportunity arises,
they will use what is in their power and within their means to
achieve their goals. Maybe it is a man thing and an inherent gender
bias to consider it a moral compromise when it comes to assessing
women.

Tanvi had an interesting and candid take that within certain limits she will take advantage of her gender to get ahead. We all do it—men and women—and so why shouldn't Tanvi. 'I have not come across anything (moral compromises to get ahead). My friend Smita (name changed), the only daughter of an Army officer, married a guy from KEM, two years our senior, and lives in a joint family in Mumbai. Smita wore anything and everything when she was at KEM, all kind of dresses. After marriage when she comes to KEM, she wears only salwar kameez and at home nothing other than sarees. They are a business family and I think this happens mostly in business families. Her husband, Ravi (name changed), is fine with Smita wearing anything. But Ravi's father is different.'

'As a doctor Ravi is still not that independent. His father has a big house, he is going to open his own pathology lab with financial help from his parents. So he doesn't want to spoil that. Smita also married him because of his money. I married Neel because I know he can give me a good life. Girls today even in a love marriage make a choice consciously. There was another senior guy who liked Smita. He was better than Ravi in every way except his wealth. But Smita chose Ravi. If a girl thinks she can use her charm to get her way, then she will do it. Within a limit even I will do it.' Tanvi is essentially saying that girls today are making more rational choices.

What I heard from Meghna was encouraging. 'I know in my class most of the children are very morally upright. Some of us in the class were planning to go for a movie. When I told this guy— our head boy—that it was A rated, he refused to go since it was morally not correct. I mean we all sneak in for A rated films. We don't think that they are that adultish. Very rarely is there any relaxation of moral values.' Maybe Meghna is just innocent; but something tells me that it is not innocence but faith and first-hand knowledge speaking here. Once again when one generally feels hopeless as we read about the daily cycle of violence, rape, torture of women and children, voices like Meghna's give us hope.

The fear of violence, socio-cultural customs and socio-economic pressures mean that India has the largest incidence of child marriages in the world. At 40 per cent India has the largest share of child marriages globally, 47 per cent of Indian girls are married off before the age of eighteen years, 22 per cent girls have given birth before they turned eighteen and the cost of lost productivity due to adolescent pregnancies in India is US$7.7 billion per annum.[148]

The number of child marriages in India is double that of child marriages even in Pakistan, a country not exactly a role model when it comes to women's rights and treatment of young girls and women. Paradoxically there seems to be a link between the success of some of the government schemes and child marriages. Vibhuti Patel, director, Post Graduate Studies and Research (PGSR) and head of the PG economics department at SNDT University pointed out the link between the success of schemes like the Integrated Child Development Scheme (ICDS) and Sarva Shiksha Abhiyan (SSA) and child marriages in a report in *The Times of India*:[149]

> SSA helps schoolgirls till Class IV, after which there are a large number of drop outs and ICDS children are in the age group of 0–6. As a result adolescent girls, who mostly drop out after Class VII as they can't cope with math, science and English, don't have to look after their younger siblings. In the absence of any programmes targeting adolescent girls in terms of vocational training or life-skill development by the state or by civil society groups, many parents are worried that these girls, who are now free of responsibility and have a lot of time on their hands, may end up in premarital relationships and turn unwed mothers,' she said (Author's note: Vibhuti Patel, director, post graduate studies and research and head of PG economics department, SNDT University). 'That's why parents in even progressive states like Gujarat and Maharashtra marry off their daughters at an early age,' said Patel.[150]

---

[148]'Marry me Later: Preventing Child Marriage and Early Pregnancy in India by Dasra', available at: www.dasra.org.

[149]'47 per cent of young Indian women marry before 18', Anahita Mukherji, available at: http://timesofindia.indiatimes.com/india/47-of-young-Indian-women-marry-before-18/articleshow/8211979.cms.

[150]Ibid.

For a girl child who becomes a child bride, life changes completely and irretrievably. As the Dasra study noted:

> She is uprooted and separated from her family, friends and everything that is familiar to her, and sent to live with her husband and his family—strangers essentially. Besides education and childhood being curtailed, she is also more likely to become a victim of domestic violence; child brides are twice as likely to be beaten and thrice as likely to experience forced sex than girls married later...adolescent girls aged 15-19 are twice as likely to die in childbirth as women in their twenties, and those under fifteen years of age are five times more likely to die. For those that survive, the chances of experiencing a still birth or new born death is 50 per cent higher than it is for women aged twenty to twenty-nine.
>
> Unfortunately, deep rooted patriarchal beliefs about the role and value of a girl, primarily as a caretaker of the household and children, and also as *paraya dhan* (wealth of another or someone else's wealth), combined with the intractable problem of poverty, sustains the problem of child marriage over generations.[151]

Slowly the marriage age is increasing.

Given that girls are considered 'paraya dhan', they are neglected in their own homes as they grow up, resulting in poor nutrition, less education on an average and an early entry into backbreaking domestic work like fetching water, cooking meals or managing siblings when their mothers are busy with other household chores. When it comes to a crunch, they are the first ones to be pulled out of schools.

The cycle of domestic violence, rape and forced sex that many of these girls endure is not only at the hands of their husband, but often also at the hands of their extended family members. Education, access to information and prosperity have helped reduce the incidence of child marriages to some extent, but the relentless cycle

---

[151]'Marry Me Later: Preventing Child Marriage and Early Pregnancy in India by Dasra', available at: www.dasra.org.

still continues. For the victims it is small consolation that these incidents have reduced.

The main driver of these customs, if they can be called customs and social practices, is a patriarchal society and deep-rooted socio-cultural beliefs. During my interviews and discussions I discovered that many girls endure insults, violence and exploitation because of lack of awareness and lack of economic independence. Tragically much of the violence is perpetrated by those well-known and close to the victims, often family members. The problem is not limited to economically challenged sections of society; the middle class often keeps quiet or hushes up incidents to protect the 'family honour'. Along with education and employment opportunities, it is the socio-cultural beliefs, behaviour and attitudes which will have to be addressed and changed. Thankfully this has started becoming part of the public discourse in recent times.

GAIR SARKARI SANSTHAYEN AUR SARKAR— NGOS AND THE GOVERNMENT

In 2005, Ramesh Ramanathan,[152] an investment banker turned social entrepreneur, told me that India is the NGO capital of the world:

> In India, unfortunately, we have a mental image that politics is very negative. This is why we are the NGO capital of the world. We tend to create societies and trusts, to do things that are the responsibility of the system or the state, rather than looking to see how we can make the system do its job better. We do care about our fellow Indians. When we see a poor person or somebody who does not have any education, our knee-jerk response is to go and adopt a school or build a hospital or buy some medicine for him. We are creating what actually is the responsibility of the state—as in the government—rather than asking why is it that the political process is not working correctly and delivering social services.
>
> We have allowed ourselves to become the Band-aids. Now, that is great as a mental solace for me—I can go to sleep at night saying that, I made a difference to the life of 300 people. But it is not solving the underlying problem. In other countries, which are more evolved and with democracies that are more evolved, the non-profit sector is invariably all about making the government more responsible, and making a process of engagement with the

---

[152]Ramesh along with his wife Swati have co-founded Janaagraha, a non-profit institution aimed at improving the quality of public governance by deepening democracy. More details about their excellent work can be found at: www.janaagraha.org.

government more effective. While I am not decrying somebody who adopts a school, there also needs to be a role to ensure the state does its job better.[153]

C Madhukar, co-founder of IPRS[154] along with M R Madhavan, had the same belief that institutions of democracy and governance need to be deepened and made sustainable and that this will impact the lives of hundreds of millions. Madhukar told me that it is much better to ensure that Rs100 billion is spent properly by the government and to help in that effort rather than to spend time in thinking and planning on how to spend a few hundred thousand rupees for a very just and noble cause. Again his views were not to deride or belittle the efforts of grassroot social entrepreneurs. As a corporate professional, for long even I have believed in the scalability, sustainability and replicability of any effort for it to really move the needle as far as impact is concerned in a country as vast and diverse as ours.

During research for this book the importance of the work that grassroot social entrepreneurs do dawned on me. In this country we need both kinds of social entrepreneurs to function in parallel. We cannot afford to wait for the institutions to start functioning, and while people like Ramesh, Swati, Madhavan and Madhukar are building institutions of governance and trying to make them more accountable,[155] social entrepreneurs like Supriya, Vinayak,[156] Parul and thousands of others are engaged in yeoman's work to help the underprivileged and disenfranchised.

---

[153]Anirudha Dutta, Anupam Gupta, Anshu Govil, (2006), *A Few Good Men: Overcoming India's Key Structural Problems*. CLSA Asia Pacific Markets, September.

[154]Institute of Policy Research & Services (IPRS) was founded by C Madhukar and M R Madhavan. Since its inception in 2006, PRS has emerged as the foremost research institution in the country catering to the research requirements of Indian MPs and also the foremost information source on parliamentary performance.

[155]One of Janaagraha's initiatives is ipaidabribe.com.

[156]Vinayak Lohani is the founder of Parivaar, the largest residential hostel-cum-school for orphaned, abandoned and destitute children in West Bengal.

The stories of Daksha in Bhavnagar, Tehseem in Hyderabad, Sunita in Noida, Priya in Ahmednagar and Saira in Mumbai all have one thread in common—the intervention by and involvement of a NGO that supported them. Without this intervention and involvement, in all likelihood these girls would have been married off and would have most likely become mothers in their teens or early twenties and their only identity would have been as someone's wife or daughter-in-law or mother. NGOs working over years and decades build a trust quotient within their ecosystem that is of paramount importance. Without this trust no Daksha's parents would listen to the sage advice and counselling being given.

Tehseem's mother was under pressure from her relatives to marry off Tehseem and if Farzaana had not found them, Tehseem would certainly be married by now as it would have been impossible for her mother to fight the socio-economic forces aligned against her. Daksha's story would also have been similar. She was nearly married off. Falgun and Parul had to intervene personally and spend hours with her parents over several days to convince them that Daksha should not be married off. It required tremendous convincing before they succeeded and by no means is that battle over. I am pretty sure they will have to go through the same routine once again one of these days, maybe with another Daksha.

This is where the role of the grassroot NGO is so important. Anita's story made me once again realize how important it is to have intervention by a grassroot NGO for change to happen. Anita was small in appearance, probably from lack of proper nutrition in her childhood, but had large, bright eyes and was very confident, articulate and self-assured. She dropped out of school when she could not clear her Class XII board exams. Anita stayed in a slum—Siddharth Nagar—in Worli along with her parents, elder brother and younger sister. Tina and I took the steps up from Annie Besant Road—the right side had a temple and then suddenly we entered a dark, narrow alley where even on a bright sunny day, there was very little hint of sunlight. Congested, families lived cheek by jowl as we walked past open narrow drains. A strong smell of garlic, cooking oil and spices assaulted our nostrils as cooking was in progress in many of the homes. The pathway was probably always wet, small children were playing around and as we walked to their house we could peep into anyone's house in the neighbourhood; a few gave us curious looks and this was not surprising given that both of us were so obviously out of place. As we sat speaking to Anita and her sister, a cat walked in. Then a little girl peeped in with a request to have her hair braided. Clearly the doors of houses in the slum were open to everyone all day long.

By Anita's own admission, she doesn't like to study. 'I just don't like it,' she told me. As she told me later, she lost interest in her studies once she started working and earning some money from the age of fifteen. That was necessitated due to her family's financial situation. But her sister passed her Class XII exam and wants to study further. Anita told us that her sister wants to become a doctor. This comment showed lack of awareness and knowledge about what her sister had studied so far and what she could aim for since her sister had not studied science but commerce. Bridging the lack of information and knowledge is a vital function that NGOs fulfil.

Anita's sister, Jyoti, wanted to be a chartered accountant (CA). A brief conversation with her and both Tina and I realized that she had a very slim, if any, shot at becoming a CA. Her performance in Class XII was quite poor, she had no idea what it takes to become a CA and she had virtually no knowledge of English. The latter is least critical, and it would be a mistake to fault her for her naiveté or lack of knowledge. The problem was that her basic grounding was very weak and that was because both the sisters had studied in local municipal schools where, according to them, classes were held irregularly, and teachers, when they came to school, had hardly any interest in teaching. It's not Anita's or her sister's fault that their basic grounding in education is so poor and that at this late stage they falter when they finally have to sit for exams.

I now firmly believe that the lives of girls like Anita and her sister could have been very different if they had come in touch with a good NGO, as some of the girls we met in this book had. As Tina and I walked back from Anita's house, our observations gravitated towards a common arc. Anita, who had failed in Class XII, was the smarter of the two sisters but possibly because she had to start working early she lost interest in her studies. Or maybe she appeared smarter and more intelligent because she has been working from a very young age. She certainly appeared to be the smarter of the two sisters. The sister who had passed Class XII didn't seem to have any spark in her. She had achieved a modicum of success by their standards and so she was not willing to do any household chores to help the family.

The challenges that these young girls face require case by case interventions over a reasonably prolonged period of time by social workers and entrepreneurs. These girls need career counselling at the right stage to ensure that they achieve their potential. This is not scalable and cannot be driven by systems and processes. Falgun and Parul had to personally speak with Daksha's parents for hours over many days before they could convince them to let Daksha complete her education before she got married. Farzana not only had to do pretty much the same but she also had to find a job for Tehseem's mother.

It is a slow grind, one girl after another, one day after another, one year after another. And Falgun and Parul often get blamed for leading the girls 'astray' or making them independent enough where they can stand up for their rights or question their families' decisions. I asked Falgun whether attitudes in society were changing and if they saw their work ending over the next ten or fifteen years. I mean wouldn't that be the biggest measure of the success of organizations like Shaishav if they were not needed in a few years' time?

Falgun told me, 'In our society there is no place for girls. Their views are never considered, their opinions are not asked for and they are not even educated. Shaishav is a place where girls can talk freely, express their views and opinions; they develop a relationship with the karyakartas (the volunteers at Shaishav)—the relationship is one of an elder and younger sister. We encourage the children to take on more responsibilities.'

'Society is changing. We have different programmes that have strengthened the leadership qualities of our girls. Now within families this is being accepted and their views are taken into consideration even for marriages. A girl can now voice her opinion whether she likes a boy or not. Even now they do not speak to their parents at first; they speak to one of the karyakartas who in turn raise these issues with their parents and then the girls slowly open up. If they do not like the marriage proposal or want to study more, then they speak up to their parents; but they express their views with respect and not as rebels. In the last 10–15 years, this has been the development and achievement.' Most women in urban well-to-do homes and other countries would consider this scenario normal; but this is a major achievement in a semi-urban or rural setting in India; it's a victory like no other.

But even as Falgun sounded hopeful, he dampened my expectations with a reality check: 'There have been problems in some families and some parents feel that we have caused trouble. But most parents want good for their girl child, but they bow down to pressure from society at large. And we do not see our work ending over the next fifteen years!'

Falgun doesn't see Shaishav's work ending in even the next fifteen years. This only means that while they have been able to change the lives of probably a few hundred girls over the last two decades or so, it will be the same slow grind for the next two as well. One is almost tempted to conclude that nothing has changed in socio-cultural terms from one generation to the next. This is what Ramesh and Madhukar stress on—to make changes permanent, institutional and socio-cultural attitudinal changes are very important. Otherwise even over the next hundred years Shashiav's workload will not decrease.

It is therefore encouraging to see the present Prime Minister raise some of these issues, which hardly ever garner attention at a national level. He is not only speaking of tall targets but is trying to engineer a social partnership between the people and the government. On 15 August 2014 Prime Minister Modi said:

> Whether after independence, after so many years of independence, when we stand at the threshold of one and half decades of twenty-first century, we still want to live in filthiness? The first work I started here after formation of government is of cleanliness. People wondered whether it is a work of a Prime Minister. People may feel that it is a trivial work for a Prime Minister but for me this is big work. Cleanliness is very big work...it will be 150th birth anniversary of Mahatma Gandhi in 2019. How do we celebrate 150th birth anniversary of Mahatma Gandhi? Mahatma Gandhi had cleanliness and sanitation closest to his heart. Why don't we resolve not to leave a speck of dirt in our village, city, street, area, school, temple, hospital, and what have you, by 2019 when we celebrate 150th anniversary of Mahatma Gandhi? This happens not just with the Government, but with public participation. That's why we have to do it together.

I asked Sohini in Delhi as to how she expects her work to change or rather how her work had changed as she had been working for over two decades in the social sector in different roles. Sohini believes that the nature of her job and areas of priorities will change in the coming years. 'In some areas I hope it will be over—we might have proper representation of women in Parliament, early marriages as a practice might reduce significantly and sex selective elimination might be a thing of past in the next 20-30 years. But power structures and centuries old patriarchy are difficult to get rid of in a few decades. My daughter's daughter or son might see a different world.'

What are your thoughts on women's empowerment in India I asked her. 'The three pillars of women's empowerment are mobility, security and decision-making power. All three are arguably low in India. The biggest block is patriarchy that exists in our society which overshadows the thoughts of even highly educated people. Women's empowerment in India is negatively impacted by the pervasive discrimination that women endure within the family and in the community.'

She continued, 'Discrimination against women in most parts of India emerges from the social and religious construct of a woman's role and her status. As such, in many parts of India, women are considered to be less than men, occupying a lower status in the family and in the community. Women and girls have restricted mobility, access to education, access to health facilities and lower decision-making power, and experience higher rates of violence. Political participation is also hindered at the panchayat level and at the state and national levels, despite existing reservations for women. Deprivation at rural levels is higher since poverty is higher,' she added.

As we are aware, urbanization is a key driver of change not only because it drives prosperity but also because it provides empowerment through better access to information. It is also easier for social organizations to reach out to people in more urban settings and also to force the institutions of democracy and society to act instead of remaining mute spectators or hostage to centuries old socio-cultural norms.

The socio-cultural construct or contract coupled with poverty is the key driver of lack of empowerment of women and discrimination against them. This discrimination between genders starts early, as we have seen with sex selective abortions. Said Sohini, 'In India, discrimination against a girl begins before her birth with some of the more affluent states in India recording high incidences of sex-selective elimination of female foetuses. Discrimination from birth, inadequate nutrition, lack of education, forced dropouts, early marriages, reproduction before the body is able to handle it are just some of the manifestations of the gender inequality which come out clearly. On the other hand, incidences of domestic violence, sexual harassment at the workplace, sexual assaults, reproductive rights, trafficking or commercial sexual exploitation, violence faced by victims of religious intolerance add upto the general discrimination of women.

In rural India, women's economic opportunities remain restricted by social, cultural and religious barriers. Rural women, particularly those from a lower caste and class, have the lowest literacy rates and most often are engaged in the unorganized sector, in self-employment or in small scale industries. Self-help groups (SHGs) are a widely practiced model for providing social and economic mobility by NGOs and the government.

Sohini makes a very important point—economic empowerment is the key. In urban areas, education leads to knowledge and economic empowerment given the relatively better opportunities that exist in both the organized and unorganized sectors. Even without much education the chances and potential for economic empowerment in urban areas are much higher than they are in a rural setting. But in rural areas there are very few employment or economic opportunities outside of agriculture, as I saw when I met Chhavi. Despite her list of contacts and high profile, the only 'jobs' she was able to bring to the women of Soda were a few embroidery assignments from some stores in Jaipur. This is not enough. The biggest chunk of women workers who migrate out of rural areas in search of livelihood mostly work in the construction sector or as domestic help in homes. Both these segments are unorganized and construction work is also dominated by thekedars or contractors making the women vulnerable and open to exploitation.

SHGs and MFIs are playing a critical role in providing opportunities to these women at their doorsteps. Job creation in rural areas for women will be critical for their empowerment. According to Sohini SHGs provide women with an opportunity to manage loans and savings that can be used by members for varying needs. SHGs are also used for promoting social change among their members and the community. Members of SHGs have used their experiences as leverage to enter other local institutions such as panchayats and micro-finance units. Rural, low-caste, poor women also make up 75 per cent of domestic workers in India—a sector that is totally unorganized, riddled with discriminations, low wages, bad working conditions, no standardization and often ill-treatment, abuse and violence.

Sohini holds a mirror to all of us since stories of exploitation and torture of domestic workers in affluent households are heard with unerring regularity. SHGs play a very important role and the success of SHGs in Andhra Pradesh and Tamil Nadu, for example, may explain better social outcomes of government schemes and even good gender ratios. This is the kind of partnership needed between government institutions and grassroot NGOs to drive permanent change.

What should the government be doing or what can it do? Booz & Co in its 2012 study of 128 countries found that countries that have not approached the issue or problem of women's empowerment systematically have performed worse in terms of outcomes.[157] According to the report:

> These countries also have more of a scattered and nonlinear relationship between inputs and outputs—in other words, there are many ways to get it wrong, and they are not far enough along in their efforts to see a clear correlation. They can clearly learn from and apply the best practices of more forward-thinking countries regarding specific policies and practices to economically empower women, and how best to implement those policies.[158]

According to Sohini, 'As a result of a vibrant women's movement in the last fifty years, policies to advance human rights for women in India are substantial and forward-thinking, such as the Domestic Violence Act (2005), and the 73rd and 74th Amendments to the Constitution that provide reservations for women to enter politics at the panchayat level. There are multiple national and state level governmental and non-governmental mechanisms such as the Women's Commission to advance these policies, and the implementation of these policies is decentralized to state and district level authorities and organizations that include local non-governmental organizations.'

Is gender budgeting an answer to some of the issues I asked Sohini. 'Gender-based budgeting is only one mechanism to ensure

---

[157]Booz & Co., (2012), *Empowering the Third Billion: Women and the World of Work.*
[158]Ibid.

that there is money to be spent for women. Who decides where that spending needs to happen? The policy and practice gap in India cuts across all sectors and initiatives as a result of rampant corruption and lack of good governance practices. Empowerment for women in India requires a cross-cutting approach and one which addresses the diversity of social structures that govern women's lives. It is not only about services but also looking at several layers that cut across the question of empowerment like caste, class and religion.'

Sohini's laundry list of important things that need to be done is long and expectedly much of it revolves around socio-cultural changes. These changes can happen only over a long period of time and need the partnership between people and the government. Some of the action points in Sohini's list are:

- Kids need to learn to respect women and understand that men and women are equal.
- Gender studies need to be included in school curriculum, in the curriculum of police forces, in IAS officers' training.
- At school and at home practices need to reflect this.
- We need a sustained behaviour-change campaign to create awareness and suggest change. Men need to be the focus of such campaigns along with women.
- Along with a sustained effort to put girls through school, there has to be an effort from the government to stop practices like sex-selective eliminations and early marriages. The government has to put in place a machinery to handle grievances, cases and complaints.
- Laws for women need to be formulated and existing laws need to have implementable mechanisms—quick and recurrent action can contain sexual harassment and abuse.
- Urban planning needs to take into account the safety and security of women—well lit bus stops, frequent service, bus stops which are closer to each other—all these will help bring down crimes against women.
- Access to education for girls not only in terms of services like making more schools for them but also addressing the inherent

preference for a son which makes families discriminate between a daughter's and a son's education.

- Implementation of national and state level policies to ensure that women workers have equal pay and are free from exploitation.

As I look at the issues and challenges confronting us, I believe the work will have to be at multiple levels. The government has and will continue to have a very important role to play in educating and empowering women, whether through its policies, laws or funds, in the implementation of extant laws and policies and in driving socio-cultural change. Then there will be an external effort by NGOs, the media and other independent institutions to drive policy changes, have the right laws, ensure implementation of the laws and ensure that existing or new institutions function.

There is a deep gap between intent, policy and implementation or practice. Unfortunately the institutional mechanism at the state level is usually corroded and dysfunctional. Erstwhile correspondent of *Financial Times* and *The Economist*, John Elliott, writes:

> Jugaad and chalta hai do India more damage on a macro level. They build fault lines that undermine and erode established institutional systems that are central to the functioning of a society and economy. They contribute to India's failures to operate efficiently...[159]

Lastly, but very importantly, we will need non-scalable models of hundreds of social entrepreneurs who will work at the grassroots to change one life every day. We will need grassroot institutions and individuals till the public institutions and governments do not function and public officials do not do what they are supposed to do.

I have absolutely no doubts any longer about the need for grassroot organizations. While the larger institutions will continue

---

[159]John Elliott, (2014), *Implosion: India's Tryst with Reality*, HarperCollins Publishers India, chapter 3, p. 40.

to work towards holding the government accountable and building institutions of democracy that deliver to the people, it is grassroot NGOs that have to deal on a case to case basis with individual girls, their families and their immediate surrounding ecosystem to ensure that they have a much better future than what their mothers and grandmothers had. They have to slowly chip away at long held social beliefs of a patriarchal society that keep girls suppressed and also exploit them. Many of these NGOs will have to start working with boys and men since fostering an attitudinal change in them is equally if not more important in our society.

This raises the obvious question of what is the government doing, if anything. Callous, insensitive statements by political leaders, give an impression that the state, its institutions and its leaders are completely dysfunctional. Many government actions get labelled as tokenism. But even then slowly things are changing. I mean who could have predicted the far reaching impact of the Right to Information (RTI) Act on transparency in government operations? RTI arguably is one of the foremost empowerment tools in the hands of NGOs, the media and the common men and women in the country.

One of the most important legislations in recent years has been the reservation for women in panchayats, the local government at the village level. The primary criticism against reservation of seats for women in panchayats has been that it is the men, mostly husbands, who control the women sarpanchs and the women are heads only in name. That is true to a large extent; or at least that was the case to begin with. I have travelled into villages where the husband is the one who sits in the panchayat office taking all decisions and conducting all meetings, including with outsiders like me. The lady, if she is at all present, does not open her mouth and the man is referred to as sarpanch pati (husband of the sarpanch). But nobody is in any doubt about who is the real sarpanch.

Do such measures remain largely symbolic and if yes, then what is the use of having them? This is where the story gets interesting.

Research is showing that slowly the women sarpanchs are assuming not just the titular role but also taking charge of decision making. According to a report on Panchayati Raj Institutions (PRIs),[160] the empowerment of women has been quite significant. The report notes:

> A survey of 165 Gram Panchayats (GPs) in Birbhum district of West Bengal confirms earlier findings that female Pradhans elected to reserved seats deliver more on drinking water infrastructure, sanitation, and roads than their non-reserved counterparts. However, reservations have a much broader impact across sectors than previously thought. Continuing to push drinking water investments, women elected in the second term under a reserved seat also invest more in 'male issues' such as school repair, health centre repair, and irrigation facilities. Further, while women elected in reserved GPs do differ from their male counterparts in their experience as leaders, they are able to increase female participation in the political process and make different policy decisions...A study in Bihar shows an interesting case where majority of Elected Women Representatives are into infrastructure development and providing irrigation facilities or constructing pucca roads.

In another study Raghabendra Chattopadhyay and Esther Duflo,[161] compared the local infrastructure available in reserved and unreserved villages just two years after women's reservation was introduced in panchayats. They found that women invested much more of their budgets in the local infrastructure that they wanted, as compared to villages that had no reservations. In West Bengal, it was more in roads and drinking water and less in schools. The same study replicated in Rajasthan found that women wanted closer sources of drinking water since they had to otherwise fetch water from long distances whereas the men wanted roads. In villages

[160]'Towards Holistic Panchayati Raj', 1 (24 April 2013).

[161]Abhijit V Banerjee and Esther Duflo, *Poor Economics: A Radical Thinking of the Way to Fight Global Poverty*, pp. 250–51.

where women were panchayat leaders more money was spent on drinking water and less on roads. To quote Abhijit and Esther:

> Further studies elsewhere in India have made it clear that women leaders almost always make a difference. Furthermore, over time, women also appear to be doing more than men with the same limited budget and are reported to be less inclined to take bribes...many women are quietly taking charge.[162]

Sometimes there are unintended consequences. Schemes that have helped in the ownership of pucca houses, access to roads, tap water, cooking gas and rural electrification have gone a long way in improving the health and productivity of women. Some of these are also helping girls to remain in school longer. Over the last ten years, the number of households with access to electricity went up from 43 per cent to 67.2 per cent,[163] access to drinking water went up from 39 per cent[164] to nearly 47 per cent[165] and access to toilets went up from 28 per cent to nearly 47 per cent.[166]

In India there are more mobile phones than toilets with 53 per cent of the total population and 60 per cent of the rural population still resorting to defecation in open spaces. A study by Dasra[167] in 2012 noted that 'sanitation brings the single greatest return on investment of any development intervention—for every $1 spent on sanitation at least $9 is saved in health, education, and economic development.' Due to lack of basic sanitation facilities in India, 1,600 children die daily before reaching their fifth birthday, 24 per

---

[162]Ibid.

[163]Census of India's House listing and Housing Census Data Highlights, 2011.

[164]'Households with Access to Drinking Water 2001', available at: http://censusindia.gov.in/2011-Common/NSDI/Houses_Household.pdf.

[165]'Households with Access to Drinking Water 2011', available at: http://www.censusindia.gov.in/2011census/hlo/Data_sheet/India/HLO_Indicators.pdf.

[166]'Households with Access to Toilets 2011', Census of India's House listing and Housing Census Data Highlights, 2011.

[167]Squatting Rights: Access to Toilets in Urban India, September 2012, Dasra, p.2.

cent of the girls drop out of school and more than 30 per cent of marginalized women face violence every year. All this costs India Rs 2.4 trillion (about US$40 billion) every year or 2.2 per cent of its GDP.[168]

The World Bank estimates that India loses approximately Rs 24,000 crores[169] (US$4billion) annually due to lack of toilets and sanitation facilities. The issue of lack of toilets has huge implications not only for health and associated costs to the country but also on the safety of girls and women. Assault and rape of women, especially in rural India and urban slums happen when they go out, especially in the cover of darkness either very early in the morning or after dusk.

The rape and murder of two teenage girls in Katra Sadatganj village, district Badaun, Uttar Pradesh in May 2014 once again highlighted this. The two cousins had gone out after dusk to relieve themselves, as they usually did in groups of two or three. Another cousin was saved as she did not go out that night since she was having her monthly periods and found it embarrassing to step out. Shanti Devi, a resident of the village, was quoted in a report in the *Indian Express* as saying, 'The men watch us and pass comments. We have requested our local leaders to provide toilets and electricity, but no one listens to us.'[170] This village reportedly gets electricity for one hour every day. And in this case as in many others the police refused to file a First Information Report (FIR), let alone start an investigation or send a search party when the mother of one of the first went to the police station to report that the girls were missing.

As the news made headlines Sulabh International[171] announced

---

[168]Squatting Rights: Access to Toilets in Urban India, September 2012, Dasra.

[169]http://www.newslaundry.com/2013/10/04/holy-shit/.

[170]*Indian Express*, (2014), 'Badaun gangrape: I flashed torch, I saw them drag my niece by her hair, says uncle of killed girls', 31 May.

[171]Sulabh International: Sulabh International Social Service Organization, a non-profit voluntary social organization founded in 1970 by Dr Bindeshwar Pathak, which is dedicated to the Gandhian ideology of emancipation of scavengers. More information can be found at: http://www.sulabhinternational.org/.

that it will build toilets in the concerned village. The need of the hour is toilets in every village and in every school. Thankfully, although belatedly, some of our leaders are paying attention to this urgent issue. Jairam Ramesh of the Congress forcefully spoke about the need for toilets when he was the Rural Development Minister under the UPA II regime. Encouragingly during the 2014 election campaign, the present Prime Minister Narendra Modi said that 'we need toilets before temples.' That is probably one of the boldest statements made by a politician, especially one whose party at one point was certainly very keen to build temples.

Thankfully Narendra Modi remembers his priorities. In his speech on 15 August 2014 he said:

> Brothers and sisters, we are living in the twenty-first century. Has it ever pained us that our mothers and sisters have to defecate in open? Whether dignity of women is not our collective responsibility? The poor womenfolk of the village wait for the night; until darkness descends, they can't go out to defecate...Can't we just make arrangements for toilets for the dignity of our mothers and sisters?...I, therefore, have to launch a 'clean India' campaign from 2nd October this year and carry it forward in four years. I want to make a beginning today itself and that is—all schools in the country should have toilets, with separate toilets for girls. Only then our daughters will not be compelled to leave schools midway. Our parliamentarians utilizing MPLAD fund are there. I appeal to them to spend it for constructing toilets in schools for a year. The government should utilize its budget on providing toilets. I call upon the corporate sector also to give priority to the provision of toilets in schools with their expenditure under Corporate Social Responsibility. This target should be finished within one year with the help of state governments and on the next 15th August, we should be in a firm position to announce that there is no school in India without separate toilets for boys and girls.

Immediately following the speech large companies and corporate groups like Tata Consultancy Services, Hindustan Unilever, Dabur, the Adani group and Bharti Foundation among others pledged to build toilets and sanitation facilities with firm targets. TCS and Bharti Foundation have committed Rs100 crores (about US$60 million) each.[172]

No amount of private sector funding and involvement of NGOs can solve this problem unless the government gets involved. Along with spending more money better governance and socio-attitudinal changes are also needed. The village where these two girls were raped and later hanged has 3,500 families of which 173 have toilets, seventy-three of them only on paper.[173] The tragedy or irony is that there are at least three government schemes funded jointly by the central and state governments for sanitation and in 2010, the Badaun district under which the village falls won the best performance award under one such scheme, the 'Sampurna Swachata Abhiyan' for building toilets.[174]

Some reports suggest that the funding was inadequate and therefore the funds disbursed in the village were diverted for constructing proper houses. Further the beneficiaries were incorrectly identified and many deserving poor families did not get any funds. The government's identification of beneficiaries suffers from various problems based on local power equations, families are included and excluded, non-existent beneficiaries are included and funds siphoned off, targeted beneficiaries are excluded and sometimes the lists of poor families are not updated for a long time.

The UPA II government's Aadhaar based direct benefits transfer (DBT) was laudatory because it gave the poor an identity, the power to exercise choice and helped weed out ghost and double beneficiaries from government lists. Nandan Nilekani as the chairman of UIDAI and his team did an exceedingly commendable

---

[172]http://articles.economictimes.indiatimes.com/2014-08-19/news/52941994_1_csr-sanitation-india-inc.

[173]*Indian Express*, (2014), 'Badaun gangrape: Why the Badaun girls didn't have a toilet they could call their own', 3 June. Recently further investigations have raised questions about whether the murder of the two girls was rape or honour killing.

[174]Ibid.

job to roll out Aadhaar in a period of less than five years and now 700 million residents in India have an Aadhaar number and by December 2015 a billion residents will have it.

As former prime minister Rajiv Gandhi famously said that only 15 paise of every rupee spent by the government reaches the intended beneficiary. The rest is lost—stolen by corrupt officials, ghost beneficiaries, duplicate claims and other leakages. Aadhaar is not a panacea for all the ills that plague the delivery of government programmes, but it is certainly a big step forward in effective delivery of government subsidies and spending programmes to its targeted beneficiaries. It is encouraging that the new government led by the BJP that came to power in May 2014 has decided not only to continue with Aadhaar and DBT but also expedite its roll-out.

It is not just about spending more money and building toilets, but about a deeper social change so that the toilets are maintained and used. In many parts of India people do not build toilets at home because it is considered unclean. Sangita Vyas, Associate Director of Sanitation at RICE, an organization focused on research and policy advocacy around issues affecting child and maternal health in India, recently wrote:[175]

> Over the past six months, we have visited over 3,500 rural households across six states in northern India, talking to people about where they defecate and what they think about it. What we have found is that sanitation is just not a priority among many rural households. Many Indians don't think that using a toilet is good for their health: half of the respondents in our survey who don't have a toilet believe that defecating in the open is the same or better for health than going in a latrine...Sanitation policy needs a radical restructuring in India. Although there are some people, for instance, the elderly and disabled, who would use a toilet if the government built them one, just building toilets

---

[175]'Most rural Indian can afford a toilet but don't want one', Sangita Vyas, available at: http://www.business-standard.com/article/opinion/sangita-vyas-most-rural-indians-can-afford-a-toilet-but-don-t-want-one-114061001295_1.html.

won't work for most people because a lack of money is not the main barrier to adoption, people's attitudes are. What India needs is a concerted effort to change the attitudes and behaviours of its citizens to get them out of the fields and into the simple but sanitary toilets they can already afford.

Dr Bindeshwar Pathak, founder of Sulabh International says, 'There exists a blatant lack of awareness amongst people—I have come across numerous people that actually prefer defecating in the open than within the four walls of their home. These mental blocks against sanitation are a feature unique to India.'[176] Culture and religion based mores probably explain why only 41 per cent of Hindu households have toilets, as compared to 74 per cent Sikh, 70 per cent of Christian and 60 per cent Muslim households.[177] Of course, there is the additional issue of space when it comes to urban areas and slums. A campaign like the one that was run to enrol children in schools has to be initiated to bring about a social revolution.

It is encouraging to see stray news items where girls are refusing to get married in a household where there are no toilets. Maybe this needs to be converted to a mass movement. How many more girls will be raped and hanged before the mass movement starts? Sohini, Parul, Falgun, Vidya, Dasra and hundreds and thousands of them have their work cut out for the next decade ahead and possibly more, as has Narendra Modi, the Prime Minister and the entire political leadership. The nature and focus of some of the things they do may change, but there is still a long long way to go.

---

[176]Squatting Rights: Access to Toilets in Urban India, September 2012, Dasra.
[177]Ibid.

LADKON KO KYA SIKHNA HAI—WHAT BOYS NEED TO LEARN AND THE IMPACT POINTS

As I transcribed the interviews and thought through my conversations, it was very evident that in the coming decade we will see greater participation of women in the labour force, we will see a more educated work force especially amongst women and these will have far reaching socio-economic implications like later marriages, lower fertility rates, better human development indicators and a greater degree of consumerism. Boys and men will have to respect the changes, accept the changes and adapt to live with the changes. It will be the new normal and will leave many maladjusted and bewildered.

During the course of my interviews through 2013, I often felt that the girls I met were more driven, more ambitious, more confident and generally doing better in most of the things that they were engaged in as compared to the boys in their community. It struck me quite forcefully when Satindra and I sat speaking to a small group of volunteers at Shaishav in Bhavnagar. The girls in the group were so much more confident and bubbling with ideas while in comparison the boys seemed shy and bereft of ideas. Even when specifically asked to contribute, most of them fell short of their colleagues. Is this a pattern? This question had been there at the back of my mind for sometime and I wondered what the implications of this were.

I met Roy Sudhir Kumar in Hyderabad at one of the centres of DRF. It was my last meeting that day before I headed back to Mumbai. We sat in the centre head's room, which was quite small and cramped with a large table, an almirah and a few chairs squeezed in. Outside the room there was a regular class going on and the sounds from there and the pedestal fan in our room constantly interrupted our conversation. Roy sported long hair and a goatee, much like Amitabh Bachchan, India's much loved and most well recognized Hindi film actor. He was dressed in denims, had a fancy digital watch with a large dial ('given by the landlord where we live and in whose house my father works,' he informed me) and was passionate about automobiles.

Roy's father is a driver and his mother works in the same house; they live in the outhouse. Roy was 22-years-old and had studied up to SSC (Class XII). His brother also completed his SSC, had no interest in further studies and now worked as a salesman in a retail store. But his sister was interested in studies and is now studying for her undergraduate degree. Roy comes across as a nice person although still rooted in tradition. He would not like his wife to work but would not mind a wife who is more educated than him since she can take better care of their children. However, he did say that the choice would be finally his wife's. 'My wife can take up any job that she wants; it should be her choice.'

I asked Roy about the girls of his age. 'In and around me, the girls study more. Boys get influenced by friends and do not study much. Out of thirty girls who were in my class in school, twenty girls are working, and about fifteen have already got married. I have friends who drink and smoke. None of the girls drink or smoke.' Disappointingly Roy did not have a very good idea of the content of his course or what DRF meant by life skills. As we finished the interview and got into our car, Tina told me, 'Girls would eat him alive. Did you see he asked us for some advice? None of the girls we have met ever asked us for that! All the girls asked was what have you studied, where do you work, what work do you do, why are you asking us these questions, what does your husband do etc. etc.' Tina is right.

This is a recurring pattern—the boys watch more TV, buy more expensive things (Roy's most expensive purchase was a branded suit for a friend's marriage), spend more time playing outdoors with friends and study less. Girls are the exact reverse. I asked about these issues and more to Ranjana Guha, who has been a high school teacher in Mumbai for over two decades and teaches English. When I met her in her school staff room she was less than a year away from retirement. 'Recently I gave tuitions to a few girls and boys—all commerce students—and a few science students from the higher strata of society. Aspirations of the girls? All of them are very focused on education and career. Boys—except 2 per cent—are not as focused. They are happy and want to party. Girls will never ask to be left early. Boys are given too much freedom compared to girls, even in affluent families.'

I asked Ranjana about the boys in her school and how they make their choices. The government aided school where she teaches is an all-boys school in a lower/middle income locality of central Mumbai and that is reflected in the background of the students. 'In my school the boys come from a very different background—mothers are maidservants, fathers are drivers, cooks etc. Mostly lower middle class. There are some boys—very few—from well to do families. How have they changed? I feel they have changed for the worse. I feel the mall and cell phone culture has been thrust upon the students. They try to show a false kind of bravado—we have been there and done that. They are in for a harsh let down because life is not easy. The aspirations are high in terms of what they listen to and see like Facebook, Twitter. But they do not have enough knowledge to be part of this world even if they have enough money.'

She continued, 'A large part of the problem is the education system—continuous promotion up to Class IX without failing anyone. They literally do not know anything. They do not know even Marathi. They want a good life and at the same time they are not sure what they mean by that. Their thinking is very superficial; there is very limited sincerity and integrity. Now the youngsters think that we will get to do something with or without education—there is a misplaced confidence within them. The political parties also tell these youngsters that you are local boys, who will not give you a job...thus, the ethics is getting destroyed. They are encouraged to participate in political activities. Local level political activities and community engagement in sports and religious activities are a big distraction for the boys and divert their attention from the pursuit of education or vocational training. On the other hand, girls have a greater urge to get educated.' Why do you say so, I asked Ranjana? 'Looking at the state of society, girls are a little desperate to get established. They have seen women who are not financially independent, they have seen their mothers being mistreated...I see that all girls want to have a career and financial independence.'

Throughout the interviews that I conducted across cities and across socio-economic strata, the message was very consistent. Girls have an urge to excel and are getting ahead. This is also reflected in the results of school board exams year after year when newspaper headlines scream how girls have performed better than boys. We have seen how more girls are graduating out of colleges than ever before and how they make up a third of the workforce in leading IT and financial services companies.

This is not to say that boys do not do well at all. Meghna for one doesn't see any difference in the attitude of boys and girls in her class towards academics or achieving excellence or in their ambitions. According to her, boys got serious a little late in her class but they started performing at par and often better than the girls. I think part of the explanation lay in family background, immediate influences and the fact that Meghna and her friends study in very good private schools in Mumbai. But overall the trend of better performance by girls is clear.

The impact of being more educated and smarter is already being felt when it comes to marriage. Indian parents are obsessed with the marriage of their children, girls and boys alike. With girls getting more educated and more ambitious, many of them will find it harder to find partners within their present socio-economic communities. Men will find it harder to handle a confident young woman who knows her mind and is unwilling to live by the earlier tenet of an *adarsh bhartiya naari*. In many of the stories that I have chronicled, I saw that girls were getting married to men who were less qualified. Give it another few years and many girls will not be willing to do so.

The challenges of finding a right partner will also cut across socio-economic strata. At one end is the mental conditioning, as we saw with Meghna and other girls, where they would like their husbands to be at least as qualified as they are, if not more. Saira told me that she would find it difficult to find a husband from her immediate community. She said, 'Yeah, I think so (it would be difficult to find a husband). It will be impossible in the area in which I live as nobody there has studied more than Class X; mostly they have studied upto Class VII only. My husband has to be more educated than me and at least a graduate. So I will escape from my area when I start working and go to some other place. Till now I have scored good marks. My neighbour's son always fails in school. Girls are doing better because boys are more interested in playing and in games and not so much interested in studies. Girls in general are more ambitious. Not all, but as compared to boys, girls are more ambitious. Girls are more hard working—they work inside the house and then go and work outside. Whenever I open our window, the boys are playing cricket the whole day. My brother can come home at any time but I cannot. If I want to go out then my mother shouts at me.'

This is what I heard from Ranjana and many others. A report in *The Times of India* quoted a match maker as saying, 'There is an acute lack of suitable matches for girls as they are well-educated.'[178]

A well-known market researcher and consultant told me how she and her husband were finding it difficult to find a groom for their daughter. Busy in her studies that took her to UK and then to USA, their daughter returned to India and probably did not have enough time on her hands to put the effort to date and find a

---

[178]*The Times of India*, (2013), 'Muslim women are overqualified', Mohammed Wajihuddin, 9 April.

suitable life partner. So unlike her mother, she has left the choice of a groom to her parents. And they cannot find a suitably qualified match in India who could be compatible with their daughter. One proposal came from a person well settled in USA working for a leading multinational company. The girl refused and said she had not returned to India only to go back to the US again after marriage. This market researcher knows of many such young girls in affluent sections of society.

The skewed gender ratio in states like Haryana—and therefore brides being imported and trafficked into the state—is well known. In neighbouring Punjab, grooms' families are now even paying for prospective brides' education and immigration costs to secure jobs in another country. But in a reversal of roles some such prospective brides are now ditching the boys once they settle down in a job in some European country. To quote a report in the *Hindustan Times*:

> Left counting his losses, both financial and emotional, Hardeep's father Mukhtiar Singh claims to have spent Rs 25 lakh (Rs 2.5 million or US$400,000) on his estranged daughter-in-law. 'We paid for her course, language classes, bank deposits and visa fee. We have all the receipts as my daughter made the payments through bank. But Kamaljit turned her back on our son after getting a permanent job there. My son went into depression, and is now under treatment for heroin abuse,' says the father of the 30-year-old.[179]

But some locals claim that the import of brides from other parts of the country is not only due to the skewed gender ratio but also due to the fact that the girls in their states are getting more educated. A newspaper report says:

> Many men in Haryana, however, claim that the shortage of brides is not caused by the skewed sex ratio as much as the rising levels

---

[179]'Men pay for visas, nursing courses to get brides in Punjab', Sukhdeep Kaur, 4 September 2014, available at: http://www.hindustantimes.com/punjab/chandigarh/nursing-foreign-dreams-punjabi-men-fund-contract-bride-s-courses-visa/article1-1259767.aspx.

in women's education. 'Women here study much more than men do. And she obviously will want to marry a man who has studied at least as much as she has, if not more. This is making it increasingly difficult for lesser educated men to find brides,' says Vinod Bala Dhankar, a social activist and woman khap leader based in Jhajjar district of Haryana. Moreover, bringing in a molki, or purchased bride, actually works out cheaper. 'Even if you are poor, you would give a bride from Haryana gold worth at least Rs 1.5 lakh (Rs 150,000 or US$2,500) plus clothes and other gifts. But for a molki you only pay for a mangalsutra and a gold ring,' says Dhankar.[180]

When I think of the girl instructor I saw in the *Siasat* office in Hyderabad, it is clear that it will be a challenge for her to find a boy from within her immediate social circle and community who will be similarly qualified, have her kind of confidence and will support her ambitions. Tehseem, if she does get educated as she wants to be, will never settle for an abusive husband as her mother had to face. These girls are not only better qualified than the boys in their neighbourhood, but they are also breaking the shackles of tradition that their mothers followed without questioning. Roy may not have much choice but to marry a girl who is more qualified than him, but will the girls be willing to make the same 'compromise'?

Daksha in Bhavnagar wants to get married only after graduation, and her precondition is that she should be allowed to work. Some potential marriage proposals do not progress because of this precondition. Sooner or later pressure will build up on her parents to fix her marriage, and I wonder what compromises Daksha will be forced to make at that stage even as I pray that she does not have to make any. Left to herself, Daksha would rather not get married, as she told me. Or consider Deepika in Bengaluru, whose mother is clearly despairing as Deepika turned thirty recently.

[180]'Human trafficking caters to demand for brides', Ashwaq Masoodi, 3 September 2014, available at: http://www.livemint.com/Politics/7cSn08nD9gvIEAbZcQrP7I/Human-trafficking-caters-to-demand-for-brides.html?utm_source=copy.

It is evident that the marriage age will rise, motherhood will be delayed, fertility will reduce and more women will start working in paid jobs outside their homes. Almost every girl I spoke to during this research said she would like to have two children, as against the fertility rate of 2.59 children per woman as per Census 2011, which itself is a decline of 18 per cent in a decade. The only girl who wanted to have three children is Anita and her reason was that even if one dies, she will be left with two. She lost a sibling in her childhood and her own family's experience is guiding her decision. Encouragingly with a reduction in teen weddings, incidence of teen motherhood has come down by over 32 per cent in a decade, with three quarters of all children being born to women in the age group of twenty to twenty-nine years.[181]

In 2007, CLSA, the investment bank that I worked in then, did two surveys among employees in the IT sector and financial services sector.[182] The surveys found that among the respondents 54–57 per cent had spouses who were home makers and not engaged in full-time employment. However, among unmarried respondents, 84 per cent said that they would look for a working spouse and would prefer their spouse to be in full-time employment. What was particularly interesting was that preference for a working spouse remained unchanged between respondents from the top seven cities versus the other 240+ cities.

The picture that emerged from the surveys is very clear. In this decade and over the next, women's participation in the labour force will rise, both in urban and semi-urban areas. This will drive two trends. The first one is that men will have to share more household chores. Traditionally the world over, women do the lion's share of work in their homes. Even today in developed

---

[181]*The Times of India* (2014), 'In new India, women want late marriage, fewer kids', Subodh Varma, 12 January.

[182]'Chain Reactions: Indian IT's impact on economy, consumption and GDP, February 2007' and 'Chain Reactions 2: India's financial services boom and its economic impact', September 2007. The two surveys had 46,000+ respondents who were employed by leading companies in these two sectors.

societies like the US, working women do the major share of the work in their homes. As Sheryl Sandberg wrote in *Lean In*, 'I still struggle with the trade-offs between work and home on a daily basis. Every woman I know does...'[183] And Indra Nooyi, PepsiCo CEO, recently said that women can't have it all which sparked a lively debate in the media.[184]

The west is much better at it than India where boys in a majority of the households are still brought up thinking that they are special and do not need to do any household chores, which is the primary job of girls and women. Families will need to ensure that boys participate in household chores as much as the girls do. Interview after interview, the girls said that they expect their partners and husbands to share in household chores. Training for this will have to start not during dating or after marriage, but much before that. This is what Tina meant when she told me that Indian mothers will need to teach their sons how to change nappies.

Changes at the societal level are not just about finding equal and supportive partners but they also need to drive attitudinal and behavioural changes among men and in society at large towards girls and women. It has been seen that childhood experiences of abuse and violence are associated with the perpetration of violence in most countries.[185] Therefore, change has to start early and will have to happen at the family and local community levels. Once again the role of governments and more importantly grassroot NGOs will be critical.

Another trend will be of the increasing number of house-husbands or husbands in temporary or part-time jobs as their wives

---

[183]Sheryl Sandberg, *Lean In: Women, Work and the Will to Lead*, p. 135.

[184]http://www.forbes.com/sites/moiraforbes/2014/07/03/power-woman-indra-nooyi-on-why-women-cant-have-it-all/.

[185]'Why Do Some Men Use Violence Against Women And How Can We Prevent It?' Quantitative findings from the United Nations multi-country study on men and violence in Asia and the Pacific, UNDP, UNFPA, UN Women, and UNV, September 2003.

have high flying careers. Already in metros it is easy to see fathers dropping their children to school or attending parent teacher meetings because their wives are travelling on work. There is nothing non-masculine about it. Men the world over are doing it although the change is very slow.

Shreya Sen Handley, a prolific blogger and contributor to different newspapers and magazines across the world including *National Geographic*, recently wrote:

> And it's still frowned upon for men to become stay-at-home dads. Between 1993 and 2007, the number of stay-at-home dads had gone up by a huge 83 per cent in the UK. By 2007, in the US, homemaking dads made up approximately 2.7 per cent of the nation's stay-at-home parents, triple the percentage from 1997, and up every year since 2005. In India, according to a 2006 study, as much as three percent of all urban fathers were stay-at-home dads, which would have been unacceptable and unheard of a decade before that. And yet, in every case, it is a very small percentage of the male population, because this is a 'role reversal' that frightens most men and many women.[186]

Sheryl Sandberg in *Lean In* says that of her batch of MBAs from Harvard, nearly 50 per cent of the women had dropped out of the workforce in twenty years. She writes:

> But more than twenty years after my college graduation, the world has not evolved as much as I believed it would. Almost all my male class mates work in professional settings. Some of my female classmates work full-time or part-time outside the home, and just as many are stay-at-home mothers and volunteers like my mom. This mirrors the national trend.[187]

A 2007 survey of Harvard Business School alumni found that in less than ten years after graduation only 81 per cent of the women

---

[186]Shreya Sen Handley, 'Men we can love', available at: http://blogs.timesofindia.indiatimes.com/witchs-brew/men-we-can-love/.

[187]Sheryl Sandberg, *Lean In: Women, Work and the Will to Lead*, p. 14.

who graduated continued to work full-time and in fifteen to twenty years the number declined to 49 per cent.[188]

This is important to mention since girls who were pursuing MBA in Harvard had presumably decided to have a career and must have been among the brightest and most ambitious within their cohort. In USA, 74 per cent of professional women who drop out of the workforce return to work in any capacity and only 40 per cent return to full-time jobs,[189] as they change their focus to having a family and then on supporting their husbands and their children. In India the problem is also acute since the participation of women in the labour force is low to begin with and then a large number of women drop out from the workforce to bring up their families.

Women make up only 24 per cent of India's workforce and only 5 per cent of them reach the top as compared to the global average of 20 per cent. A recent study found that 36 per cent of Indian working women take a break; this proportion is similar to USA and Germany.[190] Interestingly they take shorter breaks at an average of 11 months as against 2.7 years in the US and 1.9 years in Germany, with 58 per cent returning to full time jobs.[191] What is different is that in India women take breaks for childcare and also for elder care; but while childcare is slowly being outsourced, elder care still is not. According to Infosys, while competitive career opportunities is the top reason for men who leave, for women it is personal reasons and attrition among women is higher than it is among men.

Experiences of companies like ICICI Bank show that women are not only as productive as their male counterparts but are also excellent leaders. To realize their potential, corporate policies will have to be designed to support and keep women in the workforce

---

[188]Ibid.

[189]Ibid.

[190]http://forbesindia.com/blog/business-strategy/why-indian-women-leave-the-workforce/#ixzz2PjePqfHM.

[191]Ibid.

for longer. Some of the obvious measures are flexible working hours, longer maternity leave, generous childcare support, paternity leave, quality childcare services and support close to place of work or larger housing complexes in cities like Mumbai and Bengaluru. If the intent is right, more creative solutions will emerge.

As more girls start working, the marriage age will be pushed upwards and coupled with the trend that more girls by choice or otherwise will possibly remain single, we are likely to see lower fertility rates, more adoption of children and better child and maternal health. Within my circle of friends I know of at least two couples who have decided not to have biological children and have opted for adoption in the last decade. One of the prominent role models that has emerged is Sushmita Sen, model, actor and former Miss Universe, who as a single parent has adopted two daughters. There are many more couples I know who have decided not to have any children so as not to compromise with their careers or their lifestyles.

Later marriages and better education will mean better maternal and child health. Coupled with slightly better governance in the public space this will mean dramatic improvements in social and human development indicators. Between 2007 and 2010, the institutional birth percentage increased from 47 per cent to nearly 61 per cent.[192] Two Government of India initiatives—Janani Suraksha Yojana (JSY) and the Mother and Child Tracking System— are credited with success in driving increased institutional births. JSY is also one of India's first experiments with conditional cash transfers. This has obviously had a role to play in lower deaths during pregnancy or childbirth and also in lowering infant mortality, although it still remains embarrassingly high. In all these areas government policy and intervention are of paramount importance and this is where better governance comes in. Aadhaar will further facilitate conditional cash transfers to the targeted population.

---

[192]*Business Standard*, (2012), '16-fold increase in safe institutional deliveries in India', 1 August, available at: http://www.business-standard.com/article/pti-stories/16-fold-increase-in-safe-institutional-deliveries-in-india-112080100615_1.html.

Societal changes and the trends discussed in the previous chapters have wide ranging implications for all stakeholders. Let me start with the government, policymakers and NGOs. As times have changed their approach and priorities have to reflect new societal realities and they have to think about how to engage with the target group more effectively. For example, staid old government communication and advertisements no longer work. I do not profess to have all or even some of the answers but hopefully the issues that are thrown up will help redirect thinking.

Societal changes or changes to social norms and behaviour are extremely difficult to bring about and take a long time. Social norms and beliefs of generations have to be changed to address some of the gender related challenges or even other causes like the necessity to have more toilets within homes for the greater safety of women and for better health and hygiene. Trying to drive such changes in a traditional society is not only complex but can also get controversial, as we in India realize whenever the issue of sex education in schools comes up from time to time.

Sometimes help comes from unexpected quarters as the law of unintended consequences kicks in. In Brazil, the state has stayed away from family planning. In the 1980s fertility among Brazilian women started dropping rapidly, whereas till 1970 an average Brazilian woman had almost six children. The drop was attributed to access to television and popular soap operas known as telenovelas, where most female characters under the age of fifty had no children and the rest had only one child each.[193] Right after the soap operas became available in an area, the number of births started dropping and children started being named after the main characters in the soap.

For many decades the government's priority has been to try and get school going age children enrolled in schools and it has also achieved some noteworthy success. However, learning outcomes

[193]Abhijit V Banerjee and Esther Duflo, *Poor Economics: A Radical Thinking of the Way to Fight Global Poverty.*

have been pathetic. As a result we have an army of literate and semi-literate youngsters who have limited skill sets to get and succeed in most jobs. Many NGOs like Akanksha in Mumbai and Head Held High in Bengaluru try and fill this gap but their efforts are a drop in the ocean.

The Brihanmumbai Municipal Corporation (BMC or Municipal Corporation of Greater Mumbai) engaged McKinsey to advise it in its policy of running municipal schools and has handed over the infrastructure of municipal schools in a few instances to NGOs like Akanksha, Aseema and Muktangan. I visited the Muktangan School in the BDT Chawl in Worli. Muktangan uses one floor of the school and while adhering to the state board's syllabus, it uses its own proprietary pedagogy, which will in all likelihood lead to better learning outcomes. The teachers seemed more motivated than what we see in municipal schools and they belonged to the local communities. The children sat in bright well-equipped classrooms which displayed colourful charts and models. The teacher-student ratio in Muktangan School will be the envy of most reputed private schools in Mumbai.

Muktangan's pedagogy and teaching methodology is being used in various teacher training colleges. More such public-private partnerships are necessary throughout the country. Perhaps the government needs to focus on teachers' training for better learning outcomes on one hand and on vocational training to make youngsters more employable on the other. This is not a call for greater privatization since as per an ASER study, the performance of private schools is better, although in absolute terms the results are not very encouraging, and much of the difference can be explained by family backgrounds and incomes.

In 2009, the percentage of students in Class V who could read Class II level textbooks was just over 60 per cent for private schools and 50 per cent for government schools. By 2012, the same percentages were 60 and 40 per cent respectively.[194] For math, the

---

[194]Annual State of Education Report (Rural) 2012, available at: http://www.pratham.org/file/ASER-2012report.pdf.

percentage of Class V students who could do division was 46 per cent for private schools and 36 per cent for government schools. By 2012 the numbers had dropped to 39 and 20 per cent respectively.[195] Performance of both government and private schools leaves a lot to be desired, although the decline in the performance of government schools is much sharper than that of private schools. Clearly private schools are not the panacea.

Abhijit Banerjee and Esther Duflo in their book *Poor Economics* highlight Pratham's work to show that government school teachers can provide improved outcomes. They evaluated Pratham's programme which involved recruiting unpaid volunteers in villages in Jaunpur district in Uttar Pradesh who after a week's training were holding evening classes in their neighbourhood. Abhijit and Esther write:

> By the end of the program, all the participating children who could not read before the program could at least recognize letters (in contrast, only 40 percent of those in the comparison villages could read letters by the end of the year).[196]

There is another interesting experiment by Pratham that Abhijit and Esther write about:

> In Bihar, Pratham organized a set of remedial summer camps for school children in which the teachers from the government school system were invited to come and teach. The results from this evaluation were surprising: the much-maligned government teachers actually taught, and the gains were comparable to the gains from the Jaunpur evening classes.[197]

Government schools can become better once their customers have choice and the staff have the right incentives and motivation.

---

[195]Ibid.

[196]Abhijit V Banerjee and Esther Duflo, *Poor Economics: A Radical Thinking of the Way to Fight Global Poverty.*

[197]Ibid.

Whether it is learning outcomes or whether it is vocational training, the challenges are humungous in the entrenched system and seem almost insurmountable. What is sure is that there will not be one single solution directed by some ministry in the central government. Multiple efforts are going on at every stage of education and vocational training. Even as Delhi University reeled under a controversy over withdrawing its Four Year Undergraduate Programme (FYUP), which was hastily introduced in 2013, Ashoka University launched by eminent private citizens and young entrepreneurs like Ashish Dhawan and Sanjeev Bhikchandani among others, is launching a four-year undergraduate programme in liberal education in humanities, social sciences and natural and applied sciences.

Another person who is thinking about transformational change and not incremental change is Nandan Nilekani, co-founder and ex-CEO of Infosys and ex-chairman of UIDAI. He is thinking of how to leverage technology, sub-US$100 smart phones and gaming technology to change how children learn and in turn improve their learning outcomes. In a model being envisioned by Nandan Nilekani, several million children from economically and socially challenged backgrounds will be able to improve their learning outcomes in applied literacy and numeracy. While the Azim Premji Foundation works with the government schools' ecosystem, Nandan Nilekani would like to work to complement the public school ecosystem and leverage technology to deliver the desired outcomes. Then there is Neil D'Souza, founder of Zaya Learning, who is using his experience in Mozambique to see how his company can help schools deliver better learning outcomes. The government, policymakers and traditional NGOs need to start thinking of disruptive and transformational solutions.

According to data from the National Sample Survey's (NSS) sixty-eighth survey,[198] the labour force participation rate (LFPR) in

---

[198]NSS, conducted by the National Survey Sample Office (NSSO) under the Ministry of Statistics and Programme Implementation (MOSPI) has arguably the best data in India on employment and consumption.

the age group of 15–59 years for the entire population was 58.3 per cent.[199] The numbers for men and women were 83 per cent and 33 per cent respectively. Even today nearly 70 per cent of women not in the labour force are engaged in domestic duties and a lesser percentage are in education and/or retired. The numbers for rural and urban India are starker.

While LFPR for men in urban and rural areas was 81 per cent and 84 per cent respectively, the numbers for women were 22 per cent and 38 per cent respectively. This is another paradox. Given more opportunities in urban India and better qualifications (higher education and better skill set development opportunities), one would naturally have expected that the labour force participation rate would be higher in urban India than in rural India. But that is not the case. This is possibly due to the fact that in rural India a larger proportion of women engage in manual labour in the fields or in construction, whereas in urban India, led by higher economic standards, women have access to office or domestic jobs, which are smaller in number; many may choose not to enter the job market.

In most manufacturing jobs the proportion of women employed is miniscule and it is only with the growth of the services sector that new job prospects have opened up for women in larger numbers. Around 50 per cent of employees in TV news rooms in India are women. Between 2000–06, the newly registered chartered accountants were 45 per cent larger than the total number of women enrolled between 1990 to 1999 and thus, the presence of women chartered accountants increased to 13.1 per cent in 2006 from 5.2 per cent in 1995.[200]

Another reason could also be that after childbirth or due to family issues more women in urban areas tend to drop out of the workforce, either of their own volition or otherwise. A likely third reason is that in urban areas the growth of single family households,

---

[199]Based on principal status and secondary status.

[200]Roopa Purushothaman, Everstone Investment Advisors, *XX Factor: The Impact of Working Women on India's Growth, Incomes and Consumption.*

nuclear families as opposed to traditional joint families, means that women have less support from the extended family, even as outside childcare facilities are inadequate, and this probably keeps many women out of the workforce. Whatever be the reason, men in the years to come will have to step in to share household work and duties to ensure that their partners start pursuing or continue to pursue a career.

A fourth reason is that as women get more educated, as is evident from school enrolments and their proportion in colleges and universities, their entry into the workforce is delayed and thus, it will not be surprising to see the labour pool shrink in certain age groups even as the overall quality of the labour pool improves significantly. A positive consequence of this upgradation in the quality of the labour pool is that childcare has become more parent intensive with greater involvement of both the parents. Further, better educated women now compensate for the massive failure of the school system, as evident from ASER studies, by engaging in their children's education.[201] I did hear this as one reason why men now want educated brides, even when they do not want their wives to work.

As per the 66th round of NSS,[202] in 2009-10, 40 per cent females in rural India and 48 per cent of women in urban areas were engaged in domestic duties. The survey had several other interesting findings:

- Of the women aged fifteen years and above usually engaged in domestic duties, about 33 per cent in rural areas and about 27 per cent in urban areas were willing to accept work if it was made available at their household premises. They constituted about 19.1 per cent and about 17.5 per cent of the women of age fifteen years and above in rural and urban India, respectively.

[201]*Indian Express*, (2013), 'Missing them, again', Pratap Bhanu Mehta, 24 May.

[202]Participation of Women in Specified Activities along with Domestic Duties, NSS sixty-sixth round (July 2009-June 2010), Report No. 550 (66/10/5), February 2013.

- Among the women aged fifteen years and above who reported willingness to accept work at the household premises, about 93 per cent in rural areas and about 95 per cent in urban areas preferred work on a regular basis.
- About 70 per cent women in rural and urban areas preferred 'part-time' work on a regular basis while about 23–26 per cent wanted regular 'full-time' work.
- Among women aged fifteen years and above willing to accept work at the household premises, about 43 per cent in rural areas and about 30 per cent in urban areas reported the need for initial finance on easy terms to take up their desired work.

This list provides a lot of food for thought and also potential solutions. To improve women's participation in the labour force more jobs will have to be generated closer to home, there has to be a quantum leap in day care facilities for children close to home and close to places of work and increased opportunities for women to work from home and with flexible working hours, if necessary. These are issues that policy makers need to think about as we prepare for a period when women's participation in the workforce is bound to increase. I remember listening to Professor Nirmalya Kumar[203] many years back speaking about Zara's manufacturing model in Italy. Zara had organized local women's co-operatives in different localities in what was a win-win situation. It meant that Zara could still keep a part of its production in a country like Italy when most garment manufacturing was moving to China and other emerging countries without losing its cost competitiveness due to tax and other benefits, and for the women it meant working in small groups close to home.

In India there are small entrepreneurs, NGOs and some companies like Fabindia which follow the same model but this has to be scaled up to make a difference as millions of women are employed in this way. Flipkart, India's largest online retailer and

---

[203]Of London Business School; Nirmalya Kumar is now a member of the Group Executive Council of Tata Sons and is responsible for group strategy.

market place, is planning to link traditional craftsmen and artisans to customers through its platform. A pilot project has already been started in Varanasi. The kind of work that was most preferred by women who were willing to accept work at their household premises was tailoring in both the rural and urban areas. The 66th NSS survey report said, 'Among women of age fifteen years and above, about 10 per cent in rural areas and about 11 per cent in urban areas were willing to accept the work of tailoring at their household premises.' There will possibly be other opportunities outside of tailoring and handicrafts as well.

In the previous chapters I discussed how and why women's participation in the workforce is going to increase. Appropriate policies and conducive environment can further accelerate women's participation in the workforce. While a reasonable amount of discussion is beginning to take place on how to harness India's demographic dividend, there is hardly any discussion on how to increase women's participation in the workforce. This is an urgent requirement. Policy makers, the government, NGOs and institutions working for issues related to women have to think of how to work with the new generation of girls and women who are better educated, aspirational and better informed.

This tectonic shift of better educated, more aspirational girls and their increase in the workforce will present huge opportunities for a wide range of companies and service providers. A report titled 'XX Factor: The Impact of Working Women on India's Growth, Incomes and Consumption'[204] published in 2007 estimated that increased women's participation in the workforce, XX trend, could make Indians 12 per cent richer by 2025 than otherwise projected. When the report was published, the author had estimated that the XX trend 'could add US$35bn to GDP, lifting incremental demand by 10 per cent'.

This coupled with the fact that the coming generation will be

---

[204]Roopa Purushothaman, Everstone Investment Advisors, *XX Factor: The Impact of Working Women on India's Growth, Incomes and Consumption.*

relatively more resource rich and time constrained will provide an opportunity for suppliers of different products and services. Once women start working and gain some amount of independence and control over their economic well-being and finances, they will have a larger say in the savings and consumption of households. Across a range of household expenditures, working women spend more than non-working women given that they have more control over their finances and better say in how they spend and what they earn. At times this is also helped by the fact that routine household expenditures are still primarily met from the income of their fathers or husbands. These women will spend more on their children and one reason could be better spending power and the second to assuage their sense of guilt of spending less time with their children.

Which sectors will benefit from this rise? Multiple sectors will be big beneficiaries. Given that women focus more on the education and healthcare of their families, clearly education and out of school classes will be the first beneficiaries. Retail financial services will find a new cohort of consumers and they will need to tailor-make their products in some cases to address this group of consumers as it becomes significant in numbers. Credit cards, debit cards, personal loans and savings products will all have to start targeting this specific segment. Personal care, home care and packaged foods will be large beneficiaries of this trend. As more women start working demand for all FMCG products will get a boost and the culture of eating out and takeaway food outlets will also increase. Similarly travel and tourism will also get a boost with higher disposable incomes in double income families.

Products and services that can help save time or free up time for leisure and quality family time will be lapped up. This takes me back to a conversation I had many years back with Andrew Levermore, then CEO of Hypercity. He said that no amount of consumer market research will be good enough to predict consumer behaviour in India. Every focus group discussion and research had told him that cut and packed vegetables would have very limited off-take in India where housewives want to make fresh food for their families and a key part of this process was selecting and cutting fresh vegetables.

But the cut and packed vegetables started flying off the shelf from day one of the first Hypercity opening in the suburb of Malad in Mumbai. I very knowledgably nodded my head and said, 'Yeah, this (Malad) is BPO country and all the young twenty-somethings would value convenience.' I was completely wrong. Andrew told me that the twenty-somethings did not cook at home but ate out. It was the young and middle-aged couples who were rapidly switching to cut and packed vegetables. Go figure. A big beneficiary would be online retail and it is easy to understand why online retailers are growing at near or over a few hundred percent every year.

However, this is not one uniform market. Like any other consumer market, this market will have multiple segments and price points to cater to, and in a country as diversified as India there will be additional challenges of regional differences. For example, one research found that almost 50 per cent of working women in Mumbai shop alone for groceries, but only 18 per cent of working women in Bengaluru shop alone.[205]

With more families becoming double income, delayed marriages and having children at a later age will mean greater demand for leisure and entertainment, increased travels and holidays, holidays for single men, women and elderly people, packaged food, elder care facilities or old age communities, childcare facilities and increased spending on apparel, accessories, footwear and communication. More families will keep pets and niche areas like pet grooming will see robust growth.

Women have always shopped more or so goes the stereotype; very soon women in India may have more to spend as well. Then demand for domestic help, drivers and child care facilities will continue to increase. In Mumbai, for example, I have seen that the salaries of domestic helps and drivers are higher in the new sky

---

[205]Roopa Purushothaman, Everstone Investment Advisors, *XX Factor: The Impact of Working Women on India's Growth, Incomes and Consumption.*

rises—where suddenly demand has increased and a higher proportion of families are double income—than say in some of the more traditional neighbourhoods where demand is steady. This will be true of Bengaluru, Pune and Delhi as well. The trends that I have highlighted are multi-decadal in nature and these are changes that are already underway. Companies and businesses that identify and cater to these trends will be big beneficiaries and long term winners.

EK NAYEE SHUROOAT—A NEW BEGINNING

In the first week of June 2014, Indra Nooyi, PepsiCo CEO, made some very candid confessions on the challenges of a working woman who has to balance her role of a professional with that of a home maker. In response to a question at the Aspen Ideas Festival Monday Indra Nooyi said, 'I don't think women can have it all. I just don't think so. We pretend we *have* it all. We pretend we *can* have it all. My husband and I have been married for thirty-four years. And we have two daughters. And every day you have to make a decision about whether you are going to be a wife or a mother, in fact many times during the day you have to make those decisions. And you have to co-opt a lot of people to help you. We co-opted our families to help us. We plan our lives meticulously so we can be decent parents. But if you ask our daughters, I'm not sure they will say that I've been a good mom. I'm not sure. And I try all kinds of coping mechanisms.'[206]

Predictably a fairly lively debate raged on Facebook and elsewhere after Indra Nooyi's statement. On a friend's Facebook wall, one of her friends commented, 'Women like to feel guilty and beat themselves up. I do that all the time. This media hype around superwoman labels needs to stop and people like Sandberg need to mind their own business instead of creating this myth that you can have it all. No something's got to give and people have to choose their priorities based on their individual life situations. Hope women learn to chill more.'

---

[206]http://www.theatlantic.com/business/archive/2014/07/why-pepsico-ceo-indra-k-nooyi-cant-have-it-all/373750/#ixzz36hrjKqJg.

Lipika De, a batchmate from my engineering days who is now working with Tata Consultancy Services (TCS) in New Delhi had this to say:

The past week has been dominated by unabashed feminism. Images of Facebook COO Sheryl Sandberg's visit to India, PepsiCo CEO Indra Nooyi declaring that women cannot have it all and Dame Wendy Hall crowned as the most influential woman of UK IT was all over the print as well as the digital media. And no one seemed to complain. So I thought a bit of introspection maybe in order.

To begin with, let me admit I wanted to have it all, a bit more perhaps than many and everything seemed to go as per design. A career as a member of the faculty at IIT Delhi, a house well-spruced with tit-bits acquired from all over the world, a dramatics group to entertain my life-long passion in dramatics, weekend parties with co-actors who also doubled as willing guinea-pigs for my culinary experiments as well as baby-sitters for my son while I attended conferences and above all a spouse who was an equal partner in all the above activities barring the culinary ventures. Parents pitched in whenever necessary. And of course India being the land of surplus labour, life was a breeze.

However, age does not stand still. As I grew older so did others around me. Students graduated. A cute little baby grew into an argumentative teenager. Husband succeeded and continued to climb the proverbial ladder. Parents aged. Household extended. And to accommodate all, I was soon running a household with more than double the number of helping hands as the number of members.

I changed my job. I could now afford to hire a battalion of helping hands just to ensure that my life remains a perfect symphony, both professional and personal synchronized and in harmony. I wanted to be an achiever. I became the bandmaster of my home orchestra. I gave detailed instructions for the orchestra before I left house every morning. The breakfast was on the table, the cooking instructions written in laboured Hindi hung on a cloth blackboard behind the kitchen door, details of what to serve to whom during lunch repeated multiple times before I stepped into the car with my cup of coffee.

And then, with the house virtually on seige while I am away, the inevitable happened. A series of unsolved mysteries waited for me each day. Who broke the Japanese vase? How come the new sofa is torn? Why is the school dress not pressed? If I sincerely wanted to know the truth behind each of these, I would have to additionally hire Hercule Poirot. But that would be of little use, since I could not really afford to charge any of them of any misdeed and antagonize the said person. The next replacement would be no better. I gave up.

I rather concentrated on the daily report: 'no oil to cook tomorrow, rice may or may not last for two more days, the milk-man had not come today, the doctor has prescribed a new medicine for mother-in-law, a gift is needed for Divya's birthday tomorrow...' And much like the PepsiCo CEO, I would dash out to the nearest market, just so that the music doesn't die from my life! The only difference being that, since I was not a CXO and never hope to be one, I do not have a secretary at work who would check whether my son had completed his home-work before he went out to play, which in turn would inevitably mean that around 10 p.m. when I insisted that the school-bag be packed for the next day, there would be work to do.

And what happened to the accommodative spouse? Well, somewhere down the line, this became my household. The maids are mine, the nurses are mine, the kitchen is mine, the menu is mine, the grocery is mine, the garden is mine—I am the queen of all I survey! A queen who is asphyxiated and wants to break free from all the earthly possessions!

As the new academic year is about to begin, I have been requested to address a batch of fresh entrants about time—management, work—life balance, women in Engineering and so on. I am wondering where to begin. Should I say, 'Girls, don't try to have it all—leave something for the boys! Boys, don't let the girls take over and then happily crib that you are an outsider in your own home! It's not going to work for long! Agree to meet your partner half-way. If that does not work—just quit!'

I wish it was as simple as that! Life is not about quitting. Sometimes life can be about endless endurance, and still dreaming about the rainbow that would stretch from horizon to horizon when the thunderous clouds are blown away.

Lipika grew up in a small industrial town in West Bengal, but the urge to have it all was there in her. Having cursorily known her in college I would never have classified her as very ambitious. But as it turns out, she seems to be one ambitious lady who has managed her work-life balance quite well. Every woman who goes out to work irrespective of the country she is in faces the same issues. Maybe women should stop being too self-critical. Maybe they should stop trying to get it all perfect. Knowing that you can't get it all perfect, decide on your priorities and maybe it won't matter if the wardrobe is not perfectly arranged every evening or if there is a bunch of newspapers strewn across the living room.

We will follow the way the developed world has moved even as we keep our ties to our *parampara* and *sanskriti*. And it will be important for men to start changing. We have seen this movie before in some of the western countries. As *The Economist* said a few years ago, '"WHY can't a woman be more like a man?" mused Henry Higgins in *My Fair Lady*. Future generations might ask why a man can't be more like a woman.'[207] Indeed why can't a man be more like a woman? For this change even boys will need the right role models at home and in society.

To quote Sheryl Sandberg:

> True partnership in our homes does more than just benefit couples today; it also sets the stage for the next generation...A more equal division of labour between parents will model better behaviour for the next generation...women provide more than twice as much care not only for their own parents, but for their in-laws as well. This is an additional burden that needs to be shared. And children need to see it being shared so that their generation will follow the example...The revolution will happen one family at a time.[208]

This is the beginning of that change. As per the 2011 Census the number of additional literate women at 104.6 million was more

---

[207]'A Guide to Womenomics', available at: http://www.economist.com/node/6802551.

[208]Sheryl Sandberg, *Lean In: Women, Work and the Will to Lead*, pp. 119, 120.

than the 98.2 million additional men for the first time. This is a very important milestone, and the gender gap is slowly closing. Somewhere over the next fifteen to twenty years the gender gap in literacy will vanish. Along with that I strongly believe that the gender gap will narrow considerably in every other sphere as well.

While improved and increased literacy is immediately not driving significant increase in labour force participation, it will be a natural consequence with at best a few years time lag. I believe economic rationale, cost of living, aspirations for a better lifestyle and assertiveness of independence by girls and women will drive increase in labour force participation.

The first major impact of this trend will be felt on economic growth and consumption. There will barely be any segment of consumption and consumerism that will not be impacted. Equally important will be the social changes that we will see over the next decade or two. Initially at least the patriarchal society will resist the changes but the resistance in my view will be futile although for sometime gender based violence will increase and we may see increase in trafficking of girls and women. Over a period of time it will lead to better gender sensitivity, less violence, increase in the average marriage age, lower fertility rates and better social and human development outcomes. Aspirations of some girls will not be met and there will be disappointments, but their struggle will inspire others to move ahead.

No less an impact of this megatrend will be on boys and men. Long used to being pampered and mollycoddled they will have to bear an increasing share of the household work and will have less control over their female relations. While young educated women will face the challenge of finding suitable life partners, the same will be true for men and boys. They will also have to learn to live and cope with less power and authority than their fathers and grandfathers have been used to. There will be a rising trend of stay-at-home dads. I am sure we will see the day when mothers will ask their sons to serve a glass of water to their sisters and wives. Then hopefully boys and men will be as confident as the women in their lives. While the tide in this war has turned in the right direction, there is still a long and uphill battle ahead. The biggest challenge will be to change social attitudes.

I finished this book after about a year and a half since I put the outline on paper. It was an emotional roller coaster for me. At one end was the exhilaration of seeing young, ambitious girls who were doing so well in life, overcoming numerous challenges and at the other, the heart rending stories of abandoned families, daughters and wives being beaten, a father shot dead in front of his little daughter. I also realize that there is so much more interesting research that can be done on the subjects that I have discussed.

As I drew to the end of the book, I was curious about what some of the girls had done in the past one and half years.

Reena, from Bhavnagar, graduated with over 70 per cent marks and has enrolled in a journalism course at Gujarat Vidyapeeth. Meanwhile she has also got married.

Daksha, from Bhavnagar, is in the second year of her graduation course and has recently got engaged. The marriage will take place by the end of the year. Her would-be husband is also studying and her in-laws have told her that she will be allowed to complete her studies and then take up a job.

Sunita, from Noida, is in her second year of engineering in a reputed private engineering college and is doing very well. She is regularly in touch with Supriya.

Salva, from Hyderabad, has got married and is working in aircraft maintenance. She still hopes to fly a commercial aircraft one day. She has come a long way from the time when her mother had to sell off her earrings to fund Salva's studies. Her husband works in a Honda dealership after completing his BSc and then a diploma in automobile engineering.

Meghna, from Mumbai, completed her Class XII with excellent results and has decided to pursue her undergraduate studies at the University of California at Berkeley, choosing the university over a few others that she had secured admission in. Meghna's mother has once again taken up the job of a full-time teacher.

Priyanka, from Munger, completed her MBA and had some trouble finding a suitable job. Finally she took up an assignment with a real estate company in Delhi in sales and marketing.

Sanchita's daughter in Sweden is preparing to apply to leading universities across the world for undergraduate studies in 2015. She spent the summer of 2013 at Yale University attending a programme on global strategy and leadership. In the summer of 2014, she spent a month at a science oriented programme in Sweden called Research Academy for Young Scientists (RAYS).

Deepika, from Bengaluru, received her passport after what seemed like an endless wait and has travelled to Sweden twice in the last one year. She continues to perform well at her job and is yet to get married.

Anita, from Mumbai, took up a job in a call centre close to her home since her father would not allow her to work in a nursing home slightly far away. She found the job very demanding in terms of targets and deliverables and quit after four months. Her parents are now looking for a groom for her.

Saira, from Mumbai, completed her Class X and is pursuing her studies in a junior college. She dropped out of Avasara and is now associated with only Aseema and its after school program.

Meanwhile when I open the daily newspaper the atrocities on girls and women continue unabated. A used car dealer shot his wife nine times with his license revolver in Delhi. A 29-year-old girl working for a multinational, daughter of the principal of a very well-known school in Delhi, committed suicide. A 3-year-old girl was raped in a school in Bengaluru. It's another day in the life of India.

Again it's not just another day. Girls continue to outperform boys in school leaving and other competitive exams. An auto-rickshaw driver's daughter in Mumbai achieved the top rank in the Chartered Accountancy exams in 2013. A butcher's daughter topped the post graduate course in chemistry in Bangalore University and won six gold medals. Her father had studied till Class VII and mother till Class II. Six newly-wed women in Uttar Pradesh walked out of their husbands' homes when they found that their homes did not have toilets. A woman in Chhattisgarh divorced her husband as he failed to build a toilet in their home. Today is better and brighter than yesterday and there is hope that tomorrow will be better and brighter than today; and in many homes, mothers and wives are teaching their sons and husbands how to change nappies and how to cook.

SOME OF THE NGOS MENTIONED
(IN ALPHABETICAL ORDER)

Akanksha Foundation, http://www.akanksha.org/, The Akanksha Foundation is a non-profit organization with the vision of equipping all students one day with the education, skills and character that they need to lead empowered lives. Akanksha works primarily in the field of education.

American Indian Foundation, www.aif.org, focuses on bringing together Indian and American citizens to contribute to India's social and economic development and in bridging the gap between the world's two largest democracies.

Aseema, http://www.aseema.org/, is a Mumbai based non-governmental organization with a mission of providing underprivileged children with a nurturing and stimulating educational environment that helps them recognize their limitless potential.

AskHowIndia, www.askhowindia.org, is an initiative driven to improve the quality of political debate in India and hence finding solutions to India's social, economic and political issues.

Avasara Leadership Academy, https://avasaraleadershipfellows. wordpress.com/, was started by the India Leadership Initiative Fellow Roopa Purushothaman to provide education and leadership experiences to girls across all economic strata in India.

Breakthrough, www.breakthrough.tv, is a global organization which aims to eradicate violence against women by creating multimedia campaigns to inspire and equip them to stand up for their rights and build a world in which all are equal.

Caring Friends, https://sites.google.com/a/caringfriends.in/caring-friends/home, Caring Friends (CF) Mumbai, is an informal group of friends who have come together to act as a bridge between outstanding NGOs and donors. It does due diligence—visit, assess and assist NGOs—so that every rupee that a donor contributes is used optimally. CF is presently associated with more than thirty NGOs in ten states in India.

Cashpor Micro Credit, www.cashpor.in, is a not for profit company which provides microfinance facilities to women who live below the poverty line in Uttar Pradesh and Bihar.

Dr Reddy's Foundation, http://drreddysfoundation.org/, is a non-profit partner of Dr Reddy's Laboratories. DRF acts as a catalyst of change that fosters, develops and promotes initiatives at individual, group and organizational levels to achieve sustainable development.

Head Held High, http://head-held-high.com/, is a social enterprise that unleashes the power of rural youth through skills, entrepreneurship and technology to drive their socio-economic prosperity.

Imlee Mahua, http://www.imleemahuaa.org/, is a not for profit educational institution run by Prayaag Joshi in the heart of Chhattisgarh to educate tribal children, most of whose parents are forest gatherers or subsistence farmers, in villages where there is no power and less than 3 per cent of the population is literate. The school had forty-five children in 2014.

Institute for Policy Research & Studies (IPRS), www.prsindia.org, is a not for profit institution that tracks the functioning of the Indian Parliament and works with MPs from the Lok Sabha and Rajya Sabha across political parties and MLAs from various states. PRS provides a comprehensive and credible resource base to access Parliament-specific data, background information on Parliamentary and governance processes and analysis of key legislative and policy issues. (Author's note: The author is a director on the board of IPRS.)

Janaagraha, www.janaagraha.org, is a not for profit foundation which collaborates with both the people and the government to improve the standard of living in Indian towns and cities.

mMitra, http://www.armman.org/mmitra, is a free mobile application developed by NGO Armman to provide information about prenatal care and motherhood to women in rural India.

Muktangan, http://muktanganedu.org/, is a new model of education providing quality, child-centred, inclusive English-medium schooling to thousands of underprivileged children in Mumbai. It is truly 'education for the community by the community', integrating the training of teachers from the same neighbourhoods as the students, creating empowered change agents.

Parivaar, http://parivaar.org/, Parivaar is a non-denominational, humanitarian organization based in West Bengal. For over ten years, Parivaar has worked towards total care and overall development of children who are highly vulnerable to exploitation, victimization and trafficking, including orphans, street children, abandoned children and extremely impoverished children from tribal areas.

Shaishav Child Rights, www.shaishavchildrights.org, is based in Bhavnagar and aims to eradicate child labour and empower children through quality education enabling them to fight for their basic rights.

Sulabh International, www.sulabhinternational.org, is a social service organization which has been working towards providing viable sanitation options, reducing social discrimination against 'scavengers' and preventing environmental pollution.

Vidya & Child, www.vidyaandchild.org, reaches out to socio-economically challenged children through non-formal and after school support centres in northern India.

SWIKRITIYAN—ACKNOWLEDGEMENTS

It was Asis Ranjan Hore, my friend and father-in-law, who told me decades back that I must write, an idea that I had never entertained before. I guess the seed of the desire to write was planted then in the late 1980s. However, my first public attempt at writing is thanks to Nirmal Jain, wholly supported by R Venkataraman, my colleagues and co-founders at India Infoline (IIFL). They pushed me to start a daily column called 'Point Blank' on our website www.indiainfoline.com. Without that column I would never have experienced the highs of interacting with readers that any author experiences; writing this column I also got some confidence that maybe 'I can'.

By the time I left IIFL, the writing bug was in me. Subsequently CLSA Asia Pacific Markets gave me the opportunity to travel and the canvas to write as I wanted to. The seeds of this book were sown during those travels within the country and what I heard and saw. I am immensely thankful to CLSA. One person who egged me on to tell the human side of the India story is Frances Dydasco. Frances always believed that there was a book in what I was writing; I am grateful to her.

When I seriously started thinking about this book in 2013, Alok Vajpeyi pushed me to get serious and remain focused, probably knowing better than me that my laziness might get the better of me. He also introduced me to Ritu Vajpeyi Mohan, and my thanks to Ritu for accepting the idea of the book over the phone one February morning in 2013. Once she said yes, I had no choice but to move forward. Dharini Bhaskar of Rupa has been the word processor and

Wren & Martin combined and without her quick turnaround, this book would probably have been in the works for many more months. Meghna Dasgupta readily agreed to help with data analysis and research, which helped me complete the book on time. Tina Vajpeyi conducted a few of the interviews with me and shared her insights from her long association with different NGOs. My thanks to all of them.

My thanks to Patrick Foulis and Simon Cox for being generous with their time and suggestions about the outline of this book and to Patrick for reading the draft and giving his valuable feedback, which certainly makes this book richer. The trips to Delhi and Bihar with them were fun and of great importance to me. I am also grateful to Nandan Nilekani for giving some specific suggestions to my initial outline. My thanks to Lopa Banerjee for suggesting a number of useful research papers and reading material for my project and also for a most enjoyable afternoon at her home in New York. Saurabh Mukherjea, Sohini Bhattacharya, Bhavtosh Vajpayee, Hemant Bakhru, Neelkanth Mishra, Sandeep Mahindroo, Nimesh Sumati, Roopa Purushottaman, Zaheeruddin Ali Khan, Anindra Haldar and Suprio Guha Thakurta went out of their way to help me during my research and I am grateful to them.

During the course of my research, I met many incredible people—young girls, women and some boys—who without hesitation opened up their minds, hearts and hearths to me without any preconditions and were very candid in their discussions. To all of them I am grateful because the book is essentially their stories and is mostly told in their words; I am a mere messenger. As a result of my two-year project, my admiration for less privileged people in our society grew immensely. I also had the good fortune of interacting with many social entrepreneurs and my respect for them too increased manifold. My sincerest thanks to all of them. Having always been an admirer of scale, the absolute necessity of grassroot NGOs belatedly dawned on me. NGOs have been separately listed elsewhere and I would encourage readers to consider giving support to them. I may have missed out a few names inadvertently but that is more due to my memory and age.

My thanks to Sita Giri, for those cups of tea early in the morning, and Spout, our beloved pug, for letting me tickle his ears in between my writings and for his company during those early morning or late night trysts with the laptop. And last but not the least, my everlasting gratitude to my parents and sisters for all the sacrifices that they made personally and/or endured to ensure I am what I am today and to Shom, the better of the two halves in our partnership, and Siddhant and Avantika, our two children, for keeping me grounded and reminding me from time to time that there is life beyond a job and a book.

www.ingramcontent.com/pod-product-compliance
Lightning Source LLC
Chambersburg PA
CBHW050231270326
41914CB00033BA/1871/J